D1430975

A Strange Freedom

editors

WALTER EARL FLUKER & CATHERINE TUMBER

A Strange Freedom

The Best of

Howard Thurman

on Religious Experience

and Public Life

BEACON PRESS | BOSTON

BX
6495
.T53
A25
1998

Beacon Press
25 Beacon Street
Boston, Massachusetts 02108-2892
www.beacon.org

*Beacon Press books are published under the auspices
of the Unitarian Universalist Association of congregations.*

© 1998 by Howard Thurman
© 1998 annotations by Walter Earl Fluker and Catherine Tumber
All rights reserved
Printed in the United States of America
Excerpt from Olive Shreiner, *From Man to Man* (1927) by permission of HarperCollins Publishers.

03 02 01 00 99 98   8 7 6 5 4 3 2 1

Text design by Lucinda L. Hitchcock
Composition by Wilsted & Taylor Publishing Services

LIBRARY OF CONGRESS CATALOGING-IN-PUBLICATION DATA

Thurman, Howard, 1900–1981.
    A strange freedom : the best of Howard Thurman on religious experience
and public life / edited by Walter Earl Fluker and Catherine Tumber.
        p.   cm.
    Includes bibliographical references and index.
    ISBN 0-8070-1056-1 (cloth : alk. paper)
        1. Christian life—Baptist authors.   2. Experience (Religion).
3. Race relations—Religious aspects—Christianity.   4. Meditations.
I. Fluker, Walter E., 1951–   .   II. Tumber, Catherine.   III. Title.
BX6495.T53A25   1998
277.3'082—DC21   97-49410

LONGWOOD COLLEGE LIBRARY
FARMVILLE, VIRGINIA 23901

To

the Graceful Memory of

SUE BAILEY THURMAN

"Ring Out Wild Bells . . ."

IT IS A STRANGE FREEDOM to be adrift in the world of men without a sense of anchor anywhere. Always there is the need of mooring, the need for the firm grip on something that is rooted and will not give. The urge to be accountable to someone, to know that beyond the individual himself there is an answer that must be given, cannot be denied. The deed a man performs must be weighed in a balance held by another's hand. The very spirit of a man tends to panic from the desolation of going nameless up and down the streets of other minds where no salutation greets and no friendly recognition makes secure. It is a strange freedom to be adrift in the world of men.

Always a way must be found for bringing into one's solitary place the settled look from another's face, for getting the quiet sanction of another's grace to undergird the meaning of the self. To be ignored, to be passed over as of no account and of no meaning, is to be made into a faceless thing, not a man. It is better to be the complete victim of an anger unrestrained and a wrath which knows no bounds, to be torn asunder without mercy or battered to a pulp by angry violence, than to be passed over as if one were not. Here at least one is dealt with, encountered, vanquished or overwhelmed – but not ignored. It is a strange freedom to go nameless up and down the streets of other minds where no salutation greets and no sign is given to mark the place one calls one's own.

The name marks the claim a man stakes against the world; it is the private banner under which he moves which is his right whatever else betides. The name is a man's watermark above which the tides can never rise. It is the thing he holds that keeps him in the way when every light has failed and every marker has been destroyed. It is the rallying point around which a man gathers all that he means by himself. It is his announcement to life that he is present and accounted for in all his parts. To be made anonymous and to give to it the acquiescence of the heart is to live without life, and for such a one, even death is no dying.

To be known, to be called by one's name, is to find one's place and hold it against all the hordes of hell. This is to *know* one's value, for one's self alone. It is to honor an act as one's very own, it is to live a life that is one's very own, it is to bow before an altar that is one's very own, it is to worship a God who is one's very own.

It is a strange freedom to be adrift in the world of men, to act with no accounting, to go nameless up and down the streets of other minds where no salutation greets and no sign is given to mark the place one calls one's own.   — HOWARD THURMAN, from
The Inward Journey

CONTENTS

FOREWORD

SAINTS OUGHT TO BE HARD TO LOCATE. Their saintliness keeps them from being stained by the muck of particular places; dust should not fall on them, nor mud cling to them. Yet we find that the deep ones, the saintly saints, did indeed have sleeves rolled up and calluses on their hands, reaching out to beggars and kings alike. Howard Thurman would qualify for their ranks, would he not have been too embarrassed by our nominating him for such company.

As for mystics, in whose company Thurman is consistently and reflexively located, but where he is never confined, we have to ask how to "locate" them? Mystics might be dusty and muddied by their surroundings in caves or abbeys, but it would not be noticed because they are closed up in hermitages or inaccessible in their silences. Why locate them? Because for all their search for the *unum* – for participation and absorption in the One, the Whole, or God-life – they tend to use the raw material of particular traditions. They not only partly transcend these traditions but rework them into idiosyncratic visions that, when they appear to be valid at all, turn out to be universal in grasp. We speak of Buddhist or even Japanese Buddhist mysticism, of Italian or Tibetan mysticism. We might locate mystics in time—medieval or modern—or in ecclesial slots, as in Catholic or Protestant or Orthodox mysticism. So we busy ourselves locating and placing Thurman.

Yet we find it as hard to squeeze him into local, temporal, or ecclesial categories as we find it hard to dislocate him from the places and traditions on which he drew in his preaching, writing, and influencing. Is he perhaps, in the tradition of saints, Howard of San Francisco, of Boston, of the United Nations? It is important to ponder these kinds of questions if we want to get some sort of handle, find some sort of frame, with which to grasp this extraordinary figure.

Catherine Tumber and Walter Earl Fluker, in their important introductory essay are of considerable help (don't skip it in haste to get to the vital words they have transcribed and edited from Thurman). Their biographical sketch is studded with proper nouns, signals of places Thurman worked or visited in his lifelong quest to take experience – note the word in the subtitle of this book – and move it from the particular toward the universal.

He drew, more than the African-American exclusivists of a generation ago acknowledged, on the black church tradition and the experience of suffering and hope that that tradition embodied, and it shows.

Thurman also drew on the Quaker tradition, which at times he seems to have stumbled upon and at other times looks like such a natural fit that he seemed predestined to have been found by it.

He drew on the nonviolent tradition of Gandhian India, a tradition he chose to encounter as an experience and not merely to read about or wish and claim to be influenced by.

He drew on the depths of the Christian tradition. But wherever he was and whatever it was upon which he drew, he was a mystic with a love of the concrete, the particular, the empirical, the experiential. Note the subtitle's word "experience" once more.

The editors take pains to rescue Thurman from evaporation in New Age spirituality, where good intentions often lead people, and good intentions gone astray can mislead them into vapor. In that crowd, which confuses the soul-search of the sort Thurman undertook with gaseous and self-invented spirituality that is easily marketable and consumable, he lasts only momentarily and has only superficial ties and influences. He is too demanding, too historically rooted, too Jesus-centered to remain the guru of choice through the years.

What is the nature of Thurman's spirituality? Above all, it is "moored," as opposed to "unmoored." That is, Thurman's spirituality offers an anchor, a harbor from which one departs for the high seas and to which one returns, changed. Thurman visited many ports, spiritually, but he is safely at home in the one that gives him access to the figure and scope of Jesus of Nazareth.

Thurman's is also a "prophetic" spirituality, as opposed to the self-preoccupied, almost narcissistic variety found in too many of the volumes sold in the mega-book marts. Prophetic spirituality is of the sort that is realized in movements and actions that inconvenience enemies of the good in the human city. Thurman's is definitely of the prophetic sort.

Fortunately, his mooring was not at such a small pier in such a narrow harbor that he cannot be found beyond it. Fortunately, his prophetic spirituality does not shame or defeat us even as it challenges and inspires us. Again, the editors are helpful here. One can read between their lines some impatience with those who want to push him back into battle lines where racial "integrationists" and "separatists" encountered and dismissed each other. One also senses the editors' impatience with those who want to show that Thurman was irrelevant to the struggle for racial justice on one hand, or those who, on the other hand, want to rewrite him into a place in the front lines of the Civil Rights movement's activist ranks. Times have changed, and framing the debate over locating Thurman in older contexts is not as productive as is the effort to take him from his time and place and apply his ideas to our own.

That is where this book comes in, because more than anything we have seen—maybe even more than some of his own discursive books—we get Thurman in the mixture of passion and reflection that he brought to the pulpit and the rostrum. Yes, one can get some of that immediately from taped sermons and televised interviews. But one wants to do some underlining and annotating, cross-referring and rereading, to let Thurman sink in. What becomes apparent in such an exercise is that he lives on these pages, as one who informs "religious experience" and "public life" alike. In addressing the *unum* and in searching for the American soul, he is likely to do once more what he so often did to hearers and readers in the past: reach *their* souls in astonishingly fresh ways.

Martin E. Marty
Chicago, Illinois

Editorial Policy Statement

HOWARD THURMAN BEGAN a prolific career of journal publishing and public speaking when he was a student at Morehouse College in the early 1920s. However, he did not begin publishing books until 1949, when he brought out *Jesus and the Disinherited.* In the same year, he also initiated the practice of audiotaping his sermons and other public presentations; much of this taped material eventually made its way into his books, some of it did not. Walter Fluker and Catherine Tumber have collected this audiotaped, unpublished, and obscurely published material, together with Thurman's correspondence, and are editing selected documents for publication in a three-volume documentary edition entitled *The Sound of the Genuine: The Papers of Howard Thurman* (South Carolina University Press). The editors drew from the 58,000-record database created for this larger project to select the pieces that appear in *A Strange Freedom.*

The documents selected for publication here represent what the editors regard as the best of Howard Thurman's public writings and recorded oral statements. The volume consists of chapters excerpted from Thurman's books, supplemented by articles that warrant republication and two transcriptions of audiotaped lectures. With this volume, the editors have brought together for the first time a representative sample that spans the course of Thurman's entire career and covers the defining features of his thought. The editors also have tried to balance the qualities of freshness of expression against maturity of thought and to provide examples of Thurman's written and oral styles before various audiences.

Because this collection draws from a variety of sources – books, journals, archives – editorial procedure has varied slightly with each venue. The editors have taken the liberty of regularizing minor editorial discrepencies that appeared in the originals to ensure an undistracting presentation of Thurman's words. They also have silently corrected typographical errors or inconsistencies of usage within a given text (e.g., "He" and "he" to refer to Jesus Christ), on those rare occasions when they have been encountered. Otherwise, the texts presented here have been transcribed faithfully from the originals.

Howard Thurman, like many preachers and other public figures working under the press of time, had the habit – exasperating for editors working long after the fact – of frequently quoting sources without providing citations. His literary sources were also often obscure. The editors have made considerable effort to trace all of Thurman's quoted sources. But they have left quotations uncited where the obscurity of the source, combined with its relative insignificance for understanding the context of Thurman's meaning, did not warrant searching beyond standard reference works. Biblical citations are included and explained only if Thurman's meaning is unclear.

Thurman did not use inclusive language with regard to gender, and to preserve the lyrical flow of his prose, his words have not been altered.

Introduction

The fact that the first twenty-five years of my life were spent in Florida and in Georgia has left deep scars in my spirit and has rendered me terribly sensitive to the churning abyss separating white from black. Living outside of the region, I am aware of the national span of racial prejudice and the virus of segregation that undermines the vitality of American life. Nevertheless, a strange necessity has been laid upon me to devote my life to the central concern that transcends the walls that divide and would achieve in literal fact what is experienced as literal truth: human life is one and all men are members one of another. And this insight is spiritual and it is the hard core of religious experience. [1]

IN A SPEECH GIVEN at the University of Redlands in 1976, Howard Thurman observed that America was in search of its soul. As the nation celebrated its bicentennial in the aftermath of the Vietnam War and Watergate debacles and the Civil Rights movement's decline, Thurman called for a renewal of its spiritual foundations. In considering his theme, Thurman chose not to dwell on equality of rights or freedom of self-expression, which by the mid-seventies were already showing signs of degeneration into identity politics and the therapeutic quest for "empowerment." Instead, he pointed to Christian concepts of moral freedom and spiritual equality as the ethical wellsprings of a vibrant democratic culture. In this respect he remained more true to the original moral genius of American democracy than had those who viewed the ideals enshrined in the Declaration of Independence and the Constitution in strictly legal and rationalist terms. Moreover, Thurman held that America's search for its soul was also a search for a usable past. For Thurman, a national rebirth that achieved the highest ethical ideals of equality and freedom would come about only through a relentless retrieval of our past and a bold daring to re-appropriate it for the present. American history, he believed, was not simply the monolithic past of the "Founding Fathers," but a rich amalgam of many voices and cultural traditions, each contributing its parcel to the national character. Thurman himself drew deeply from the African-American Christian tradition in which he was reared.

Howard Thurman's response to the spiritual and moral climate of America twenty years ago resonates with the crisis of national character that is today dramatically playing out at all levels of society. Our purpose in assembling this collection of his published and unpublished writings is to present Thurman as a public intellectual who influenced some of the most important social justice movements of the mid-twentieth century, and whose work continues to reward careful scrutiny. Thurman's meditative prose and poetry have received deserved recognition, but arguably at the expense of his focused critique of culture which, we believe, merits equal attention. Here, we seek to flesh out the limited caricature of Thurman as a detached and evasive mystic. We have therefore selected documents for this volume that illustrate Thurman's prophetic denunciation of social practices that militate against a vigorous democracy and his deep commitment to character, civility, and community in American life. Three critical angles of vision introduce the reader to the definitive elements of Thurman's thought and we have organized the selections presented here accordingly: Finding God in Private Life, Religious Experience and Ethical Life, and "Community and the Will of God" – the title of one of Thurman's lecture series. We have also included a final section under the heading, Meditations for "Apostles of Sensitiveness." It is our hope that this final section will, in Thurman's words, meet "the need for materials of refreshment, challenge and renewal for those who [are] intent upon establishing islands of fellowship in a sea of racial, religious, and national tensions."² In making our selections, we have paid particular attention to Thurman's formative experiences as African-American intellectual and pastor, his serious philosophical engagement with liberal modernity, and his deep, abiding faith in the possibility of a democratic republic that takes seriously the plight of what he often called, "the disinherited." It is our hope that *A Strange Freedom* will inspire in its readers a renewed commitment to democratic community and a spiritually self-disciplined love of the world.

I

In order to grasp the essentials of Thurman's theological and ethical thought one must understand the ways that he made of his own long and varied life what he called a "for instance" of his ideas. Thurman was born in Daytona, Florida, on November 18, 1899 to a family mired in the frustrations of the working poor. Finding in the protective fold of his neighborhood and in nature his "windbreak against existence," Thurman showed early signs of mystical engagement with the world for which he would later become famous. Reared by his beloved Grandma Nancy, a former slave, young Thurman regularly read the Bible aloud to her as a child. From her he learned not only of the trials of slavery, but also of the slaves' deep religious faith, which profoundly shaped his later vision of the transformative promise of African-American Christianity. Grandma Nancy's intellectual and spiritual tutelage helped to mold young Thurman's natural gifts and prepared him to take seriously his formal education. Facing nearly insuperable financial obstacles, Thurman managed to break through the formal barriers that prevented Daytona's black children from reaching high school and attended Florida Baptist Academy in Jacksonville from 1915 to 1919. In 1923, he completed his undergraduate education in economics and government at Morehouse College, where he won nearly every available literary prize, purportedly read every book in its library, and graduated as valedictorian of his class. Thurman had spent the summer of 1922 studying philosophy in residence at Columbia University, where he attended classes with white students for the first time. But it wasn't until 1923, when Thurman filled one of two placements allotted to black students at Rochester Theological Seminary, that he began to explore the possibilities of interracial communion. At first he was panicked by the prospect of being thrown from an all-black into an all-white environment. But by his second year Thurman and two white classmates had arranged to rent an on-campus suite together, bypassing school strictures against interracial living. At Rochester, the intellectual center of the Social Gospel, Thurman began to forge the outlines of a distinctive interracial ministry and engaged in formal studies of the Bible, liberal theology, and comparative religion. In 1926, he earned a Bachelor of Divinity degree having served as student government president and, again, graduating as valedictorian of his class.

Instead of pursuing a doctorate, as many of his teachers urged him to do, Thurman decided to delve into the ministry he had started as a seminarian with single-minded purpose, serving his first pastorate in Oberlin, Ohio. As a youth movement leader prominent in YMCA circles in the mid- to late 1920s, he became the most articulate and visible theological translator of the youthful rebellion of that period. A regular on the "Y" lecture circuit during the height of segregation, he was the student movement's most popular speaker before interracial audiences. With his close friends Mordecai Wyatt Johnson, Benjamin Mays, William Stewart Nelson, and Frank T. Wilson, Thurman helped pioneer the introduction of theological education at black colleges and universities, and worked to wrest control of black seminary training from white leadership. In the late 1920s, he was appointed the first African-American board member of the pacifist Fellowship of Reconciliation (FOR). By the end of the twenties, Thurman had emerged as a leading voice on the changing ministry of the Black Church.

Between 1928 and 1932, Thurman returned to the South to serve as Professor of Religion and Director of Religious Life at Morehouse and Spelman Colleges and to enable his mortally ill first wife, Kate Kelly Thurman, to be close to her family. She succumbed to her illness in 1930. During this deeply painful period of his life he spent the spring of 1929 studying at Haverford College under the Quaker mystic Rufus Jones from whom he acquired a critical method for affirming the truths found in mystical experience without negating the claims of the social world. In 1932, Thurman married international Christian student movement leader, musician, and poet Susie Bailey, who became his "companion at the gate" for the rest of his life. In the same year he was appointed chairman of the Committee on Religious Life and professor of Christian Theology at Howard University. Four years later he was appointed the first dean of Howard University's Rankin Chapel. During these years, as the New Deal unfolded and the United States prepared to enter World War II, Washington, D.C., was the Civil Rights movement's center of gravity. Thurman worked quietly with many of the early movement's leading figures, including Mary McLeod Bethune, Nannie Burroughs, and A. Philip Randolph. He was also associated with Howard University intellectuals Abram Harris, Mordecai Wyatt Johnson, Alain Locke, and E. Franklin Frazier, as well as with Atlanta-based W. E. B. Du Bois, who acted as advisors to the movement.

In 1943 A. J. Muste, longtime colleague and National Secretary of FOR, invited Thurman to recommend a student to help establish and copastor the Church for the Fellowship of All Peoples in San Francisco – the first multiracial, intercultural church in the United States. With African Americans migrating to San Francisco to work in the defense industry while Japanese Americans were being forced into federal internment camps, the city was simmering with racial tension and seemed to require a new vision of ministry. To Muste's surprise, Thurman resigned his tenured position at Howard University and volunteered himself to assume the copastorate of this new and creative venture in interracial and interreligious fellowship, a position he held from 1944 to 1953. Through the establishment of the Church for the Fellowship of All Peoples, Thurman brought together people of different faiths, races, and classes in acts of common worship and fellowship. Fellowship Church is now a national historic landmark, recognized for its ecclesiological experimentation and pioneering social vision.

Thurman's ministry at Fellowship Church had been deeply influenced by his leadership between 1935 and 1936 of the first all black American delegation to make a Christian youth movement "pilgrimage of friendship" to India, Ceylon, and Burma. On this voyage he had met Mohandas K. Gandhi. By all accounts, Thurman's conversation with Gandhi represented the first formal exchange between an African-American religious leader and the great Indian prophet of nonviolent revolution. An outspoken critic of traditional Christianity, Gandhi believed that western interpretations of Christianity contributed to racial, economic, and sexual discrimination and led to segregation of the world's peoples. In formulating his response to Gandhi's critique of Christianity, Thurman integrated the Gandhian principles of unity and nonviolent social change into his own Christian pacifism and mysticism.

The Gandhian ideas that took shape in the years just before and during Thurman's tenure at Fellowship Church received a larger audience through the publication of his most famous book, *Jesus and the Disinherited* (1949), which deeply influenced leaders of the Civil Rights struggle in the 1950s. Exploring the "anatomy" of fear, hate, and deception to which the oppressed can so easily fall prey, Thurman here articulated the vision of spiritual discipline that later informed the intellectual and moral basis of the black freedom movement in the South. As a FOR board member, he urged the selection of his former student James Farmer to chair FOR's Interracial Committee and encouraged Farmer to establish the separate organization, the Congress of Racial Equality (CORE), upon whose board he also sat. He also sat on the board of the National Association for the Advancement of Colored People (NAACP). Thurman regularly advised leaders of these organizations such as Martin Luther King, Jr., Jesse Jackson, Vernon Jordan, James Farmer, Whitney Young, and Bayard Rustin about matters both political and spiritual, always preferring quiet pastoral counsel and intellectual guidance to political visibility.

The years at Fellowship Church also prepared Thurman for what was to be another daring adventure in his search for "common ground." In 1953, at the invitation of President Harold Case, Thurman resigned as minister-in-residence of Fellowship Church to become the dean of Marsh Chapel at Boston University and professor of Spiritual Disciplines and Resources in the School of Theology. This pioneering move was not without great inner struggle and deliberation, but Thurman marveled at the opportunity to translate the idea of an inclusive fellowship – which he had successfully demonstrated in San Francisco – to a large university setting, where there was potential for greater outreach and dissemination. He also felt that the move had significant social implications for he would be the first black man to hold such a position in a white university setting. In a short time, his popularity reached far beyond the university. Thurman's services attracted students and faculty not only from the university and surrounding schools, but from the greater Boston community as well. Before long he was heard over the university radio station, WBUR, and became a regular contributor to a local television series entitled *We Believe*. Thurman's Marsh Chapel ministry confirmed his belief in the power of religious experience to overcome the religious, cultural, class, and racial barriers that militate against community. Several years before his formal retirement from Marsh Chapel in 1965, Thurman therefore launched what he referred to as his "wider ministry." He and his wife, Sue Bailey Thurman, took two trips around the world. They traveled to Nigeria where he served as visiting lecturer in philosophy and religion at the University of Ibadan. They also journeyed to Israel, Japan, the Philippines, Egypt, and Hawaii. These trips abroad, taken during the peak of the cold war, had a profound effect on Thurman's international perspective and his view of the United States' responsibility as a leader among nations.

Thurman's latter years were devoted to the "wider ministry" of the Howard Thurman Educational Trust, which he founded in San Francisco in 1965. Under Thurman's direction, the Trust was a charitable and eleemosynary foundation that provided a channel for the enlistment and disbursal of funds in a carefully planned program of support for religious, charitable, scientific, literary, and educational programs. The Thurman Trust also housed Thurman's private library and more than 800 tapes of meditations, sermons, addresses, lectures, and discussions which represented over forty years of his spiritual pilgrimage toward community. Much of this material was duplicated and made available through Howard Thurman Listening Rooms established throughout the United States and in seventeen countries. As this volume goes to press, the Howard Thurman Educational Trust is being transferred to Morehouse College, Thurman's distinguished alma mater, where it will be nurtured and reconfigured for future work.

The Trust marked Thurman's last formal endeavor to create a place where his dream of community could be realized. After a long illness, he died at his home in San Francisco during the early morning hours of April 10, 1981. At a posthumous public tribute to Thurman, Jesse Jackson spoke for a host of civil rights activists, pacifists, and black educational and clerical leaders when he proclaimed Thurman a "teacher of teachers, a leader of leaders, a preacher of preachers." His vision of a "friendly world underneath friendly skies" continues in his rich legacy of the written and oral word.

II

W. E. B. Du Bois once remarked, "[W]hat Howard Thurman really believes I have never been able to find out." Du Bois's trouble with Thurman may not have been with what he really believed, but rather, with his understanding of the relation between religion and politics, which hardly conformed to what many activist scholars wanted and expected to hear.[3] In today's postmodern intellectual climate, Howard Thurman is, if anything, an even more enigmatic figure. Many students of African-American history view him as a vague mystic who had abandoned the communal solidarity and Christocentrism of the Black Church. Others regard him as an integrationist who did not grasp the realities of institutional power and cultural estrangement that have historically marked American race relations. Likewise, Thurman is too readily embraced by the denizens of New Age spirituality. They are attracted to his intercultural and liturgical experimentation, his pacifism, and, of course, his mysticism, often without reckoning with the historical foundations and tragic dimensions of his thought, or its relationship to politics.

    Few committed to the project of democratic renewal are even aware of Thurman's theocentric cultural criticism as a rich and lively resource for their work. This oversight reflects the diminished fund of moral imagination, political will, and intellectual honesty wrought by the liberal left's dubious alignment with postmodern criticism over the past thirty years. While the so-called culture wars have proceeded apace, Thurman's subtle voice has, as it were, dispersed into thin air. As critics from Harold Cruse to Christopher Lasch to Cornel West have argued, twentieth-century

American intellectuals, both black and white, have been historically am-
bivalent about their role and responsibilities as intellectuals. Setting great
store by the state, modern technology, and mass politics, they floundered
when these inventions of modernity no longer served as adversarial tools.
As intellectuals have since retreated into the academy to war over "essen-
tialism" and "social constructivism," the corporate market has proceeded
uninhibited, assuming unprecedented global proportions and creating
greater class stratification. Today the crisis in black intellectual leadership is particularly painful. The divisions it reflects – between those
with wealth and fame and those in poverty, between liberals and neo-
conservatives, and especially between communitarian black nationalists
and integrationists – throw into bold relief the ethical flummoxing of
American social criticism in general, yet the consequences for impover-
ished inner-city communities are so acutely lethal.[4]

Howard Thurman never shirked from his identity or responsibilities as
an intellectual. Moreoever, he was arguably the most thoroughgoing integrationist of his generation, a pastor who brought the integration ideal
right into the institutional heart of black and white society: the church
worship service. Yet ironically, Thurman has as much wisdom to impart to
a serious black nationalism now as he did to the integrationist goals of the
mid-century Civil Rights movement. Indeed, Thurman's approach may
help us cut through the many impasses that place our democratic experiment in jeopardy. Above all, Thurman was insistent that black Americans
claim their American heritage. Though he was sympathetic to black nationalists' longing for self-determined community, Thurman was impa-
tient with efforts to dispense with what he regarded as the grandest experiment in democracy in the history of the world. His reasons for holding so
fiercely to American democratic ideals were rooted in his theological understanding of community. For Thurman, the search for common ground
or "community," which he equated (somewhat ambiguously) with "wholeness" and "harmony," was grounded in the moral order of a universe designed by a loving Creator. Democracy was, in Thurman's view, the greatest and yet the most demanding political effort to find common ground in
human history, and – beyond the ancient Greeks, Locke or Rousseau – Jesus of Nazareth provided essential spiritual resources for democracy's

moral foundations. The religion of Jesus rightly understood, Thurman believed, renders every individual soul sacred and thus endows each human personality with tremendous moral responsibility rooted in obligation to God. Jesus thus teaches us to place equal value on the power of loving wholeness and the truth that our search for common ground is an inherent good that must abide in the face of inevitable disappointment. Human suffering is a part of God's mind "coming to itself," according to Thurman, and is experienced when the longing for community, or "wholeness and harmony," encounters the limits – physical and moral – that God has also woven into the texture of human life. Thurman does not offer a view of redemptive suffering per se, but regards suffering as an occasion to experience the magnitude of God. And suffering, along with other glimpses we have of God's intent both within and outside of ourselves, refortifies us in our search for God. Another way of putting it is that democratic culture approximates both the best means and the best end in the human quest for God.

But God is present even when democracy is not, and here Jesus had a word of peculiar significance for the disinherited. Thurman drew heavily on moral traditions embedded in African-American Christianity to argue not only for the fundamental reality of the beloved community, but for equality and freedom as the highest ethical ideals. By equality, he had in mind his Grandma Nancy's loving admonition that he was not a "nigger," a taunt constantly hurled at young Thurman by hostile whites in the segregated south, but "a child of God." This countervailing childhood reminder that he was equal to his self-appointed social superiors in the eyes of God held him steady. If anything, in youth he treated white people indifferently, and cast them outside the scope of his "magnetic field of morality."[5] It was later in life, when he found himself immersed in northern white society, that Thurman came to understand freedom as the freedom to choose not only the character of one's actions, but the emotional and spiritual quality of one's *reactions*. The three "hounds of hell" that dog those "with their backs against the wall" – fear, hate, and deception – must be mastered, Thurman insisted, and prevented from ripping out the heart of self-respect. It was the *will* to segregation – not necessarily separation itself – that kept moral poisons alive on both sides of the racial "wall."

Thurman believed in integration not only because he was convinced that the historical moment demanded it, but because he believed so deeply in spiritual discipline against resentment – which was for him the most valuable end in any case. Cultural transformation – which was promoted in his own day by the spiritual disciplines associated with integration – must accompany political and legal change, Thurman maintained, if institutional rearrangements were to have any depth and longevity.

III

The current crisis in black leadership is made all the more pressing by the economic and moral anarchy imperiling inner-city communities. But both have roots in the ethical impoverishment of the entire nation as it nears the end of the "American Century" leading the world into a new phase of global corporate expansion. Thurman's work stands as a critical resource for the cultivation of ethical practices at this historic juncture. Thurman offers at least three ways in which we might begin to think about closing the divides that threaten to engulf us, drawing not only from African-American Christianity, but from mystical and "traditional" liberal protestant traditions as well. First of all, his ethical theory was rooted in the mystical experience of unity – the profoundly moving, if fleeting, "creative encounter" with the realization that all life is one. As religious intellectual and pastor, Thurman sought, quite simply, to breathe new life into the essential integrity of religion itself as a form of knowledge. This aspect of Thurman's thought and ministry looms so large that it is easy to miss. By the time he was a seminarian in the mid-twenties, the churches, both black and white, had been overtaken with social gospel humanitarianism, expensive programs of massive church building, or in response, with a growing dependence on otherworldly salvation schemes. Churchgoers were losing touch with the widespread moral and aesthetic derailment taking place around them. The youthful rebellion, the rampant materialism of mass consumer culture, the growing spiritual appeal of secular political ideologies were all signs of the evaporation of an authentically reliable religious life. Thurman committed himself to restoring to those who would walk with him the essential religious core of human experience.

But he did more than this. The experience of mystical unity, he argued, made it possible to activate the Christian injunction to "put yourself in another's place." By this he did not mean that we should lose our identity in, or worse, project our own self-image onto others. Rather, mystical experience, he held, both strengthens and impels us to exercise the moral imagination to understand another human experience. If we know and love God, nothing human, however foreign or repugnant, should be utterly alien to us. Moreover, the moral essence of vital religious experience prepares those most engaged in sustaining democracy with the inner core not to yield uncritically either to conventional social pressures or to the cultural expectations often exerted by alternative social movements. In his later life, he made this self-revealing observation:

> I didn't have to wait for the revolution. I have never been in search for identity – and I think that [all] I've ever felt and worked on and believed in was founded in a kind of private, almost unconscious autonomy that did not seek vindication in my environment because it was in me.[6]

Undoubtedly, Thurman would have had no truck with the epistemological radicalism prevalent in our own day. In the tradition of Emerson, Thurman sought to preserve and transmit to future generations the democratic habits of a spiritually grounded self-reliance.

A second contribution Thurman's work makes to a religiously inspired and ethically grounded public life assigns an important, yet circumscribed role for ministry and the church. Thurman was steadfast in his insistence that the church not become a vehicle for a particular socioeconomic ideology. The social mission of the church was that of an exemplar of community and to that end, he argued, the church must not be exclusive. But it must serve primarily as a resource for those engaged in the creation of a loving and just society – those he often called "apostles of sensitiveness." As he said of Fellowship Church,

> [I]t was important that individuals who are in the thick of the struggle for social change would be able to find renewal and fresh courage in the spiritual resources of the church. There must be provided a place, a moment, when a per-

son could declare, "I choose!" . . . [T]he true genius of the church was revealed
by what it symbolized as a beachhead in society in terms of community, and as
an inspiration to the solitary individual to put his weight on the side of a society
in which no person need be afraid.[7]

Thurman's pastoral ministry, in other words, extended beyond the public
sphere to personal encounters with individuals who found in his presence
a cove to experience "the literal truth of God." This was part of the ministry performed for so many who had to deal with the harsh and often brutal
realities of living in a society that rendered them either invisible or the objects of scorn. This dimension of Howard Thurman was one of the peculiar graces of the man. Somehow, he was able to dig deep into the inner re-
cesses of one's being, in the places which for others seemed unreachable,
and to find the hidden treasures of the soul – the lost dreams wandering
about as forsaken ghosts in the wastelands of the heart, the shattered
hopes that had ricocheted off the hard realities of living and being in the
world, the flickering visions of yesteryear whose white heat had once irra-
diated glowing ideals and made living an adventure – this, too, is part of
the vibrant legacy that he bequeaths to us. For the quiet counsel and reflection he offered to Martin Luther King, Jr., Vernon Johns, James
Farmer, Whitney Young, Vernon Jordan, Jesse Jackson, Otis Moss, and a
host of others passing through the "dark night of the soul" in the thick of
social struggle, Thurman was widely recognized as the pastoral leader of
the Civil Rights movement. In the understated words of his late wife, Sue
Bailey Thurman, "he helped to move the stumps out of the way for so
many people."[8]

The third contribution Thurman makes to a renewed spiritual basis for
ethical public life is a deep appreciation of the world's faith traditions.
Thurman was fond of saying, "What is true in any religion is in the religion
because it is true; it is not true because it is in the religion."[9] But Thurman
did not herald a vague syncretic "spirituality." On the contrary, he was an
eloquent defender of the "religion of Jesus" as a vibrant religious philosophy that captured the funded insights of the world's historic spiritual
quest. Nonetheless, he could not support the tactics of overseas Christian
missionaries, who in his day sought to eviscerate the native cultures that

gave rise to the world's great religious traditions. Thurman's sustained and eloquent religious argument for democracy, it must be said with emphasis, did not extend to western democracies' historic alliance with imperialism. It was no coincidence that the questions that informed his pastorate of Fellowship Church grew out of his criticism of western cultural imperialism:

> Is the worship of God the central and most significant act of the human spirit? Is it really true that in the presence of God there is neither male nor female, child nor adult, rich nor poor, nor any classification by which humankind defines itself in categories, however meaningful? Is it only in the religious experience that the individual discovers what, ultimately, she or he amounts to?[10]

At stake for Thurman in these questions were not simply the economic, political, and social forces that mitigate the life chances of the disinherited. Rather, his critique struck at the religious nucleus of a culture which nurtures and sustains inequality. Thurman believed that the Jesus of Eurowestern interpretation carries fundamental presuppositions about the nature of the right, the good, and the beautiful.[11] As a result, when Jesus is viewed as a religious object, his worship becomes a tool of divisiveness and oppression and lays the ground for a principle of exclusiveness which impedes the possibility of intercultural fellowship. International peace, Thurman contended in a century engulfed in both hot and cold war, genocide, and the terror of nuclear weapons, could come about only through the exercise of moral imagination required to respect and understand the religious truths embodied in cultures around the world.

IV

Our failure to uphold the religiously based ethical ideals of American democracy, and to insist on their adherence both personally and publicly, has played out most tragically in the nihilism of the young, particularly in the violent youth culture embraced by so many inner-city children and young adults. The horrific death, crime, and imprisonment statistics among young black men, which should not have to be recounted here, stand as testimony to the urgency of Thurman's many-layered message. Thurman spent most of his career in student ministry in which he sought to ground the young in the religious sources of a rich inner life to enable them to develop their natural gifts and to cultivate responsible and historically appropriate action in the world. If we have the courage to reckon with Thurman's subtle challenges, we might have the means to cultivate character, civility, and community – so fragile, yet so pivotal to a vital democracy – in ourselves and in our children.

Character, civility, and community, from Thurman's point of view, have no meaning without an appreciation of human limits. For Thurman, character rests on one's inner moral authority and integrity, which are garnered from the tragic and often unbearable exigencies of life. In the crucible of suffering one experiences the opportunity to choose between fate and destiny. Fate – the natural and social circumstances shaped by the keepers of power – is a given. But destiny is what one does with his or her fate. In the throes of suffering and evil, we are called to cultivate spiritually self-disciplined habits and practices, which enable us to courageously exercise moral and practical choices as we make our way through the world. Civility, for Thurman, arises out of the fundamentally personal and individual experience of one's encounter with God. To experience the sacred in private girds us to go into the public world with humility, gratitude, and an "abiding enthusiasm." Our rights and our freedom to express ourselves, in other words, are always circumscribed by the historical locations in which we find ourselves. We are "time-binders and space-binders," as Thurman was fond of quoting from one of his favorite prose poems. Another way of putting the point, as he did in his eulogy to Civil Rights leader Whitney Young, "The time and place of a man's life on earth is the time and the place of his body, but the meaning or significance of his life is as far reaching and redemptive as his gifts, his dedication, his response to the demands of his times, the total commitment of his powers can make it."[12] Through the agency of morally-anchored character and transformative acts of civility we are enabled and required to engage in the creation of beloved community. The "world" – God's world – includes the public arena of human action in which we seek harmony, excellence, and beauty with the hopeful assurance that our own little lives, with all their frustrations and disappointments, do not exhaust the possibilities of God's purposes. The growing edge of human possibility, for him was at once God's possibility and the ground of hope.

V

The growing edge, the ground of a hopeful future, was the spiritual well-spring of Howard Thurman's intellectual vision of human community and American democratic renewal. In the midst of a confused and fragmented narrative about the meaning of American character and destiny, he challenged citizens to learn the miracle of social patience and the wisdom of listening to what he called "the sound of the genuine" for new insights into the possibility of our continued existence in this nation and on this planet. For him this meant a return to the hard work of moral imagination and spiritual discipline so that a new center of common consciousness might emerge – that indeed a new word might be spoken. The modern Civil Rights movement, for him, exemplified what is possible in a land where a unique gathering of all races, ethnicities, religions, and worldviews are present at one place and one time. For one swirling historical moment, however brief and anxious, Thurman felt that a significant minority listened to the sound of the genuine in the grandiloquence of the event – in an imaginative public language filled with hope and possibility. The decline of the Civil Rights movement, for Thurman, was but "a time of bivouac on a promontory" overlooking a long and difficult future for the Western world. But in that movement he saw the precursor to a larger ecumenical movement which combined the distilled wisdom of ancient prophets with the fresh inclinations of young ambassadors in search of a city where the builder and maker was God. Many of these new voices, he believed, would come from beyond the culturally constrained moral syntax of Western Christianity. In fact, he felt that a new religious and public narrative was in the making – and his only regret was that he might not be around to witness it.[13]

What might this new public language sound like? If Thurman was correct, then certainly it will bear some affinity to the biblical narrative from which he drew his own imaginative public language. Our challenge will be to look beyond the entrenchments of religion, race, class, and gender, to see the face of others who call our attention to common ground and acts of moral imagination. For this time, a fresh and vibrant articulation of hope in human agency is needed to furnish answers that proceed from encounter with a truth that moves at levels undisguised and uninhibited by religious formulae and dogma.

Darrell Fasching has appropriately described Howard Thurman as "the holy man for the coming millennium." Fasching has not been alone in his recognition of Howard Thurman's peculiar genius and many, only partially realized, contributions to the religious and public life of twentieth-century America. Long heralded as a stellar exemplar of American religious leadership, a theoretician of nonviolent direct action, and a cultivator of spiritual insight into the ethical dimensions of community, Thurman's steady insistence on the search for common ground between diverse cultures finds creative resonance at this critical impasse of American history.[14] The therapeutic and managerial discourses prevalent in the public square will not resolve the tensions of religion, race, class, and gender that have grown deeper and even more insidious with the increased concentration of corporate power. Nor will the often violent, hate-filled warrants for moral action found in what we used to call the Right and the Left deliver us from our contemporary moral quagmire. But Howard Thurman's gentle wisdom and clear analysis of how strange democratic freedom really is and what it requires of us may lead us to a religiously inspired public ethic that does not pay homage to greedy, grinning gods of postmodernity.

Catherine Tumber
Walter Earl Fluker

Rochester, New York

Section One

FINDING GOD IN PRIVATE LIFE

Meditation | *The Idol of Togetherness*

If thy soul is a stranger to thee, the whole world is unhomely.

THE FIGHT FOR THE PRIVATE LIFE is fierce and unyielding. Often it seems as if our times are in league with the enemy. There is little rhythm of alternation between the individual and the others. Land values are so high that breathing space around the places where we live is cut away. We flee from the crowded city to the quiet of the countryside. But the countryside becomes jammed with the sounds, the noises, the sights, the pressures which were left behind. Sometimes we escape into the city from the country.

Because of the disintegration of the mood of tenderness that has overtaken us, we falter in our understanding of one another. There is a certain kind of understanding abroad – it is understanding that invades, snoops, threatens, and makes afraid or embarrasses. The craftsmen of the public taste move in upon us, seeking to determine the kind of food we eat, the soap we use, the make of car we drive, and the best way to brush our teeth. What has become of the person, the private wish?

We have made an idol of togetherness. It is the watchword of our times, it is more and more the substitute for God. In the great huddle we are desolate, lonely, and afraid. Our shoulders touch but our hearts cry out for understanding without which there can be no life and no meaning. The Great Cause, even the Cause of Survival, is not enough! There must be found ever-creative ways that can ventilate the private soul without blowing it away, that can confirm and affirm the integrity of the person in the midst of the collective necessities of our times.

There is within reach of every man a defense against the Grand Invasion. He can seek deliberately to become intimately acquainted with himself. He can cultivate an enriching life with persons, enhancing the private meaning and the personal worth. He can grow in the experience of solitude, companioned by the minds and spirits who, as Pilgrims of the Lonely Road, have left logs of their journey. He can become at home, within, by locating in his own spirit the trysting place where he and his God may meet; for it is here that life becomes *private* without being *self-centered,* that the little purposes that cloy may be absorbed in the Big Purpose that structures and redefines, that the individual comes to himself, the wanderer is home, and the private life is saved for deliberate involvement.[15]

CO | *Barren or Fruitful? (1932)*

Thurman preached "Barren or Fruitful?" at Plymouth Congregational Church in Washington, D.C., just before assuming his teaching duties at Howard University in the fall of 1932.[16] *The sermon text is Jeremiah 17, in which the great prophet warns against basing self-respect on the good opinion of others and admonishes us to seek security in commitment to God. Thurman's encounter with black elite culture as a student and professor at Morehouse College, along with the challenge of preaching to spiritually and politically complacent audiences in the late 1920s may explain why this was one of Thurman's favorite biblical texts during the early period of his career. The prophetic denunciation of social elitism remained a consistent theme throughout his life.*

THERE ARE TWO remarkable pictures given us by the Prophet Jeremiah. With these two pictures as a background, I want each of you to think seriously about this question: To what do I appeal when I want to convince myself that I am somebody?

I

First – a curse on him who relies on man, who depends upon mere human aid. For he is like a desert scrub that never thrives; set in a salt solitary

23

place in the steppes – a striking picture! A certain kind of man likened unto a desert scrub – undeveloped and underdeveloped, undernourished and emaciated, stubby, and stunted, acting on the theory that to breathe is to live! What a character analysis!

He is thus, says Jeremiah, because he relies on man. He has a false sense of security. When such a man wants to convince himself that he is somebody, his appeal, most often, is to those things that are of temporary and passing significance.

I am putting the question quite personal[ly] this morning: In what do you find your security? I shall review, in outline, three of the more commonplace bases of appeal. You may supply others and out of your experience make a fuller rendering of the details of the three which I shall mention.

In the first place, there are those who appeal to family connections and social position. They are quite proud of family background and take keen sweet delight in pointing out the fact that the leaves of their family tree are always green. A friend of mine has written some lines depicting such a man –

> He was proud of descent
> For he came from one of
> The best families.
> But as a man, he was
> Worth exactly forty cents an hour.

It is a very desirable thing to come from a good healthy vigorous family stock. But in the last analysis Life is not interested in the accident of birth. Life does not care who your father was or how far back you can trace your mother's roots! What about you? Every man must stew in his own juice. If your basic security is found in your family connections, you are leaning on a broken stick. A desert scrub that never thrives!

There are others who appeal to their training, their education. Education is very useful and necessary. More often, a good education is a commodity that has a very definite exchange value. For instance, a doctor charges a fee for his services, unique to him because of specialized training. In other words a doctor rents his skill to the public, for which he receives varying degrees of economic security. Superficially viewed, this may seem to be a true basis of security.

Very often when a man's stock begins to go down or the ground is being cut away from beneath his self-respect, the fact that he is educated does give him a certain sense of security. There *is* something marvelously sustaining about genuine education. But a man who appeals to the fact that he is a college graduate or a professional school graduate in order to convince himself that he is somebody—well, such a man is sailing under false colors. Life does not ask you from what college do you come, or if you have been to college at all. It wants to know *basically* what you are and in what direction you are going. Very often in the most rigorous and elemental experiences of life the differences between men resulting from training and background melt away. And behold, where are they? He who thinks to the contrary is fooled—a desert scrub that never thrives!

And then there are those who appeal to the peculiar quality of their righteousness. They are "I thank God I am pure" people. Jesus dramatized this quality very effectually in His picture of the two men who went up into the temple to pray. One man said in substance: "O God, I thank Thee I am not as other men. I pay my vows. I attend all temple services. I give of my means to charity. I thank Thee God that it is with me as it is. I pause in my busy life to let Thee know how good I am."

In an obscure part of the temple another man prayed. He dared not lift his head above, but with deep contrition cried aloud, "Lord, Lord, have mercy on me, a sinner!"

The tragedy of a self-righteous man is that he has an ideal that he can live up to—he has a goal that he has reached already. He who turns to his self-righteousness for security is doomed to fundamental defeat. In utter amazement he will discover one day that his life is barren—a desert scrub that never thrives!

What a revealing experience it is to step aside and see yourself go by. Try it! It will certainly make you humble!

Is your life barren? When you are most yourself do you know yourself to be a "desert scrub," a spiritual[ly] undernourished and moral[ly] emaciated individual—narrow, selfish, puny-souled, bigoted, living under a false sense of security?

II

The second picture is most inspiring. The prophet pictures the man who depends on God, who has God for his confidence, as a tree planted beside a stream sending his roots down to the water. He has no fear of scorching heat, his leaves are always green. He goes on bearing fruit when all around him is barren and lives serene. In other words such a man looks out on life with quiet eyes!

Perhaps, in the last analysis the only thing to which a man may appeal for basic security is the high quality of his dedication and the supreme worth of that to which he is dedicated. If a man dedicates his life to the highest that he knows, that dedication at once gives to his life added worth and significance.

A man cannot dedicate himself to that which is outside of the realm of his experience at every point. I cannot conceive of that which does not have its roots within me. If you have no conception of the meaning of the word "fly," I could not explain the aeroplane to you. "If you have no thought of your own, those of other men will find nothing to which they can fasten themselves." So when a man dedicates himself to God, the Highest, the fact and the experience cannot be foreign to him originally but in some genuine sense it must be already present in him.

A man came to Jesus seeking help for his son. (Pathos is revealed in utter rawness when a strong man finds that his strength is powerless to help where his love dictates.) Jesus said to him, "It will be as you desire if you have faith." It was then that the man said, "I have faith – help Thou my lack of faith." *The consciousness of a lack of faith springs out of faith itself.* If I had no faith in God, I could not know that I had no faith in Him. When a man dedicates himself to God it means that that dedication springs out of a genuine God-consciousness.

Your fundamental security then is not family, training, piety or the like but rather the supreme quality of your dedication to the highest there is in life – God.

To say, "I affirm my faith in God with my total personality" is one of the supreme affirmations of the human spirit.

The real atheist is not necessarily the man who denies the existence of God; but rather the man who, day after day and week after week, subscribes to a faith in God with his lips while *acting* on the vital assumption that there is no God.

I have deep respect for the man who with great sincerity reaches the conclusion that life has no meaning for him. Full of years he might conclude, no God, no sin, no future life – nothing but the survival of the fittest and every man for himself. To him I can only say, "Such is not my experience." Such a man, however, is not an atheist in the sense that many church-goers are. "They honor Me with their lips but their hearts are far from Me." Acting every day as if there were no God while doing lip service to God.

Suppose we dare start today believing in God to the extent that wherever we went the Kingdom of God would be at hand. In a very short time the entire complexion of our city would be transformed!

There are three things that my faith in God teaches me about God. I shall mention these almost in outline. In the first place it teaches me that God *is*. Bear in mind ever, my friends, that faith is a way of knowing.

When Jesus prayed, all who heard Him were conscious that He was not talking to the air. When Jesus prayed He met Somebody. And when I am most myself and sigh my soul in prayer, I too meet Somebody – I know Jesus was right!

Have you ever tried to pray and could not connect up? So many details of living, so many carking cares loomed large before you that your words fell back dead.

> "My words fly up, my thoughts remain below,
> Words without thoughts never to heaven go."

And then, sometimes, as if by chance, there is kindled in the heart an upmounting desire on the wings of which one mounts to the very presence of God!

To one who has a living, leaping faith, God is. There are no ordinary proofs – one has worked one's way through all such preliminary stages. It is like growing in love. At first there are many "tokens of testing," little ways of checking, but gradually there is an awareness that proofs are unnecessary – one knows and is relaxed! My faith *teaches* me that God is!

Again, my faith teaches me that God is near. Not away off, up above the sky, on a great white throne – an aged white man with blonde angels standing in mid-air to obey his command! Not that.

Isaiah says that in the year that King Uzziah died he saw the Lord on a great white throne, high and lifted up. But Jesus funded the religious experience of all the prophets of Israel, erected a vast experimental pyramid, scaled the heights of it and brought God down out of the clouds and discovered Him pre-eminently as the main spring in the heart of man. An amazing insight it was that exclaimed, The Rule of God – it is within you!

"Speak to Him, Thou, for He heareth
And spirit with spirit may meet – "

Do you remember the words on the Railway Station: He who seeks the wealth of the Indies must take the wealth of the Indies with him?

God is here. In the midst of life, breaking through the commonplace, glorifying the ordinary, the Great, High God is near. One should tread the earth with a deeply lying awe and reverence – God is in this place!

Do not wait to hear His spirit winging near in moments of great crisis, do not expect Him riding on the crest of a wave of deep emotional excitement – do not look to see Him at the dramatic moment when something abnormal or spectacular is at hand. Rather find Him in the simple experiences of daily living, in the normal ebb and flow of life as you live it.

The final thing that my faith teaches me is that God is love. Not only that He is; not only that He is near; but that He is love. Fully do I realize how difficult this is. There is so much anguish in life, so much misery unmerited, so much pain, so much downright reflective hell everywhere that sometimes it seems to me that it is an illusion to say that God is love. When one comes into close grips with the perversities of personality, with studied evil – it might be forgiven one who cried aloud to the Power over Life – human life is stain – blot it out! I know all that. I know that this world is messed up and confused. I know that much of society stretches out like a gaping sore that refuses to be healed. I know that life is often heartless, as hard as pig iron. And yet, in the midst of all this I affirm my faith that God is love – whatever else He may be.

Why do I? The reason is not far to seek. When I love someone I seem to be at the center of all meanings and values. Life takes on a new significance and I seem to have a quality of experience which is or was the guarantor of all experience. Again, under the compulsion of love, I send my life forth to do and be things that nothing else is capable of inspiring. I do gladly for Love's sake, what no power in heaven or hell could make me do without it. Therefore, whatever else Ultimate Reality God is, He must be love.

When a man dedicates his life to God he begins at once to fulfill in his own experience the practical logic of that dedication. It is here that he finds a true basis for security. The measure of my dedication is the measure of my own stature. He who dedicates his life to God is like a tree planted beside a stream sending its roots down to the water. Its leaves are always green. It has no fear of scorching heat. It goes on bearing fruit when all around it is barren and it lives serene.

Which shall it be for you – a scrawny scrub in a desert – barren – or a fruitful tree that looks on life with quiet eyes? Which?

∞ | *What Shall I Do With My Life?* (1939)

Thurman wrote a version of this sermon, a meditation on Matthew 4:1–11, while a semi-narian in the mid-1920s and frequently delivered variations of it to student audiences throughout his career.[17] Once we establish a primary relationship with God as the foundation of our lives, he argues, we must come to a moral reckoning with the spiritual power God invests in the believer. Having faith is only the beginning of the spiritual pilgrimage, and can easily seduce us into confusing our budding religious passion with the will of God, leading to inevitable disappointment and doubt. Thurman claims to love Jesus because he faced squarely and creatively the temptations to think both too much and too little of his newly awakened spiritual energies. Before we can give shape and definition to our individual lives, Thurman instructed his youthful listeners, we must also come to terms with the moral order of things – with all its possibilities and limitations.

IN THE FIRST TEMPTATION Jesus was hungry. The fact could have doubt-less been duplicated all over Palestine with this important exception – many of his fellows were hungry through no choice of their own. They were hungry because necessity had confronted their universe with an invincible gesture. By their fellows they had been shut off from free and necessitous participation in the basic creature demands for survival. On the

30

other hand, Jesus was hungry because he had foregone these demands under the impelling power of a great concentration. He was caught in the agonizing grip of a great challenge: What shall I do with my life? What must
be for me an adequate disposition of my life?

Wrestling in the wilderness seemed strangely trivial and irrelevant.
The quest in its practical bearing was this: How fundamentally important
is bread, is feeding the hungry? It is true that man cannot live by bread
alone. He must have bread. But should this be his major concern? Only a
hungry man could face this question realistically. The danger for a hungry
man in such a reflection is that the importance of food may be greatly
overemphasized, for it is very natural to idealize possessions which we
are denied.

With reference to the problem before him Jesus reached an amazingly
significant conclusion. Man must live on bread but not bread alone. There
is more besides, and it is this that reveals the true stature of the man. Man
must have food, yes. But admitting this and seeing its practical significance in terms of actual survival, what then? He must let the bias of his
life be on the side of those needs that cannot be adequately included in
creature demands.

The problem for us is at once clear. I must not make the error of giving
myself over to the meeting of these needs alone, but even as I recognize realistically the physical needs of men, I must let my bias be on the side of
their deeper concerns; I must give priority to those of their desires and
yearnings that can never be met by a full stomach or by all the economic
security available in the world. The major emphasis must not be an either-
or one but rather a both-and emphasis with a positive bias in favor of that
which is deeper than food. My interests in creature needs must be genuine and practical, but I must see these needs as things which may stand
clearly in the way of the realization of the higher ends of life. Feed the
hungry? Yes, and always. But I must know that man is more than his physical body. There is something in him that calls for beauty and comradeship
and righteousness. I love Jesus for the shaft of light that he throws across
the pathway of those who seek to answer the question, What shall I do
with my life?

In the second temptation Jesus is facing the problem of one of life's great illusions. The tempter suggests to him that if he were to go to the pinnacle of the temple and cast himself down, he would not be hurt; in other words, the operation of what we call natural law would be interrupted in his behalf and God would perform a miracle on the spot. For, the tempter quietly whispers, the world of nature is not really orderly.

Jesus' reply was very striking. He said in substance, "If I go to the pinnacle of the temple and cast myself down I will break my neck. He who presumes to disregard the ordinary processes of nature tempts God." His choice here was on the side of the normal, natural working of the simple laws of life, demanding nothing of them that dared to stretch them out of shape. To do so would have been to deceive himself and to have created a spiritual problem for which no solution could have been found.

The bearing of this choice upon the lives of students is at once clear. I have had students who during an entire semester did not pay much attention to the simple, direct, natural operations of the classroom, who fulfilled none of the day-by-day requirements relative to their work. Then, when the day of judgment arrived, they came into the classroom, read the examination questions and expected, by some beyond-the-natural operation, to participate in complete knowledge and understanding of the questions raised. In other words, they expected a miracle. What they received was what they had rated – failure. It is a terrible truth that life does not have a habit of making exceptions in our case even though we may be good in general, even though our fathers may be great men and our reputations of outstanding merit. Let us not be deceived by the great illusions, but let us see the finger of God moving in the natural unfolding of antecedents and consequences. I love Jesus for the shaft of light that he throws across the pathway of those who seek to answer the question, What shall I do with my life?

In the third temptation the tempter strikes at the center of Jesus' dominant passion, to bring society under the acknowledged judgment of God and thereby insure its purification. More and more as he lived, Jesus became the embodiment of this great desire. He thought of himself as the example of the judgment and of the salvation of God. The tempter said to him, "Behold the kingdoms of the world. You want them to become the Kingdom of God. But they belong to me." It seems to me that the full realization of the tempter's thought came to Jesus with tremendous shock. His reasoning may have been, "God created me; God created the world of nature; God created all mankind. Therefore, God is the creator of the relationships that exist between men." At this point the devil suggested, "You may be logical, but you are not true. I made the relationships between men." In the awareness of the far-reaching significance of this fact, Jesus subsequently cautioned his disciples, "Behold, I send you out as lambs among wolves. You must be as wise as serpents and as harmless as doves." And again he said, "Rejoice when men persecute you for my sake, for it means that you are making inroads on territory that is foreign to the will of God."

It seems to me that experience reveals a potent half-truth; namely, that the world can be made good if all the men in the world as individuals become good men. After the souls of men are saved, the society in which they function will be a good society. This is only a half-truth. Many men have found that they are caught in a framework of relationships evil in design, and their very good deeds have developed into instrumentalities for evil. It is not enough to save the souls of men; the relationships that exist between men must be saved also.

To approach the problem from the other angle is to assume that once the relationships between men are saved, the individual men will thereby become instruments of positive weal. This is also a half-truth. The two processes must go on apace or else men and their relationships will not be brought under conscious judgment of God. We must, therefore, even as we purify our hearts and live our individual lives under the divine scrutiny, so order the framework of our relationships that good men can function in it to the glory of God. I love Jesus for the shaft of light that he throws across the pathway of those who seek to answer the question, What shall I do with my life?

Give me the courage to live!
Really live – not merely exist.
Live dangerously,
Scorning risk!
Live honestly,

Daring the truth –
Particularly the truth of myself!
Live resiliently –
Ever changing, ever growing, ever adapting.
Enduring the pain of change
As though 'twere the travail of birth.
Give me the courage to live,
Give me the strength to be free
And endure the burden of freedom
And the loneliness of those without chains;
Let me not be trapped by success,
Nor by failure, nor pleasure, nor grief,
Nor malice, nor praise, nor remorse!
Give me the courage to go on!
Facing all that waits on the trail –
Going eagerly, joyously on,
And paying my way as I go,
Without anger or fear or regret
Taking what life gives,
Spending myself to the full,
Head high, spirit winged, like a god –
On . . . on . . . till the shadows draw close.
Then even when darkness shuts down,
And I go out alone, as I came,
Naked and blind as I came –
Even then, gracious God, hear my prayer:
Give me the courage to live![18]

∞ | *Suffering (1963)*

Toward the end of his tenure as dean of Marsh Chapel at Boston University, Thurman published Disciplines of the Spirit.[19] *This distillation of his popular "Spiritual Disciplines and Resources" class, which Thurman taught between 1954 and 1961 during the height of the Civil Rights movement, consisted of five chapters: "Commitment," "Growing in Wisdom and Stature," "Suffering," "Prayer," and "Reconciliation." The latter three chapters are reprinted in this volume. In "Suffering" Thurman observes that it is part of human life to encounter limits – in our bodies and minds – which we always experience as pain and sometimes, evil. But suffering also occasions a profoundly solitary encounter with an "authentic adversary": the authority of God. For Thurman, life is "good" in that it includes both good and evil. Encountering God through suffering can lead either to a shriveling of the spirit – a sense of wounded pride and searing resentment – or to a deepening of our commitment to life itself. Without suffering there would be no freedom to choose our path and to risk failure and disappointment.*

SUFFERING IS UNIVERSAL FOR MANKIND. There is no one who escapes. It makes demands alike upon the wise and the foolish, the literate and the illiterate, the saint and the sinner. Very likely it bears no relationship to the character of the individual; it often cannot be assessed in terms of merit or demerit, reward or punishment. Men have tried to build all kinds of immunities against it. Much of the meaning of all human striving is to be found in the desperate effort of the spirit of man to build effective windbreaks against the storm of pain that sweeps across the human path. Man has explored the natural world around him, the heights and depths of his own creative powers, the cumulative religious experience of the race – all in an effort to find some means of escape, but no escape is to be found. Suffering stalks man, never losing the scent, and soon or late seizes upon him to wreak its devastation.

Prof. Thomas Hayes Proctor of Wellesley College, in an address delivered in Houghton Memorial Chapel in April 1940 commented in this vein:

> Men may do much with intelligence and resolute will since Nature is to some extent plastic and may be molded nearer to the heart's desire. But time and tide, disease and death, the spots of the sun and far-off galaxies are not within our power, nor will they be in any future imaginable to man. Nor is there any surety in Nature that the future will be better than the past. It may well be worse. No one who faces fact can deny the possibility of ultimate catastrophe. The values that give dignity and worth to life may be swept away; the causes that we cherish may be defeated, disruptive forces may destroy civilization; in some distant era even human life may become impossible on a cooling planet, and the whole epoch of human living be the briefest of moments between dead eternities . . . Our deepest loves are at the mercy of a wandering germ.

There is an impersonal quality about all human suffering. It humiliates and violates the person and often the very dignity of the human spirit. It seems to be utterly unmindful of consequences and blind to both good and evil. Nevertheless, there is something utterly personal and private about it; the encounter with suffering is always personal at the point of contact with the individual. An earthquake may destroy a city in a vast upheaval that seems like the temper tantrum of elemental forces. Yet to every human being who suffers loss of family, loss of limb or of life, it is a moment of naked intimacy with pain, terror, and disaster.

The setting for suffering is the world in which we live. Life is hazardous. The Master says that God makes his sun to shine on the evil and the good, his rain to fall on the just and the unjust. In Luke 13 there is a very incisive comment.

> It was at this time that some people came to tell him about the Galileans whose blood Pilate had mingled with their sacrifices. But he replied to them,
> "Do you think, because they suffered this, that these Galileans were worse sinners than the rest of the Galileans?
> I tell you, no; unless you repent you will all perish as they did.
> Or these eighteen men killed by the fall of the tower at Siloam? – do you think that they were worse offenders than the rest of the residents in Jerusalem?
> I tell you, no; unless you repent you will all perish as they did."
> — *Luke 13:1–5 (Moffatt)*

Man's journey is hazardous because the world in which he lives is grounded in order and held intact by an inner and irresistible logic, by laws that, in one vast creative sweep, encompass the infinite variety of the universe and give life its stability, but at the same time make living anywhere, at any time, a dramatic risk for any particular unit of life, be it man or plant. It is on such a stage, in such a setting, that the drama of the private life and the collective enterprises of man is played. Though suffering is a private encounter, and in the last analysis a man must deal with it in solitariness and isolation, it is ultimately reassuring if it can be placed in a frame of reference as universal and comprehensive as life itself.

Suffering is always pain in some form. A thing that is not capable of feeling pain cannot suffer. A simple working definition is that suffering is physical pain or its equivalent, with reference to which the individual may be inspired to protect himself, so that despite its effects he may carry on the functioning of his life. I have deliberately left this statement awkward; I want the basic elements to appear in a simple sentence. Let us examine the component parts.

I

Suffering is a form of physical pain. It is rooted in pain; where there is no experience of pain, there can be no suffering. Suffering has no meaning outside of consciousness, and further, the potential of the experience it-self is co-extensive with life. Pain may be experienced at a level of life that is not capable of interpreting the meaning or fact of the pain. It may be a reflex within an organism where self-consciousness, as such, is dif-fuse and general. The sense of self may be one with total consciousness, of whatever degree. The more developed the sense of self and the more acute the self-awareness, the more definite is the potential for suffering.

It is reasonable to suppose, then, that so-called subhuman forms of life do not suffer in death to the extent that human beings do. Such a supposi-tion may be entirely erroneous. To hold such a view and to be guided by it in matters of fact is to swing wide the door to all kinds of carnage and mis-ery. Under such circumstances it is easy to inflict pain indiscriminately upon others by the simple device of defining them as subhuman and therefore as nonmembers of the human family.

This is one of the functions of hate during times of war. The enemy na-tion is defined as comprised of subhuman beasts, brutes, savages; then we are free to inflict pain without a violent pang of conscience. During the war with Japan I saw billboards in California showing Japanese men as monsters with huge grotesque faces, large buck teeth, enlarged black-rimmed glasses – in short, they were not human beings at all. To destroy them would be a righteous, or at least decent, act. In a very penetrating in-sight, Olive Schreiner suggests that historical Christianity has misunder-stood or misinterpreted the teaching of Jesus concerning reverence for life in his insistence that God cares for the sparrow that falls by the way-side, for the grass of the field, the birds of the air, and even the numbering of the hairs of the head. She insists that Christianity as it has developed since the time of its founder wrongly limits the ethical concept of rever-ence for life to human personality. Once this exception is allowed, the rest is simple. Deny personality to human beings and the ethical demand no longer obtains. Much of the evil in human life and society is rationalized in this way. People who are victimized by injustices must be defined as be-ing, in Kipling's phrase, "the lesser breeds without the law." This makes conscience easy in the face of inflicted pain. When such a definition has social sanction and approval, all kinds of brutality take place as a matter of course and there is no sense of ill-doing.[20]

To illustrate how much a part of the mores such attitudes become: When I was thirteen years old and living in Florida, I worked in the afternoon after school for a wealthy white family in one of the residential areas of our town. During the fall I raked leaves each afternoon. In the family there was a little girl about five years old who delighted in following me around while I worked. She would scatter the leaves as fast as I raked them into a pile. I grew tired of this. I suggested that if she did not stop I would report her behavior to her father, of whom she had marked fear. This so incensed her that she ran over to me, took a pin out of her little pinafore and stuck me on the hand. I drew my hand back and asked her if she had lost her mind. She looked at me in amazement and said, "That didn't hurt you really! You can't feel!"

The same point is demonstrated in the moving account of Carl Ewald in his novel *My Little Boy, My Big Girl*. Let the story speak for itself.

> There is great warfare and a lot of noise among the children in the yard.
>
> I hear them yell *Jew*. I go to the window and see my little boy bare-headed out in the front line of the battle.
>
> I settle down quietly to my work again, certain that he will appear shortly and tell me all about it.
>
> Soon after he is there.
>
> He stands next to me, as is his habit, and says nothing. I steal a glance at him – he is highly excited, feels very proud and happy, like one who has fearlessly done his duty.
>
> "Such fun you had down there."
>
> "Well," he says modestly, "– it was only a Jewish boy we were beating up."
>
> I jump up so my chair turns over.
>
> "A Jewish boy – you were beating him up – what had he done?"
>
> "Nothing."
>
> His voice is not very confident, for I look so queer.
>
> But this is only the beginning. For now I grab my hat and run out the door as fast as I can and yell:
>
> "Come on – come on – we must find him and ask his forgiveness."
>
> My little boy hurries after me. He does not understand a word but he is terribly in earnest. We look in the yard, we shout and yell. We rush into the street

and around the corner. Breathlessly we ask three people if they have seen a poor, mistreated Jewish boy.

All in vain. The Jewish boy and all the persecutors have vanished.

We sit up in my study again – the laboratory where our soul is crystallized out of the big events in our little life. My brow is knit and I drum with my fingers on the table. The boy has both hands in his pockets and doesn't take his eyes from my face.

"Well –" I say, "there is nothing more we can do. I hope you will meet that boy some day so you can shake hands with him and ask him to forgive you. You must tell him that you did it because you were stupid, that if anyone tries to harm him again, you will help him and beat them as long as you can stir a limb."

I can see from my little boy's face that he is ready to do my will. For he is still a mercenary who does not ask under which flag he serves so long as there is battle and booty. It is up to me to call forth in him the staunch solider who defends his native land. Thus I continue:

"Let me tell you – the Jews are very wonderful people. You remember David whom Dirty read about in school? He was a Jewish boy. And Jesus whom everybody worships and loves although he died two thousand years ago. He was also Jewish."

My little boy rests his arms on my knees and I go on with my story.

The old Hebrews rise before our eyes with a splendor and power quite different from Dirty's Catechism. They ride on camels in their colorful clothing and with their long beards . . . Moses and Joseph and his brothers and Samson and David and Saul. Wonderful stories these are. The walls of Jericho fall before the blast of the trumpets. . . .

"And what else?" says my little boy, using an expression habitual to him when he was much younger and which still comes to his lips when he is carried away.

We hear of Jerusalem's destruction and how the Jews took their little boys by the hand and wandered from place to place, scorned, despised and mistreated. How they were not allowed to own houses or land but could be only merchants, and how the Christian robbers took all the money they had saved up. How they remained true to their God and maintained their ancient, sacred rituals amongst all the strange peoples who hated and persecuted them.

The day belongs to the Jews.

We look at old books in the bookcase which I am very fond of and which were written by a Jew with a strange name, which my little boy doesn't understand at all. We learn that the most famous man in Denmark at present is a Jew.

And when evening comes and Mother goes to the piano to sing the song that Dad loves best of all it appears that the words were written by one Jew and the melody composed by another.

My little boy is hot and flustered when he goes to sleep that night. Restlessly he tosses in his bed and talks in his sleep.

"He is a bit feverish," his mother says.

"No wonder. Today I vaccinated him against the meanest of all common blights."[21]

Physical pain is fundamental to man's experience as a creature. We do not know why, but we do know that for the most part it serves the function of a signal of danger. If a man could feel no pain, there would be no warning sensation when a particular action becomes self-destructive. Pain is man's first line of defense against death. Pain cannot protect one against it finally, but it may function to trigger a deploying tactic against death. It makes it possible in some instances for a man to have an important part in determining when he shall die. If he uses pain as a warning and seeks to ascertain its cause, he may be able to take measures that will prolong his life and thus postpone the time of his dying. In this sense death may operate on an ascending or descending scale in man's life. The operation of the law of the constant and the variable is applicable here. In response to the alert of pain, a man may approach the control of his own death as the variable approaches the constant. He may narrow the gap, but he can never close it.

In a discussion of physical pain in his book, *The Soul of the White Ant,* the South African Eugene Marais makes the interesting point that, in all of nature, the only experience of pain that is not involved in alerting the organism to danger is the pain of childbirth. He takes the rather obscure position that pain in childbirth is positive and creative because it is the alchemy of the pain that awakens mother love in the female parent. If we accept this thesis in essence, then both aspects of pain have in them elements that are positive and creative.[22]

But this does not exhaust the possibilities of physical pain. Beyond its warning function as a danger signal it often persists as a reminder that all is not well. The early pain that sends a man to the doctor for examination may lead to the discovery of cancer, but long after such a discovery, if the cancer is not rooted out the pain continues and usually increases with mounting intensity. There is a logic in the pain itself. Whatever else we may say about physical pain, it must be emphasized that what is called pain is a pattern of behavior of cells sensitized by a system of nerves that function out of an integrated center. There is an anatomy of physical pain which is orderly, precise, and definite.

In the appendix of C. S. Lewis's *The Problem of Pain,* there is a note supplied by a medical doctor from his clinical experience. He makes a distinction between the effects of short attacks of severe physical pain and long-continued pain. With the former the effect is of short duration, even though overwhelming while it lasts. When it is over, it is over and done with. With the latter, the alteration in behavior is apt to be more noticeable. Often great strength and resignation are developed in the character, with a corresponding humbling of pride. Sometimes there is an obvious deterioration in character and disposition. The telling point is made that the failures are so few "and the heroes are so many." Long illness often has the effect of wearing down the life to a slow remorseless grind. "The invalid gives up the struggle and drifts helplessly and plaintively into a self-pitying despair. Even so, some, in a similar physical state, will preserve their serenity and selflessness to the end. To see it is a rare but a moving experience."

With reference to mental pain, Lewis has this to say:

> Mental pain is less dramatic than physical pain, but it is more common and also more hard to bear. The frequent attempt to conceal mental pain increases the burden: it is easier to say "My tooth is aching" than to say "My heart is broken." Yet if the cause is accepted and faced, the conflict will strengthen and purify the character and in time the pain will usually pass. Sometimes, however, it persists and the effect is devastating; if the cause is not faced or not recognized, it produces the dreary state of the chronic neurotic. But some by heroism overcome even chronic mental pain. They often produce brilliant work and strengthen, harden, and sharpen their characters till they become like tempered steel.[23]

II

We come now to the next part of our definition – I refer to the phrase "or its equivalent." There is a transfer value in the pain experience. Because man has a mind and is in a very profound sense an experiencer of life, pain is something that is seen as happening *to* him. He is *aware* that it is happening to him. He knows that he hurts – it is a very local experience.

Thus for man suffering is possible. For him the physical pain is interpreted; it is at this point that the crucial issue of all suffering arises. What does the pain mean? What is it saying beyond the fact that it hurts? The most elementary answer to simple physical pain is not far to seek. Certain behavior brings certain results. We learn this at an early age. Put your finger on a hot stove and your finger is burned. This is painful, but in a simple sense very understandable. When we raise the question about pain in its more complex dimension, however, it tends more and more to become unanswerable. Here is a person who is afflicted with an incurable disease; he is young, full of promise, the whole world stretches out before him, boundless and unexplored. But he is assaulted, left to spend his days to the end helpless and smitten. After we answer the why of the disease itself (even supposing that we know the cause of it and how the man contracted it), the crucial problem remains untouched. The moral and psychic equivalent to the physical pain must be dealt with. In other words, the practical problem of suffering has to be faced.

It is not surprising that mankind has tried to place the source of evil or pain at a point in time that antedates history, and thus to establish grounds for its existence outside of individual human morality. Man the individual is too finite, too time-space encumbered to bear on his local shoulders the burden of evil. The responsibility has to be placed, yet God must be protected from too direct an involvement, because there must be some source beyond and outside the struggle which can yield perspective and wisdom to those who are caught in it. Here the story of the Garden of Eden meets a critical need in the struggle of Western man. Responsibility has to be placed, or all moral values in existence vanish as "snow upon the desert's dusty face." Adam becomes the figure whose action, personal in character, makes possible an impersonal involvement of all mankind, and in the story the world of nature is actively involved in disintegration and defeat. The creation of man in the first instance is an act of God. The baleful effects of man's behavior can only be countermanded by another act of God, the precipitation of Himself into time through the appearance of Jesus Christ in history. To those who accept such an appearance as authentic, a way is available for redemption from the suffering that the presence of sin or evil produces.

We are now ready to deal with the first and most practical question men raise about suffering. Is the victim being punished for something he has done? In other words, is suffering punitive? It must at once be admitted that there is punitive suffering in the world. There is such a thing as reward and punishment. We are never sure about how the scales are balanced, but one of our oldest racial memories registers the fact that man is responsible for his actions; that is, he is morally responsible. This means that he may or may not be paid in kind for his deeds, but he may be paid in quality or its equivalent. It is a very curious kind of conflict, complication, and involvement.

When I was ten years old, I broke my arm. The doctor put it in splints and a sling. This happened during the summer at the height of the wild grape season and the series of summer picnics. I researched my entire past to see what I had done to merit this kind of misfortune. I did not feel myself capable of doing a deed so monstrous that I deserved that kind of punishment.

So much turns on the interpretation given. Suppose we decide that the young man described earlier, whose future has been cut off by incurable disease, is not being punished; and suppose we decide further that the disease itself is part of what may be called the structural dependability of nature. Now what? He is still cut off from his dreams and from all the promise of his life. In other words, he is a sufferer.

Such a man has to handle his suffering or be handled by it. This brings me to the other part of the definition. The mind may work out an immunity so that the spirit of the person not only remains undefeated but is triumphant over his suffering. By "mind" I do not refer merely to the process of stimulus and response, of action and reaction, but mean to include here the individual's total sense of being: the comprehensive focal unity of the man's personality, inclusive of what he thinks and feels. I mean the *is*-ness of personality. It is this central conscious ground of personal being that is at last confronted by suffering, and in that ultimate private encounter the battle is won or lost.

The suffering may be capitulated to before the issue is so closely drawn. For instance, it may be accepted quite simply, with some disappointment but with resignation, as "one of those things," "I got a bad break," or "it was fun while it lasted." In my high school class there was an extremely beautiful and gifted girl who contracted a fatal illness. The last time I saw her we discussed the whole matter of her imminent death. She said, "I'll tell you, Howard, how I feel about it. I feel as I did when I was a very little girl and went to a play at church with my mother, and we had to go home before the play was over."

There may be hostility directed against life in the abstract; such hostility may embitter the spirit, make the individual wreak his vengeance on all and sundry. Since life is spoiled for him, he proceeds to try to spoil it for others. The people who pay the greatest price are those who are bound to him in ties of ministry and kinship from which there is no easy way of escape. The embittered person says in effect, "I'm stuck with it, but I don't have to like it," or "It's a dirty trick life has pulled and I've got to even the score any way I can – and you're elected."

But if the person comes to grips with his suffering by bringing to bear upon it all the powers of his mind and spirit, he moves at once into a vast but solitary arena. It is here that he faces the authentic adversary. He looks into the depth of the abyss of life and raises the ultimate question about the meaning of existence. He comes face to face with whatever is his conception of ultimate authority, his God.

The first thing his reflection brings to mind is that there is a fellowship of suffering as well as a community of sufferers. It is true that suffering tends to isolate the individual, to create a wall even within the privacy that imprisons him, to overwhelm him with self-preoccupation. It makes his spirit miserable in the literal sense of that word. Initially, it stops all outward flow of life and makes a virtue of the necessity for turning inward. Indeed, one of the ground rules of man's struggle with pain is the focusing of the energies of life at a single point. All of him that can be summoned is marshaled. This is true whether he is dealing with sheer physical pain or the more complex aspects of other dimensions of suffering. The pain gives his mind something else to think about and requires what approximates total attention.

One of the great preachers of another generation tells the story of a stagecoach driver who made a round trip each day between two towns. On a certain morning, halfway along, the lead horse was frightened by a large piece of paper in the middle of the road. It was all the driver could do to keep the team from running away. On the return trip he noticed at some distance the same piece of paper. Now he prepared himself. As soon as the lead horse saw the white object, his ears stood up; as he neared it, his body tensed in fear. At the crucial moment the driver flicked him on the tender part of his ear with his whip to avert a repetition of the event of the morning. The driver gave the horse something else to think about.

Thus suffering may at times seem an end in itself for generating energy in the spirit, as indeed it does. If the pain is great enough to lay siege to life and threaten it with destruction, a demand is made upon all one's resources. In this kind of concentration of spirit, the same thing operates as we observed in the chapter on commitment. The energy of life becomes available when the conditions of single-mindedness are met. It is important to hold in mind that this is the way of life – when life is attacked, it tends to rally all its forces to the defense.

In the case of human life, its forces include not only physical but spiritual resources as well. This is why very often we see people as profoundly changed by their suffering. Into their faces has come a subtle radiance and a settled serenity; into their relationships a vital generosity that opens the sealed doors of the heart in all who are encountered along the way. Such people look out upon life with quiet eyes. Openings are made in a life by suffering that are not made in any other way. Serious questions are raised and primary answers come forth. Insights are reached concerning aspects of life that were hidden and obscure before the assault.

The question remains, however, "Why is this not the experience of every sufferer?" Frankly, I do not know the answer. As already suggested, for some all resources seem to be cut off completely and the withering of the spirit keeps pace with the disintegration of the body or anguish of the emotions. There are all kinds of problems and paradoxes here. Sometimes a person who has always been generous becomes tight and hard under suffering. There are those who before the visitation have had an active religious faith and a vital Christian enthusiasm, but now become dour in spirit and withdraw themselves from all previous religious convictions. These are what the French mystic, Simone Weil, refers to as "the afflicted."[24]

I once knew such a man. All his life he had been an active teacher of religion at two colleges. Generations of students had been helped and inspired both by his example and by the wisdom of his counseling. His children were led to pursue worthy and creative goals in their lives and regarded him as the major anchor in all their journeying on the high seas of their vocational undertakings. Yet there came a time when, in his encounter with personal suffering, he seemed stripped of every resource. His prayer life became increasingly barren; none of the things that had nourished him all through the years could reach him now. All the tides flowed out and the shoals and rocks of his coastline stood exposed in a stark and ugly pattern. Yes, suffering may have this result. For such a time, for such a person, the only thing is to wait it out, to affirm with avid recollection and present insistence that the contradictions of life are never final. All contradictions are held together in an almighty synthesis that gives them, ultimately, a meaning and a context.

As to the demand upon resources created by suffering, let us examine more closely those that become available when the real issues are faced. I have referred to the fact that the individual enters a fellowship of suffering and the community of sufferers. This is obvious and need not be labored. The only point to be held steadily in mind is that, despite the personal character of suffering, the sufferer can work his way through to community. This does not make his pain less, but it does make it inclusive of many other people. Sometimes he discovers through the ministry of his own burden a larger comprehension of his fellows, of whose presence he becomes aware in his darkness. They are companions along the way. The significance of this cannot be ignored or passed over. It is one of the consolations offered by the Christian religion in the centrality of the position given to the cross and to the suffering of Jesus Christ. The theological insistence is that the love of God manifests itself in his son, Jesus Christ. The position is summarized in a telling fashion by Leslie Paul.

God did not just "appear" as a spirit in the fashion of a man, and speak to men out of the visible form to which they are accustomed so that they might not be too astonished or frightened. No, the Son of God *became* a man. He took on the burdens and cares of human existence. He became a party to human limitations. He suffered in Himself what it was to be creaturely man. Yes, and much, much more. He endured His human limitations in the greatest pain and loneliness and encountered human company at its most vile, tasting the spittle of the rabble on His lips. For the truths that He spoke, the sick that He healed, and for His very Divinity itself He was taken and done to death. We do not face only the simple, radiant, joyous revelation of God to man – would to heaven that we did! We have to reckon also with the most bitter humiliation, the very deepest human tragedy – that the Son of God was nailed on a cross by the men He had come to meet and to save.

Even if one were to call it all a myth born in the unconscious, and breathe again with relief that man had only imagined this dreadful deed, and that it had not occurred under the floodlights of day after all – one would still not be exonerated. For that man should invent this, out of nowhere – or out of nowhere in his outer world – out of, only, his deep, inner torment would itself be a cry almost too fearful to bear from man's soul, a cry telling of man's agonizing need to be redeemed from himself and find God.[25]

For many Christians the sense of the presence of the suffering Christ, who in their thought is also the suffering God, makes it possible through His fellowship to abide their own suffering of whatever kind or character. To know Him in the fellowship of His suffering is to be transformed by the glory of His life, and for these individuals this is enough – in His name they can stand anything that life can do to them. This is the resource and the discipline that comes to their rescue under the siege of pain.

III

If the sufferer is merely an innocent victim, what then? One of the characters in Margaret Kennedy's novel *The Feast*[26] suggests that the entire human race is tolerated for its innocent minority. There is a strange and awful vitality in the suffering of the innocent. It does not fall within any usual category. The mind moves very easily with the balance of the swinging pendulum; we are accustomed to equating things in terms of equilibrium. Our values are defined most easily as merit and demerit, reward and punishment. There is great reassurance for the spirit in the idea that reverses can somehow be balanced by the deeds that have brought them about. Many men are at peace with their suffering when they remember that the pain is deserved, is payment for a just and honest debt. Of course there may be a full measure, pressed down and overflowing, but the hard core of the pain is for acknowledged wrong done; the essence of the hardship is atonement for evil. All this falls into a simple pattern of checks and balances, of sowing and reaping, of planting and harvesting.

But where the pain is undeserved, where innocence prevails and no case can be made that will give a sound basis for the experience of agony, then the mind spins in a crazy circle. Always there must be an answer, some clue must be found to the mystery of the suffering of the innocent. It is not enough to say that the fathers have eaten sour grapes and the children's teeth are set on edge. This is not enough. It is not enough to say that the individual sufferer is a victim of circumstances over which he has no control. There is truth in such descriptions, but the heart of the issue remains untouched. The innocent do suffer; this is the experience of man.

Margaret Kennedy's idea is an arresting one. It is that mankind is protected and sustained by undeserved suffering – that swinging out beyond the logic of antecedent and consequence, of sowing and reaping, there is another power, another force, supplementing and restoring the ravages wrought in human life by punishment and reward. The innocent ones are always present when the payment falls due – they are not heroes or saints, they are not conscious burden-bearers of the sins and transgressions of men. They are the innocent – always there. Their presence in the world is a stabilizing factor, a precious ingredient maintaining the delicate balance that prevents humanity from plunging into the abyss. It is not surprising that in all the religions of mankind there is ever at work the movement to have the word *made* flesh, without being *of* the flesh. It is humanity's way of affirming that the innocent *hold,* while the evil men do exacts its due. "Their shoulders hold the sky suspended. They stand, and earth's foundations stay."

But what of those who have no such orientation and whose lives are not girded by such a faith – there would be no problem if suffering came only to those who had, even latently, such a resource. Are these others abandoned by God and left to languish without a witness of His love, concern, and care, or must they take time out from suffering to find the way into such assurance? One may truly say of many lives that, when they were able to burst out of the prison house of their pain, they found God in the midst of their adversity. But what of the others?

In the first place, when a man is driven by suffering to make the most fundamental inquiries concerning the meaning of life, he has to assess and re-assess his total experience. It may be that he has never seriously thought about the meaning behind the energy of a simple act. He has never thought seriously about God. He has taken his life and all life for granted. Now under the assault of pain he is led to wonder about the mystery of life. Why do men suffer, he asks himself. He sorts out the answers available to him, some of which we have touched upon. He may conclude, perhaps, that suffering is given; it is a part of the life contract that every living thing signs at the entrance. Therefore it must belong in and to life. It is no invasion from the outside. It is no strange phenomenon wandering at random among the children of men. And if it belongs, then it has to be accepted as a part of one's acceptance of life. To reject it is to reject life. This is the first thing that he pins down in his assessment.

If suffering belongs, then does it go along for the ride, or must it carry its end of the stick? Does it have a function? What would life be like if there were no suffering, no pain? The startling discovery is made that if there were no suffering there would be no freedom. Men could make no mistakes, consciously or unconsciously. The race could make no mistakes. There would be no error. There would be no possibility of choice at any point, or in any sense whatsoever. It is irrelevant to suggest that there might be a more satisfactory way to guarantee this than to make human misery in some sense mandatory. Freedom therefore cannot be separated from suffering. This, then, may be one of the ways in which suffering pays for its ride.

The ultimate logic of suffering, of course, lies in the fact of death. The particular quality of death is to be found in what it says about the future.

Death is a denial of the validity of the future. This is the logic of all suffering. It is what rallies the spirit and girds man to do battle. Suffering is the gauntlet that death throws down in the arena. All religions, since man began his pilgrimage on the planet, have been forced to deal with this central issue: they must answer the challenge of the end of man's life. Stripped of all cultural accretions and special limitations of specific historic situations, religion – regarded as fundamental to the human enterprise – says that life and death take place in a larger context, which religion calls Life. Life and death are the experience of living things, and here Life in some sense becomes identical with God. To say that man's spirit is driven to deal with the issue of death is equivalent to saying that man is driven to a face-to-face encounter with Life and its Creator, out of whom come life and death as experiences in Life. Death is seen as being an experience *within* Life, not happening *to* Life.

Why do men suffer? They suffer as a part of the experience of freedom. They suffer as a part of the growth of life itself. They suffer as a part of life. This leaves many questions unanswered: the pain of the innocent, the frustration of wasting illness of one kind or another. But at last we have a clue in the notion that without suffering there is no freedom for man, and that through it every man is faced with the necessity of experiencing in his being – not merely in his physical body – the meaning of death.

How does this happen? It may be said that the experience of death is for every man, as long as he lives, vicarious. It is a highly speculative experience so long as he is alive. But it is embodied in the reality of the world of which he is a part. All around him he sees his fellows die, sees them fail, finally, to continue as he knows them. If suffering is the logic, the intention, *of* this failure, then he knows that for him and all his kind there is a common fate. Strangely enough, it is the profound rejection of his verdict that is absolutely binding. He recognizes that death, through its part in defining duration, does establish a form or aspect of life, and in so doing gives life a meaning and a purpose. It provides a measuring rod for values to be worked out within a particular time interval. If he could settle for this kind of finality, then with death as an established boundary he would be sure that whatever meaning he is to know, whatever fulfillment he is to participate in, must be achieved between the time of his birth and the time of his death. This would enormously simplify life; it would dwarf all experience and make effective a ceiling to all endeavor. The only problem would be of possible miscalculation as to the length of a man's days. But that would be a calculated risk to be taken into account as a rider to all his strivings.

Yet this is not a true picture, for man is aware of desires, of aspirations, of projections that cannot be telescoped into his solitary life span, but are personal nevertheless. Somehow they must be contained in what he means when he considers his life. Desperate, he must establish some kind of finality to existence, some phase of man's life capable of containing not only his time-bound dreams but also capable of containing *him*. *He* must be dealt with in the equation – not merely his hopes, dreams, and aspirations. There must be an answer that confirms him, that establishes for him a basis of ultimate self-validation. This, religion insists, is found only in God. Always his God must be more than his thought about God, more than his private needs, demands, or requirements. His God must be comprehensive enough to include the whole movement of life in its every dimension and outreach. Man must be able to deal not merely with the fact of death, but also with the fact of life. He must be so confirmed in his living that he encompasses the fact of his dying.

Of course, the classic Christian reference is to Jesus of Nazareth. But there are others before and after him: Socrates, Galileo, John Brown, and others of our own time "who have dared for a high cause to suffer, resist, fight – if need be, to die."[27]

To be confirmed in life is to make even of death a little thing. It is to be robbed of the fear of living and consequently to be robbed of the fear of dying.

This answer to suffering is best seen when men act in response to love. It is only for love of someone or something that a man knows that, because of the confirmation of life in him, he can make death an instrument in the hands of life. Last summer in a town just outside of Edinburgh, a seventy-year-old man was standing on a bridge when he saw a three-year-old child fall into the water. He dove from the bridge, saved the child, but lost his own life. The problem comes home to each of us when we ask ourselves: Under what circumstances and for whom would you give up your life?

I believe that such confirmation of life in us is the work of the Holy Spirit of God. For me, the love of God nourishes and confirms us and gives to us the assurance that, because life in all its vicissitudes is contained in Him, in Him we have the sense of ultimate finality in existence that makes total existence, and our life in it, purposeful and meaningful. I cannot escape the necessity of concluding that the answer to suffering is to be found in experiencing in one's being the meaning of death. To state it categorically, it is to have one's innermost self or persona assured that the finality of death, which is the logic of all suffering, is itself contained in a more comprehensive finality of God Himself. Such a God is conceived as the Creator of Life and the living substance, the Creator of existence itself and of all the time-and-space manifestations thereof. Within the construct of this creation, He is at work pervading it with the quality of Himself. This means that, at any point in human history, no event in the life of a single person can be separated from what are, in fact, the ends of God.

This makes all formal concepts of the problem of evil, all metaphysical questions about evil, merely academic. The problem of evil is literal fact. Evil itself is specific and concrete. But what a man who is suffering wants to know is, "How may my suffering be managed or overcome? Is there any resource available that can reduce it to a unit of containment? Must I finally be overcome and destroyed by it?" The answer is to be found in the testimony of the human spirit. It is not to be found in the books or the philosophies or even in the ritual or ceremonies of religion. All of these may be helpful to the individual in sustaining him against the ravages of his experience. But the man who suffers must say yea or nay, in his utterance feeling himself sustained, supported, and confirmed, or undermined, deserted, and denied. If the answer to his suffering is to face it and challenge it to do its worst because he knows that when it has exhausted itself it has only touched the outer walls of his dwelling place, this can only come to pass because he has found something big enough to contain all violences and violations – he has found that his life is rooted in a God who cares for him and cultivates his spirit, whose purpose is to bring to heel all the untutored, recalcitrant expressions of life. Such a man knows that he cannot determine what may befall him, either as a child of nature, as a child of his time and age, or even as a child of God. He knows that suffering, the ultimate logic of which is death in life, is a part of the living stuff of his earthly adventure. He knows that even in his own strength he never quite explores the limits of his endurance, and beyond all this there is the possibility of a reinforcement of his life that transcends all the vicissitudes of his fortune and shares in a collective destiny in which God is all and in all. Wherever there is such a possibility, to miss it would be to have all sense of the future cut off and all the meaning of even the simplest values of his life disintegrate in his hands. To seek to know how he may enter into such a grand fulfillment is the essence of all wisdom and the meaning of all human striving. Of course, he may be mistaken. But to be mistaken in such a grand and illumined undertaking is to go down to his grave with a shout.

> *Heir of the Kingdom 'neath the skies,*
> *Often he falls, yet falls to rise;*
> *Stunned, bleeding, beaten back,*
> *Holding still to the upward track,*
> *Playing his part in Creation's plan —*
> *God-like in image, this is man.*

⬭ | The Negro Spiritual
Speaks of Life and Death (1947)

"The Negro Spiritual Speaks of Life and Death" was originally delivered as Harvard Divinity School's prestigious Ingersoll Lecture on the Immortality of Man on April 14, 1947.[28] *The first African American to give the talk, Thurman stood in succession to an illustrious lineage of religious intellectuals that included William James, Josiah Royce, Edgar Sheffield Brightman, William Ernest Hocking, and Alfred North Whitehead, among others. From the earliest days of his career, Thurman had frequently spoken on the spirituals under the title of "Deep River," which he privately published in 1945. But he had long before ceased discussing African-American cultural practices before white audiences because he did not wish to nourish the assumption that "black scholars were incapable of reflecting creatively on any matters other than those that bore directly on their own struggle." In the case of this elite gathering at Harvard, however, he decided to make an exception in the hope that his delineation of the slaves' spiritual resourcefulness and universalism might "deliver those in another kind of bondage into a new freedom."*[29] *Grasping the influence of the "sorrow songs," as W. E. B. Du Bois called Negro spirituals, is essential for understanding Thurman's own approach to religion and history. His early spiritual formation began in the Black Church where these songs were staples of worship and spiritual expression. Thurman's tragic understanding of the human condition distilled from the slaves' creative appropriation of Western Christianity comes through in his interpretation of the spirituals. The centrality of religious experience as filtered*

through the biblical narrative, Thurman argues, served as a primary source for the en-
slaved Africans' understanding of the cosmos and the role of faith in the construction of a
meaningful existence. Here Thurman captures the heart of African Americans' religious
quest for freedom as revealed in the enslaved singers' perspective on the theological
themes of life and death, Jesus and God, and judgment and hope. He concludes that in
the particularity of their struggles there resides a universal moral intent for inclusive hu-
man community.

THE MYSTERY OF LIFE AND DEATH persists despite the exhaustless and exhaustive treatment it has been given in song and story, philosophy and science, in art and religion. The human spirit is so involved in the endless
cycle of birth, of living and dying, that in some sense each man is an authority, a key interpreter of the meaning of the totality of the experience.
The testimony of the individual, then, is always fresh if he is able to make
himself articulate to his fellows. Even when he is not, there is the persistent conviction that in some profound sense he himself knows and understands. When the external circumstances of life are dramatic or unusual,
causing the human spirit to make demands upon all the reaches of its resourcefulness in order to keep from being engulfed, then the value of its
findings made articulate, has more than passing significance.

I have chosen, coincidentally with the suggestion of Dean Sperry,[30] to
examine the Negro spirituals as a source of rich testimony concerning life
and death, because in many ways they are the voice, sometimes strident,
sometimes muted and weary, of a people for whom the cup of suffering
overflowed in haunting overtones of majesty, beauty and power! For many
years it has been a growing conviction with me that the clue to the meaning of the spirituals is to be found in religious experience and spiritual discernment. To be sure, the amazing rhythm and the peculiar, often weird
1-2-3-5-6-8 of the musical scale are always intriguing and challenging to
the modern mind. The real significance of the songs, however, is revealed
at a deeper level of experience, in the ebb and flow of the tides that feed
the rivers of man's thinking and aspiring. Here, where the elemental and
the formless struggle to a vast consciousness in the mind and spirit of the
individual, shall we seek the needful understanding of the songs of these

slave singers. The insights disclosed are not original in any personal or private sense. The unique factor of the inspiring revelation is that, in the presence of their naked demand upon the primary sources of meanings, even without highly specialized tools or skills, the universe responded to them with overwhelming power.

In an essay included in a little book of meditations on Negro Spirituals published under the title *Deep River*, I located three major sources of raw materials over which the slave placed the alchemy of his desiring and aspiring: the world of nature, the stuff of experience, and the Bible, the sacred book of the Christians who had enslaved him. It was from the latter two that the songs of life and death originate. An examination of some of the insights to be found here is at once the purpose and proposal of my lecture.

Death was a fact, inescapable, persistent. For the slave, it was extremely compelling because of the cheapness with which his life was regarded. The slave was a tool, a thing, a utility, a commodity, but he was not a *person*. He was faced constantly with the imminent threat of death, of which the terrible overseer was the symbol; and the awareness that he (the slave) was only chattel property, the dramatization. It is difficult for us, so far removed in time and mood from those agony-ridden days, to comprehend the subtle psychological factors that were at work in the relationship between slave and master. If a slave were killed, it was merely a property loss, a matter of bookkeeping. The notion of personality, of human beings as ends so basic to the genius of the Christian faith, had no authentic application in the relationship between slave and master. The social and religious climate were uncongenial to such an ethic. Of course, there were significant exceptions to the general rule – which exceptions, by the light they cast, revealed the great moral darkness by which the period was engulfed. The situation itself stripped death of dignity, making it stark and nasty, like the difference between tragedy and melodrama. Death by violence at the hand of nature may stun the mind and shock the spirit, but death at the hands of another human being makes for panic in the mind and outrages the spirit. To live constantly in such a climate makes the struggle for essential human dignity unbearably desperate. The human spirit is stripped to the literal substance of itself.

The attitude toward death is profoundly influenced by the experience of life.

It is important then to examine this literature to see what is revealed here concerning the attitude toward death. How significant is death? Is it the worst of all possible things that can happen to an individual:

> Oh Freedom! Oh Freedom!
> Oh Freedom, I love thee!
> And before I'll be a slave,
> I'll be buried in my grave,
> And go home to my Lord and be free.

Obvious indeed is it here that death is not regarded as life's worst offering. There are some things in life that are worse than death. A man is not compelled to accept life without reference to the conditions upon which the offering is made. Here is something more than a mere counsel of suicide. It is a primary disclosure of an elemental affirmation having to do directly, not only with the ultimate dignity of the human spirit, but also with the ultimate basis of self-respect. We are face to face with a gross conception of the immortality of man, gross because it is completely exhaustive in its desperation. A radical conception of the immortality of man is apparent because the human spirit has a final word over the effect of circumstances. It is the guarantee of the sense of alternative in human experience, upon which, in the last analysis, all notions of freedom finally rest. Here is a recognition of death as the one fixed option which can never be taken from man by any power, however great, or by any circumstance, however fateful. If death were not implicit in the fact of life in a time-space dimension, then in no true sense would there be any authentic options in human experience: This concept regards death merely as a private option, private because it involves the single individual as if he and he alone existed in all the universe; option, because, while it assumes the inevitability of death as a factor in life, it recognizes the element of time which brings the inevitable factor under some measure of control.

The fact that death can be reduced to a manageable unit in any sense, whatsoever, reveals something that is profoundly significant concerning its character. The significant revelation is in the fact that death, as an event, is spatial, time encompassed, if not actually time bound, and therefore partakes of the character of the episodic. Death not only affects man by involving him concretely in its fulfillment, but man seems to be aware that he is being affected by death in the experience itself. There is, therefore, an element of detachment for the human spirit, even in so crucial an experience. Death is an experience *in* life and a man, under some circumstances, may be regarded as a spectator *of,* as well as a participant *in,* the moment of his own death. The logic here is that man is both a space binder and a time binder.

The second attitude toward death that comes to our attention is one of resignation mixed with elements of fear and a manifestation of muted dread – this, despite the fact that there seems to have been a careful note of familiarity with the experiences of death. It is more difficult for us to imagine what life was like under a less complex order of living, than is our lot. We are all of us participants in the modern conspiracy to reduce immediate contact with death to zero except under the most extraordinary circumstances. We know that death is a commonplace in the experience of life and yet we keep it behind a curtain or locked in a closet, as it were. To us death is gruesome and aesthetically distasteful as a primary contact for ourselves and our children. For most of us, when members of our immediate families die, the death itself takes place in a hospital. Particularly is this true of urban dwellers. From the hospital, the deceased is carried to a place of preparation for burial, the mortuary. When we see the beloved one again, the body has been washed, embalmed, and dressed for burial. Our exposure to the facts involved, the silent intimacies in preparation for burial are almost entirely secondary, to say the least. The hospital and the mortuary have entered profoundly into the life of modern man, at this point. The result is that death has been largely alienated from the normal compass of daily experience. Our sense of personal loss may be great but our primary relationship with death under normal circumstances tends to be impersonal and detached. We shrink from direct personal contact with death. It is very difficult for us to handle the emotional upsets growing out of our experience with death when we are denied the natural moments of exhaustive reaction which are derivatives of the performance of last personal services for the dead. Therapeutic effects are missed. Tremendous emotional blocks are set up without release, making for devious forms of inner chaos, which cause us to limp through the years with our griefs unassuaged.

This was not the situation with the creators of the Spirituals. Their contact with the dead was immediate, inescapable, dramatic. The family or friends washed the body of the dead, the grave clothes were carefully and personally selected or especially made. The coffin itself was built by a familiar hand. It may have been a loving though crude device, or an expression of genuine, first-class craftsmanship. During all these processes, the body remained in the home – first wrapped in cooling sheets and then "laid out" for the time interval before burial. In the case of death from illness all of the final aspects of the experience were shared by those who had taken their turn "keeping watch." Every detail was etched in the mind and emotions against the background of the approaching end. The "death rattle" in the throat, the spasm of tense vibration in the body as the struggle for air increased in intensity, the sheer physical panic sometimes manifest – all these were a familiar part of the commonplace pattern of daily experience. Out of a full, rich knowledge of fact such a song as this was born:

> *I want to die easy when I die.*
> *I want to die easy when I die.*
> *Shout salvation as I fly.*
> *I want to die easy when I die.*

A quiet death without the seizure of panic, the silent closing of the door of earthly life, this is the simple human aspiration here.

As if to provide some measure of contrast, the age-old symbolism of the river of death appears in a song like this:

> *Chilly water, chilly water.*
> *Hallelujah to that lamb.*
> *I know that water is chilly and cold,*
> *Hallelujah to that lamb.*
> *But I have Jesus in my soul,*

Hallelujah to that lamb.
Satan's just like a snake in the grass
Hallelujah to that lamb.
He's watching for to bite you as you pass
Hallelujah to that lamb.

In a bold and audacious introduction of still another type of symbolism which has all the graphic quality of the essentially original, revealing the intimate personal contact with death and the dying, this old, old song announces:

Same train carry my mother;
Same train be back tomorrer;
Same train, same train
Same train blowin' at the station,
Same train be back tomorrer;
Same train, same train.

There is a sense of the meaning of death as a form of frustration (for those who remain) with a dimension of realism rare and moving in this song:

You needn't mind my dying,
You needn't mind my dying,
You needn't mind my dying,
Jesus goin' to make up my dying bed.

In my dying room I know,
Somebody is going to cry.
All I ask you to do for me,
Just close my dying eyes.

In my dying room I know,
Somebody is going to mourn.
All I ask you to do for me,
Just give that bell a tone.

In the third place, death is regarded as release, as complete surcease from anxiety and care. This is to be distinguished from that which may come after death. We are thinking here of the significance of death regarded somewhat as a good in itself. The meaning of death in such a view is measured strictly against the background of immediate life experience. It is not a renunciation of life because its terms have been refused, but an exulting sigh of sheer release from a very wearying burden:

> I know moon-rise, I know star-rise,
>> I lay this body down.
> I walk in the moon-light, I walk in the star-light,
>> To lay this body down.
> I walk in the graveyard, I walk through the graveyard,
>> To lay this body down.
> I lie in the grave and stretch out my arms,
>> To lay this body down.

Man, the time binder, one with the shimmering glory of moonlight and starlight and yet housed in a simple space-binding body, is heir to all the buffetings of the fixed and immovable, yet he can lay the body down and stretch out his arms and be at one with moonrise and starlight.

The note of the transcendence of death is never lacking – whether it is viewed merely as release or as the door to a heaven of endless joys. We shall examine the place and significance of the concepts dealing with that which is beyond death at a later point in our discussion. But the great idea about death itself is that it is not the master of life. It may be inevitable, yes; gruesome, perhaps; releasing, yes; but triumphant, NEVER. With such an affirmation ringing in their ears, it became possible for them, slaves though they were, to stand anything that life could bring against them.

It is next in order to examine the attitude taken toward life, because the attitude toward death cannot be separated from the attitude toward life. Was life merely a "veil of soul-making"? Was it merely a vast anteroom to the great beyond? Was it regarded as an end in itself? Or was it a series of progressions, a pilgrimage, a meaningful sojourn?

There seem to be no songs dealing with the origin of life as such or the origin of the individual life in particular. Life was regarded essentially as the given – it was accepted as a fact without reflection as to cause or reason. They were content to let the mystery remain intact.

Given the fact of life, there is much which has to do with interpretations of its meanings, its point and even its validity. In the first place, life is regarded as an experience of evil, of frustration, of despair. There are at least two moods in evidence here – one mood has to do with an impersonal characteristic of life itself. Loneliness and discouragement – such is the way of life. One cannot escape – such experiences are inherent in the process itself. Hence:

> Let us cheer the weary traveler,
> Let us cheer the weary traveler,
> Along the heavenly way.

This has some elements similar to the philosophy of unyielding despair developed by Bertrand Russell in his essay on Free Man's Worship.[31]

> Sometimes I feel like a motherless child,
> A long way from home.

Here again is another song which reflects the same temper.

There is also the familiar note in:

> Nobody knows the trouble I've seen,
> Nobody knows my sorrow.
> Nobody knows the trouble I've seen,
> Glory, Hallelujah!

All the reaches of despair are caught up and held in a trembling wail in:

> I couldn't hear nobody pray,
> Oh, I couldn't hear nobody pray.
> Oh, way down yonder by myself,
> And I couldn't hear nobody pray.

A climactic chord in the mood of the seventh chapter of Paul's letter to the
Romans is to be found in:

> *O wretched man that I am!*
> *O wretched man that I am!*
> *Who will deliver poor me?*
> *My heart is filled with sadness and pain,*
> *Who will deliver poor me?*

The solitariness of the human spirit, the intensely personal characteristic of all experience as distinguished from mere frustration or despair is
evident in such a song as:

> *I've got to walk my lonesome valley,*
> *I've got to walk it for myself.*
> *Nobody else can walk it for me,*
> *I've got to walk it for myself!*

Here we are in the presence of an essential insight into all human experience. It seems, sometimes, that it is the solitariness of life that causes it to
move with such intensity and power. In the last analysis all the great moments of profoundest meaning are solitary. We walk the ways of life together with our associates, our friends, our loved ones. How precious it is
to lean upon another, to have a staggered sense of the everlasting arms felt
in communion with a friend. But there are thresholds before which all
must stop and no one may enter save God, and even He in disguise. I am
alone but even in my aloneness I seem sometimes to be all that there is in
life, and all that there is in life seems to be synthesized in me.

It is a matter of more than passing interest that this element of overwhelming poignancy is relieved somewhat by a clear note of triumph. Out
of the fullness of a tremendous vitality the lowering clouds are high-
lighted by an overflowing of utter exuberance:

> *I feel like a motherless child;*
> *I feel like a motherless child;*

Glory hallelujah!
Sometimes my way is sad and lone,
When far away and lost from home;
Glory hallelujah!

The same note appears in a softer key, expressive of a quiet but sure confidence:

Soon-a-will be done with troubles of the world;
Soon-a-will be done with troubles of the world;
Going home to live with God.

Or again the quality of triumph is to be found in the total accent of the song:

All-a-my troubles will soon be over with,
All-a-my troubles will soon be over with,
All over this world.

The second mood suggested in the interpretation of life as an experience of evil, of frustration, of despair, has to do with a personal reaction to the vindictiveness and cruelty of one's fellows. The mood is set in a definite moral and ethical frame of reference which becomes a screening device for evaluating one's day-by-day human relations. It would be expected that these songs would point indirectly to be sure, but definitely, to the slaveowner. But for the most part, the songs are strangely silent here. Many indeed have been the speculations as to the reason for this unnatural omission. There are those who say we are dealing with children so limited in mentality that there is no margin of selfhood remaining for striking out, directly or indirectly, in a frenzy of studied fury against the slave owner. This is arrant nonsense as the vast number of slave insurrections all through this terrible period will certify. There are those who say that the religion was so simple, so naive, so completely otherworldly that no impression was made by the supra-immoral aspects of the environment; only a simple acceptance of one's fate. Any person who has talked with an ex-slave could hardly hold such a position. There seems to be a more comprehensive answer than any of these. The fact was that the slave owner was regarded as one outside the pale of moral and ethical responsibility. The level of high expectation of moral excellence for the master was practically *nihil*. Nothing could be expected from him but gross evil – he was in terms of morality – amoral. The truth seems to be that the slave owner as a class did not warrant a high estimate of ethical judgment. There is no more tragic result from this total experience than the fact that even at the present time such injunctions as "love your enemies," etc. are often taken for granted to mean the enemy within the group itself. The relationship between slave and master, as far as both the slave and master were concerned, was "out of bounds" in terms of moral responsibility. It seems clear, then, that the second mood has to do with those "we group" relationships of the slave and his fellow bondsmen.

Such is the meaning of:

> *Down on me, down on me,*
> *Looks like everybody in the whole round world is down on me.*
> *Talk about me as much as you please,*
> *I'll talk about you when I get on my knees.*
> *Looks like everybody in the whole round world is down on me.*

> *Sometimes I'm up, sometimes I am down,*
> *Sometimes I'm almost on the ground.*
> *Looks like everybody in the whole round world is down on me.*

To refer to the refrain of one other such song:

> *Oh, this is a sin-trying world,*
> *This is a sin-trying world.*

In the second place, life is regarded as a pilgrimage, a sojourn, while the true home of the spirit is beyond the vicissitudes of life with God! This is a familiar theme of the human spirit. We are dealing with a striking theory of time. Time is measured in terms of events, actions, therefore intentions and desires. All experience, then, is made up of a series of more or less intense meaning–units that may fall in such rapid succession that the interval between is less than any quantitative value. Within the scope of an event-series all of human life is bound. Freedom can only mean, in this sense, the possibility of release from the tyranny of succeeding intervals of events. The totality of life, then, in its existential aspects, is thus completely exhausted in time. Death in such a view means complete cessation of any sense of interval and therefore of any sense of events. In short, here death means either finality or complete absorption from time-space awareness. Whatever transpires beyond death, while it can be thought of only in terms of time-space intervals, is of another universe of discourse, another quality of being.

It is in order now to raise a question as to the relation between *before* and *after* in terms of death and life. There seems to be no real break between before and after. Any notion of the continuity of life that transcends the fact of death is significant because of the advantage that is given to the meaning of life. Even though it be true that death is a process moving toward fulfillment in a single climactic event; as contrasted with life, death seems ever to be a solitary event; while life does not seem to be a single event but a process. Even at birth, the process of life seems to be well under way, well advanced. In the light of man's conscious experience with life, death seems to be a moment for the release of potentials of which the individual is in some sense already aware. Life then becomes illustrative of a theory of time that is latitudinal or flowing. On the other hand, death is suggestive of a theory of time that is circular or wheel-like.

Life always includes movement, process, inner activity and some form of irritation. Something more is implicit than what is apparent in any cycle or series of cycles that sustain all manifestations. In such a view, life takes on a definite character of timelessness. There are no isolated, unrelated and, therefore, inconsequential events or moments. Every day is fraught with antecedents and consequences the logic of which is *inner relatedness* rather than *outer seeming*. Every day is a day of judgment and all life is lived under a continuous and inner scrutiny.

To think of life, then, as a pilgrimage means that not only is life characterized by an undertow of continuity but also that the individual has no alternative but to participate responsibly in that continuity. It is this concept rooted in the New Testament interpretation of the meaning of life that is to be found in many of the Spirituals. A few such songs have been mentioned in other connections. One of the great utterances of this character is:

> Done made my vow to the Lord,
> And I never will turn back,
> I will go, I shall go,
> To see what the end will be.

> My strength, Good Lord, is almost gone,
> I will go, I shall go,
> To see what the end will be.
> But you have told me to press on,
> I will go, I shall go,
> To see what the end will be.

The goal of the pilgrimage looms large by inference in some of the songs. The goal is not defined as such in many of them – but the fact of the goal pervades the temper with which the journey is undertaken or endured. There is something filled with breathless anticipation and great strength in these lines:

> Wait a little while,
> Then we'll sing a new song,
> Wait a little while,
> Then we'll sing a new song.

> Sometimes I get a heavenly view,
> Then we'll sing a new song,
> And then my trials are so few,
> Then we'll sing a new song.

There is no attempt to cast a false glow over the stark ruggedness of the journey. The facts of experience are seen for what they are – difficult, often even unyielding:

It is a mighty rocky road,
Most done travelling.
Mighty rocky road,
Most done travelling.
Mighty rocky road,
Bound to carry my soul to the Lord.

Hold out your light you heaven-bound soldier,
Let your light shine around the world.

Of the sheer will to carry on under the compelling aegis of a great commitment, what could be more accurately expressive than:

Stay in the field,
Stay in the field,
Until the war is ended.
Mine eyes are turned to the heavenly gate,
Till the war is ended.
I'll keep my way, or I'll be too late,
Till the war is ended.

Here is still another variation of the same basic theme:

Oh, my good Lord, show me the way.
Enter the chariot, travel along.

Noah sent out a morning dove,
Enter the chariot, travel along,
Which brought back a token of heavenly love,
Enter the chariot, travel along.

What, then, is the fundamental significance of all these interpretations of life and death? What are these songs trying to say? They express the profound conviction that God was not done with them, that God was not done with life. The consciousness that God had not exhausted His resources or better still that the vicissitudes of life could not exhaust God's resources, did not ever leave them. This is the secret of their ascendency over circumstances and the basis of their assurances concerning life and death. The awareness of the presence of a God who was personal, intimate and active was the central fact of life and around it all the details of life and destiny were integrated.

It must be borne in mind that there seems to be little place in their reckoning for the distinction between God and Jesus. In some of the songs the terms God and Jesus are used interchangeably – to illustrate:

> *Did you ever see such a man as God?*
> *A little more faith in Jesus,*
> *A preaching the Gospel to the poor,*
> *A little more faith in Jesus.*

For the most part, a very simple theory of the incarnation is ever present. The simpler assumptions of Christian orthodoxy are utilized. There was no elaborate scheme of separate office and function between God and Jesus and only a very rare reference to the Holy Spirit. Whether the song uses the term, Jesus, or the oft repeated Lord, or Saviour, or God, the same insistence is present – God is in them, in their souls, as they put it, and what is just as important, He is in the facts of their world. In short, God is active in history in a personal and primary manner. People who live under great pressures, grappling with tremendous imponderables which left to themselves they could not manage, have no surplus energy for metaphysical distinctions. Such distinctions apart from the necessity of circumstances or urgency of spirit, belong to those upon whom the hold of the environment is relatively relaxed. Urgency forces a reach for the ultimate, which ultimate in the intensity of demand is incorporated in the warp and woof of immediacy.

It is the next in order to examine the large place given to the other-worldly emphasis in these songs. What is the meaning of Heaven, of the final Judgment? In such considerations we come to grips with the conception of immortality implicit and explicit in the songs, and the basis for it.

Again and again I have heard many people (including descendants of these singers) speak disparagingly of the otherworldly emphasis as purely a mechanism of escape and sheer retreat. The argument is that such an emphasis served as a kind of soporific, making for docility and submission. It is further charged that here we are dealing with a clever device by which these people were manipulated into a position which rendered them more completely defenseless than they would have been without it.

Such an argument must be examined. In the first place, the facts make clear that religion did serve to deepen the capacity of endurance and the absorption of suffering. It was a precious bane! What greater tribute could be paid to religious faith in general and to their religious faith in particular than this: It taught a people how to ride high to life, to look squarely in the face those facts that argue most dramatically against all hope and to use those facts as raw material out of which they fashioned a hope that the environment, with all of its cruelty, could not crush. With untutored hands – with a sure artistry and genius created out of a vast vitality, a concept of God was wrenched from the Sacred Book, the Bible, the chronicle of a people who had learned through great necessity the secret meaning of suffering. This total experience enabled them to reject annihilation and affirm a terrible right to live. The *center of focus* was beyond themselves in a God who was a companion to them in their miseries even as He enabled them to transcend their miseries. And this is good news! Under God the human spirit can triumph over the most radical frustrations! This is no ordinary achievement. In the presence of an infinite desperation held at white heat in the consciousness of a people, out of the very depth of life, an infinite energy took shape on their behalf.

> *Oh rise, shine, for thy light is a coming.*
> *Oh rise, shine, for thy light is a coming.*
> *My Lord says he's coming by and by.*

Do we wonder then that they sang:

> *Oh religion is a fortune,*
> *I really do believe.*
> *Oh religion is a fortune,*
> *I really do believe!*

In the second place, this religious emphasis did not paralyze action, it did not make for mere resignation. On the contrary, it gave the mind a new dimension of resourcefulness. I had a college classmate who cleared his throat just before responding to the question of his teacher. The clearing of the throat broke the impasse between his mind and his immediate environment so that he could have a sense of ascendency in his situation. It was in some such fashion as this that these religious songs functioned. (Of course, they did much more than this.) Once the impasse was broken, many things became possible to them. They could make their religion vehicular in terms of the particular urgencies of the moment. "Steal away to Jesus" became an important call to those who had ears to hear. In other words, far from paralyzing action, religion made for detachment from the environment so that they could live in the midst of the traffic of their situation with the independence of solitude. The pragmatic result for them was an awareness that against the darkness of their days, something warred, "a strange new courage." To them it was the work of God and who could say to them NAY?

We turn now to an examination of the place and significance of the notion of judgment. Taking their clue from the word picture given by Jesus in the Gospels, the Judgment was the climax of human history. This made a tremendous appeal to the imagination. The figure of Gabriel was added to the imagery of Jesus. There are many references to Gabriel:

> O get your trumpet Gabriel
> And come down on the sea.
> Now don't you sound your trumpet
> Till you get orders from me –

> I got a key to that Kingdom
> I got a key to that Kingdom
> And the world can't do me no harm.

To mention the refrain of one other song:

> Gabriel, Gabriel, blow your trumpet!
> My Lord says he's going to rain down fire.

Some of these songs are almost pure drama. Consider this very old hymn, no record of which is to be found in any of the available collections:

> *Oh, He's going to wake up the dead,*
> *Going to wake up the dead,*
> *God's going to wake up the dead.*
> *One of these mornings bright and fair,*
> *God's going to wake up the dead.*

The judgment is personal *and* cosmic so that even the rocks and mountains, the stars, the sea, are all involved in so profound a process:

> *My Lord what a morning!*
> *My Lord what a morning!*
> *When the stars begin to fall.*
>
> *You will hear the trumpet sound*
> *To wake the nations underground,*
> *Standing at my God's right hand,*
> *When the stars begin to fall.*

The matter of most crucial importance is this – a man is brought face to face with his own life – personal accountability is the keynote:

> *When the master calls me to Him*
> *I'll be somewhere sleeping in my grave.*
> *In that great day when he calls us to him*
> *I'll be somewhere sleeping in my grave.*

The deep intimacy between the soul and God is constantly suggested. Even the true name of the individual is known only to God. There are references to the fact that the designation, Child of God, is the only name that is necessary. This gnosis of the individual is an amazing example of the mystical element present in the slave's religious experience. The slave's answer to the use of terms of personal designation that are degrading is to be found in his private knowledge that his name is known only to the God of the entire universe. In the Judgment everybody will at last know who he is, a fact which he has known all along.

> *O' nobody knows who I am, who I am,*
> *Till the Judgment morning.*

Judgment takes place in time. It is a moment when the inner significance of a man's deeds is revealed. God shall deal with each according to his history. It was with reference to the Judgment that life took on a subdued character. Everybody is judged. The Judge is impartial. There is distinct continuity between the life on earth and the Judgment. Excuses are of no avail. God, the Judge, knows the entire story.

> *O', He sees all you do,*
> *He hears all you say.*
> *My Lord's-a-writing all the time.*

Judgment was not thought of as being immediately after death. There is a time element between death and final judgment. Life, death, judgment, this was the thought sequence. When the final judgment takes place there will be no more time. What takes place after judgment has a necessitous, mandatory character ascribed to it. Man can influence his judgment before death – after death everything is unalterable. This notion of the ultimate significance of life on earth is another aspect of the theory of time to which we have made reference. Here is a faithful following of the thought of the Gospels.

And yet there is more to be said concerning the idea of the Judgment. What does the concept say? Are we dealing with a matter of fact and of literal truth? If we are, then the symbolism of the Judgment is necessarily an essential symbolism. What is the literal truth seeking expression in this symbolism? It is this: The life of man is significantly capable of rising to the demands of maximum moral responsibility. That which is capable of a maximum moral responsibility functioning in the tiny compass of single events takes on the aspects of the beyond-event, hence beyond time, therefore eternal. The conclusion seems inescapable that man is interpreted as having only mortal manifestations, but even these mortal manifestations have immortal overtones. If this were not true then there would be no significance in the symbolic fact of judgment. The literal truth requires a symbolism that is completely vehicular or revelatory.

Finally, we turn to an examination of the place and significance of the fact of Heaven in the thinking of these early singers. Heaven was a place – it was not merely an idea in the mind. This must be held in mind, constantly. The thinking about it is spatial. It is the thinking of Jesus in the Fourth Gospel. "I go to prepare a place for you. If I go and prepare a place for you I shall come again, and take you into myself that where I am there ye may be also." "In my father's house are many mansions." These word pictures supplied a concreteness to the fulfillment of all earth's aspirations and longings. The songs are many, expressing highly descriptive language of this character:

> I haven't been to heaven
> But I've been told,
> The streets are pearl
> And the gates are gold;
> Not made with hands.

What a plaintive wistfulness is found here:

> In bright mansions above,
> In bright mansions above,
> Lord, I want to live up yonder;
> In bright mansions above.

Such an aspiration was in sharp contrast to dimly lighted cabins with which they were familiar. Perfection, truth, beauty, even goodness are again and again symbolized by light. This is universal.

Heaven was as intensely personal as the facts of their experience or as the fact of the Judgment. Here at last was a place where the slave was *counted in*. He had the dignity of personal registration.

O write my name, O write my name,
The angels in heaven are going to write my name.
Yes, write my name with a golden pen,
The angels in heaven are going to write my name.

Heaven is regarded as a dimension of self-extension in the sense of private possession:

I want God's heaven to be mine, to be mine,
Yes, I want God's heaven to be mine.

Who is there that can escape the irony and the triumph in:

I got a robe,
You got a robe,
All God's children got robes.
When we get to heaven
We're going to put on our robes,
We're going to shout all over God's heaven.

There will be no proscription, no segregation, no separateness, no slave-row, but complete freedom of movement – the most psychologically dramatic of all manifestations of freedom.

All of these songs and many others like them argue for an authentic belief in personal immortality. In large part it is a belief growing out of the necessities of life as they experienced it. Family ties are restored, friends and particularly loved ones are reunited. The most precious thing of all was the fact that personal identity was not lost but heightened. Heaven would not be heaven, it would have no meaning, if the fact of contrasting experiences was not always possible and evident. There was a great compulsion to know then a new and different life, which knowledge could only be real if the individual were able to recall how it once was with him. We are not surprised to find a great emphasis on reunion. There was nothing more heart-tearing in that far-off time of madness than the separation of families at the auction block. Wives were sold from their husbands to become breeders for profit, children were separated from their parents and from each other – in fact, from the beginning, the slave population was a company of displaced and dispossessed people. The possibility of ever seeing one's loved ones again was very remote. The conviction grew that this is the kind of universe that cannot deny ultimately the demands of love and longing. The issue of reuniting with loved ones turned finally on the hope of immortality and the issue of immortality turned on the fact of God. Therefore God would make it right and once again God became the answer.

This personal immortality carried with it also the idea of rest from labor, of being able to take a long sigh cushioned by a deep sense of peace. If time is regarded as having certain characteristics that are event transcending and the human spirit is not essentially time bound but a time binder, then the concept of personal survival of death follows automatically. For man is never completely involved in, nor absorbed by, experience. He is an experiencer with recollection and memory – so these songs insist. The logic of such a position is that man was not born *in* time, that he was not created by a time-space experience, but rather that man was born *into* time. Something of him enters all time-space relationships, even birth, completely and fully intact, and is not created by the time-space relationship. In short, the most significant thing about man is what Eckhart calls the "uncreated element" in his soul. This was an assumed fact profoundly at work in the life and thought of the early slaves.

This much was certainly clear to them – the soul of man was immortal. It could go to heaven or hell, but it could not *die*. Most of the references to hell are by inference. Not to be with God was to be in hell but it did not mean not to *be*.

It is in order to raise the same question about heaven that was raised previously about the Judgment. Are we dealing here with a matter of literal truth? Or are we once again dealing with necessary symbolism growing out of literal truth? In other words, what is the intrinsic meaning attached to or to be drawn out of the concept of heaven? Is this mere drama or some crude art form? Certain facts are quite evident in the picture given. Heaven was specific! An orderly series of events was thought to take place. The human spirit rests – the fulfillment of the exhausted. A

crown, a personal crown is given – a fulfillment for those who strive without the realization of their strivings. There is a room of one's own – the fulfillment of life in terms of the healing balm of privacy. There are mansions – the fulfillment of life in terms of living with a high quality of
dignity. There are robes, slippers – the fulfillment of life in terms of the
restoration of self-respect. The idea at the core of the literal truth in the
concept of heaven is this – life is totally right, structurally dependable,
good essentially as contrasted with the moral concepts of good and evil. It
affirms that the contradictions of human experience are not ultimate. The
profoundest desires of man are of God, and therefore they cannot be denied ultimately.

> *Our ship is on the ocean but*
> *We'll anchor by and by.*

To use the oft-repeated phrase of Augustine, "Thou hast made us for Thyself, and our souls are restless till they find their rest in thee."[32] There is an
order, a moral order in which men participate, that gathers up into itself,
dimensional fulfillment, limitless in its creativity and design. Whatever
may be the pressures to which one is subjected, the snares, the buffetings,
one must not for a moment think that there is not an ultimate value always
at stake. It is this ultimate value at stake in all experience that is the final
incentive to decency, to courage and hope. Human life, even the life of a
slave must be lived worthily of so grand an undertaking. At every moment
a crown was placed over his head that he must constantly grow tall enough
to wear. Only of that which is possessed of infinite potentials, can an infinite demand be required. The unfulfilled, the undeveloped only has a future; the fulfilled, the rounded out, the finished can only have a past. The
human spirit participates in both past and future in what it regards as the
present but it is independent of both.

   We may dismiss, then, the symbolism of these songs as touching life
and death if we understand the literal truth with which they have to do.
The moment we accept the literal truth, we are once again faced with the
urgency of a vehicular symbolism. The cycle is indeed vicious. To be led
astray by the crassness, the materialistic character of the symbolism so

that in the end we reject the literal truth is to deny life itself of its dignity and man the right or necessity of dimensional fulfillment. In such a view the present moment is all there is – man is no longer a time binder but becomes a prisoner in a tight world of momentary events – no more and no less. His tragedy would be that nothing beyond the moment could happen to him and all of his life could be encompassed within the boundary of a time-space fragment. For these slave singers such a view was completely unsatisfactory and it was therefore thoroughly and decisively rejected. And this is the miracle of their achievement causing them to take their place alongside the great creative religious thinkers of the human race. They made a worthless life, the life of chattel property, a mere thing, a body, *worth living!* They yielded with abiding enthusiasm to a view of life which included all the events of their experience without exhausting themselves in those experiences. To them this quality of life was insistent fact because of that which deep within them, they discovered of God, and his far-flung purposes. God was not through with them. And He was not, nor could He be, exhausted by any single experience or any series of experiences. To know Him was to live a life worthy of the loftiest meaning of life. Men in all ages and climes, slave or free, trained or untutored, who have sensed the same values, are their fellow-pilgrims who journey together with them in increasing self-realization in the quest for the city that hath foundations, whose Builder and Maker is God.

⏺ | *Prayer (1963)*

Of the five spiritual disciplines Thurman outlines in Disciplines of the Spirit, *the disci-*
pline of prayer prepares us for the most intimate communion with God.[33] *For Thurman,*
"the hunger of the heart" is itself an expression of the "givenness of God," and the univer-
sal impulse to pray suggests that the divine presence is most authentically revealed to in-
dividual souls. In prayer, Thurman argues, we experience our utter dependency on the
Creator, which is why we seek in prayer a variety of things: thanksgiving, petition, for-
giveness of sins, pure enjoyment of our love of God, and spiritual restfulness. In this
piece, Thurman not only outlines various types of prayer—and affirms the validity of
them all—but he also draws from a number of religious traditions to instruct readers in
available "aids" to prayer.

I

IT WAS THE YEAR OF HALLEY'S COMET. I was a little boy living in a sawmill
town in Florida. I had not seen the comet in the sky because my mother
made me go to bed with the setting of the sun. Some of my friends who
were more privileged had tried to convey to me their impression of the
awe-inspiring spectacle. And I heard my stepfather say one day when he
came home for lunch that a man had been down at the mill office selling

what he called "comet pills." The theory was that if these pills were taken according to directions, when the tail of the comet struck the earth the individual would be immune. As I remember it, the owner of the sawmill made several purchases, not only for himself and family, but for his key workmen – the idea being that after the debacle he would be able to start business over again.

One night I was awakened by my mother, who asked if I would like to see the comet. I got up, dressed quickly, and went out with her into the back yard. There I saw in the heavens the awesome tail of the comet and stood transfixed. With deep anxiety I asked, without taking my eyes off it, "What will happen to us when that thing falls out of the sky?" There was a long silence during which I felt the gentle pressure of her fingers on my shoulders; then I looked into her face and saw what I had seen on another occasion, when without knocking I had rushed into her room and found her in prayer. At last she said, "Nothing will happen to us, Howard. God will take care of us." In that moment something was touched and kindled in me, a quiet reassurance that has never quite deserted me. As I look back on it, what I sensed then was the fact that what stirred in me was one with what created and controlled the comet. It was this inarticulate awareness that silenced my fear and stilled my panic.

Here at once is the primary ground and basis of man's experience of prayer. I am calling it, for the purpose of this discussion, the "givenness of God" as expressed in the hunger of the heart. This is native to personality, and when it becomes part of a man's conscious focus it is prayer at its best and highest. It is the movement of the heart of a man toward God; a movement that in a sense is within God – God in the heart sharing its life with God the Creator of all Life. The hunger itself is God, calling to God. It is fundamental to my thought that God is the Creator of Life, the Creator of the living substance, the Creator of existence, and as such expresses Himself through life. This is the meaning, essentially, of the notion that life is alive and that this is a living universe. Man himself cannot be an exception to this fact.

It has always seemed curious to me that man should investigate the external world, recognize its order, and make certain generalizations about its behavior which he calls laws; that he should study his own organism and discover there a kind of orderliness of inner behavior, which he seeks to correct when it acts out of character by a wide variety of ministrations, from drugs and surgery to hypnosis and faith – and yet that he should be inclined, at the same time, to regard himself as an entity apart from all the rest of creation, including his body. Man is body, but more than body; mind, but more than mind; feelings, but more than feelings. Man is total; moreover, he is spirit. Therefore it is not surprising that in man's spirit should be found the crucial nexus that connects him with the Creator of Life, the Spirit of the living God. The apostle is utterly realistic when he says that in Him we live and move and have our being. The most natural thing in the world for man, then, would be to keep open the lines of communication between him and the Source of his life, out of which he comes and into which (it is my faith) he goes.

Prayer is a form of communication between God and man and man and God. It is of the essence of communication between persons that they shall talk with each other from the same basic agenda. Wherever this is not done, communication tends to break down. If, however, an atmosphere of trust can be maintained, then one learns how to wait and be still. It is instructive to examine the prayer life of the Master from this point of view. I am always impressed by the fact that it is recorded that the only thing that the disciples asked Jesus to teach them how to do was to pray. The references are many to His own constant dependence on prayer:

> when Jesus had been baptized and was praying, heaven opened and the holy Spirit descended in bodily form like a dove upon him   – *Luke 3:21*

> In the early morning, long before daylight, he got up and went away out to a lonely spot   – *Mark 1:35*

> after saying good-bye to them, he went up the hill to pray   – *Mark 6:46*

> and he took the five loaves and the two fish, and looking up to heaven he blessed them   – *Mark 6:41; Matt. 14:19. Cf. Mark 8:6, 14:22; Matt. 26:26; Luke 24:30*

> large crowds gathered to hear him . . . while he kept in lonely places and prayed   – *Luke 5:15, 16*

This filled them with fury, and they discussed what they could do to Jesus. It was in these days that he went off to the hillside to pray. He spent the whole night in prayer to God   —*Luke 6:11, 12*

Now it happened that while he was praying by himself, his disciples were beside him. So he inquired of them, "Who do the crowds say that I am?"

—*Luke 9:18*

he took Peter, John, and James, and went up the hillside to pray. While he was praying, the appearance of his face altered and his dress turned dazzling white . . . Now Peter and his companions had been overpowered with sleep, but on waking up they saw his glory   —*Luke 9:28, 29, 32*

The seventy came back with joy . . . He said to them, "Yes, I watched Satan fall from heaven like a flash of lightning. . . . I praise thee, Father, Lord of heaven and earth"   —*Luke 10:17, 18, 21*

"Simon, Simon, Satan has claimed the right to sift you all like wheat, but I have prayed that your own faith may not fail"   —*Luke 22:31, 32*

Then he went outside and made his way to the Hill of Olives, as he was accustomed. The disciples followed him, and when he reached the spot he said to them, "Pray that you may not slip into temptation." He withdrew about a stone's throw and knelt in prayer, saying, "Father, if it pleases thee, take this cup away from me. But thy will, not mine, be done"   —*Luke 22:39–42*

Jesus gave a loud cry, "My God, my God, why forsake me?"

—*Psalm 22:1; Mark 15:34*

Then with a loud cry Jesus said, "Father, I trust my spirit to thy hands"

—*Psalm 31:5; Luke 23:46*

To Jesus, God breathed through all that is: the sparrow overcome by sudden death in its flight; the lily blossoming on the rocky hillside; the grass of the field and the clouds, light and burdenless or weighted down with unshed waters; the madman in chains or wandering among the barren rocks in the wastelands; the little baby in his mother's arms; the strutting insolence of the Roman Legion, the brazen queries of the tax collector; the children at play or old men quibbling in the marketplace; the august Sanhedrin fighting for its life amidst the arrogances of empire;[34] the whisper of those who had forgotten Jerusalem, the great voiced utterance of the prophets who remembered – to Jesus, God breathed through all that is.

To Jesus, God was Creator of life and the living substance, the Living Stream upon which all things moved, the Mind containing time, space, and all their multitudinous offspring. And beyond all these, He was Friend and Father. The time most precious for the Master was at close of day. This was the time for the long breath, when all the fragments left by the commonplace, all the little hurts and big aches, came to rest; when the mind could be freed of the immediate demand, and voices that had been stilled by the long day's work could once more be heard; when there could be the deep sharing of innermost secrets and the laying bare of heart and mind – yes, the time most precious for him was at close of day.

But there were other times: "A great while before day," says the Book – the night was long and wearisome because the day had been full of jabbing annoyances; the high resolve of some winged moment had spent itself, no longer sure, no longer free, and then vanished as if it had never been; the need, the utter urgency was for some fresh assurance, the healing touch of a heavenly wing – "a great while before day" he found his way to the quiet place in the hills. And prayed.

II

The Master was always concerned about his Father's agenda. In reflecting on the discipline of prayer, I asked myself how I may find a clue to God's purposes in the world? How may I sense Him at work? Already I am aware of Him in the hunger of my heart; this is a crucial clue. In the depths of my own spirit, then, I may be aware of His Presence, share His Mind, and establish true communication because my will comes to rest in His Will. We shall return to this later in the discussion.

The work of God in the world is another important clue to His agenda.

If I can understand this, a rapport is established between God and me which becomes the prelude to communion or communication in prayer. This is what the Psalmist is talking about when he says,

> The heavens declare the glory of God;
>> and the firmament sheweth his handywork.
> Day unto day uttereth speech,
>> and night unto night sheweth knowledge.
> There is no speech nor language,
>> where their voice is not heard.
> Their line is gone out through all the earth,
>> and their words to the end of the world.
> In them hath he set a tabernacle for the sun,
>>> Which is as a bridegroom coming out of his chamber,
>>> and rejoiceth as a strong man to run a race.
> His going forth is from the end of the heaven,
>> and his circuit unto the ends of it:
>> and there is nothing hid from the heat thereof.

> The law of the Lord is perfect, converting the soul:
>> the testimony of the Lord is sure, making wise the simple.
> The statutes of the Lord are right, rejoicing the heart:
>> the commandment of the Lord is pure, enlightening the eyes.
> The fear of the Lord is clean, enduring for ever:
>> the judgments of the Lord are true and righteous altogether.
> More to be desired are they than gold, yea, than much fine gold:
>> sweeter also than honey and the honeycomb.
> Moreover by them is thy servant warned:
>> and in keeping of them there is great reward.
> Who can understand his errors? Cleanse thou me
>> from secret faults.
> Keep back thy servant also from presumptuous sins;
>> let them not have dominion over me:
>> then shall I be upright,
>> and I shall be innocent from the great transgression.

Let the words of my mouth, and the meditation of my heart,
    be acceptable in thy sight,
O Lord, my strength, and my redeemer.   *– Psalm 19*

Or when he bursts forth:

O Lord our Lord,
    how excellent is thy name in all the earth!
    who hast set thy glory above the heavens.
Out of the mouth of babes and sucklings has thou ordained strength
    because of thine enemies,
      that thou mightest still the enemy and the avenger.
When I consider thy heavens, the work of thy fingers,
    the moon and the stars, which thou hast ordained;
What is man, that thou art mindful of him?
    and the son of man, that thou visitest him?
For thou hast made him a little lower than the angels,
    and hast crowned him with glory and honour.
Thou madest him to have dominion over the works of thy hands;
    thou hast put all things under his feet:
All sheep and oxen,
    yea, and the beasts of the field;
The fowl of the air, and the fish of the sea,
    and whatsoever passeth through the paths of the seas.
O Lord our Lord, how excellent is thy name in all the earth!   *– Psalm 8*

Any close examination of the world of nature reveals that everything is painstakingly structured. In its functioning, nature operates on the basis of a rather definite agenda. All animals and plants live intentional lives. We cannot dismiss this fact by saying that it is blind instinct or merely a pattern of conformity on the basis of which the continuity of the particular species is guaranteed. Here the activity of an innate order is at work. When I am able to read the specifications, then I can understand the behavior. The same thing is at work in me as elsewhere in the whole process. This is why so much knowledge about our own bodies is secured from the study of other forms of life. Such study is mandatory for all who would acquire a working knowledge of the human organism. If I regard this under-standing as a part of God's – the Creator's – working paper, then I relate to it not only with my mind but also with my feelings. I react to what I ob-serve: this is the Hand of God fashioning His creation. Such a mood of reverence has a transfer value for me also. It moves me directly into the ex-perience of what Schweitzer calls "reverence for life."[35] But there is much in familiarity with technology (which is the pragmatic application of a knowledge of the behavior of particles) that stifles any mood of reverence. So rapid and astounding have been our developments in this area that there is little time for the element of reverence to emerge. I doubt very se-riously if a scientist who knew reverence as a part of his own response to what his investigation of nature revealed could ever bring himself to the fashioning of atomic or hydrogen bombs.

Now, the mood of reverence opens up the spirit to a receptivity of the greatness of God at work in the world of nature. It heightens one's sensitiv-ity to meaningful overtones of beauty that enliven the spirit and enrich the awareness of values. Here, then, is one important clue to the divine agenda or working paper. Harmony becomes a language the understand-ing of which opens up a whole world of communication between God and me.

> The universe is not dead. Therefore, there is an Intelligence there, and it is all-pervading. At least one purpose, possibly the major purpose, of that Intelli-gence is the achievement of universal harmony.
>
> Striving in the right direction for Peace (Harmony), therefore, as well as the achievement of it, is the result of accord with that Intelligence.
>
> It is desirable to effect that accord.
>
> The human race, then, is not alone in the universe. Though I am cut off from human beings, I am not alone.
>
> For untold ages man has felt an awareness of that Intelligence. Belief in it is the one point where all religions agree. It has been called by many names. Many call it God.[36]

There is an element of profound truth in the outlook of pantheism, which sees the work of God in the world of nature with such clarity as to identify God with His world; the temptation is hard to resist. But this is not enough. God must never be a prisoner in His creation. When I look carefully at my own body, I see at once that my body functions are so closely meshed and integrated that, under ordinary circumstances, I am not aware of any part of my body as such unless the inner harmony breaks down at the point of function. I do not become little-finger-aware unless my little finger no longer functions as a little finger should. When the harmony is broken, I say that the part is ill or the body is ill. The body is quite literally a dwelling place of the Most High God, Creator of the Universe. The mood of reverence applies here with telling effect upon man's whole world of values, meaning, and morality.

Further, I seek a clue to God's working paper, His agenda in the world of men, in the whole story of man's collective or social life on the planet. At first look, human relations as experienced in human history, or in the immediate social environment in which we live, seem quite chaotic. The casual view discovers no valid intent; if there be an intent, it seems more evil than good, more diabolical than benevolent. In the language of faith, the kingdoms of this world often conflict with the Kingdom of God. It cannot be denied that a part of the fact of human society is the will to destroy, to lay waste, and to spend. There is often so much that casts down and so little that uplifts and inspires. The bloody carnage of fratricide is a part of the sorry human tale. And yet always, against this, something struggles. Man does not ever quite make the madness total. Always there is some voice that rises up against what is destructive, calling attention to an alternative, another way. It is a matter of more than passing significance that the racial memory as embodied in the myths of creation, as well as in the dream of prophet and seer, points ever to the intent to community as the purpose of life. This is no mere incident of social evolution, or growth toward civilization from times more primitive. It goes to the very heart of all human striving. It is basic to the aspirations of the entire human race. The dramatic character of this phenomenon can be seen during periods of the greatest violence among men – in war. In the midst of the vast death-dealing moments of war between nations there are always voices speaking out for peace. They are not tolerated; they are taken out of circulation so that their spirit may not become contagious; but they always appear and reappear.

Occasionally there comes into view on the horizon of the age a solitary figure who, in his life, anticipates the harmony of which he speaks. No one dreamed that Mahatma Gandhi would be able to introduce into the very center of a great modern empire such as Britain a principle contrary to empire, and abide. For Gandhi to have come out of the womb of a religion outside of the Christian faith and address himself to an empire whose roots were nurtured by that faith is the most eloquent testimony of the timeless, universal character of what was working in him. It is as though there were at work in this little man an Intent by which he was caught up, and of which in some way he became the living embodiment. The moving finger of God upon human history points ever in the same direction. There must be community. Always, in the collective conscience and in the private will, this intent appears and reappears like some fleeting ghost. It is a fact that mankind fails again and again, but the sense of not being mistaken in the fundamental intention never deserts the final purpose, or the judgment that is passed upon all social behavior.

When the hunger in a man's heart merges with what seems to be the fundamental intent of life, communion with God the Creator of Life is not only possible but urgent. The hunger of the heart, which is a part of the givenness of God, becomes one with the givenness of God as expressed in the world of nature and in human history. It must be pointed out that this hunger may function merely at the level of human striving and enlightened social concern. In this sense it may be regarded simply as a characteristic of personality; only this and nothing more. In other words, it may not become personal in terms of the devotional response of the individual to Life. Or, it may be a clue to the Father's house, to the Holy of Holies, wherein the Creator of Life and the King of the Universe has His dwelling place. Prayer is the means by which this clue is pursued. The hunger cannot be separated from God. For many this is what makes any communication between God and man possible. This is the swinging door that no man can shut. This is not to say that the great God of Life is reduced to or squeezed into the hunger of the heart of man, but that the hunger is an expression of the givenness of God. I repeat: it is the trysting place where the God and the soul of man meet, where they stand on a common ground and the wall or partition between them has no status. It is what Eckhart calls the "apex of the soul – the uncreated element in the soul of man."[37] This is the citadel of encounter.

The true purpose of all spiritual disciplines is to clear away whatever may block our awareness of that which is God in us. The aim is to get rid of whatever may so distract the mind and encumber the life that we function without this awareness, or as if it were not possible. It must be constantly remembered that this hunger may be driven into disguise, may take a wide variety of twisted forms; but it never disappears – it cannot. Prayer is the experience of the individual as he seeks to make the hunger dominant and controlling in his life. It has to move more and more to the central place until it becomes a conscious and deliberate activity of the spirit. When the hunger becomes the core of the individual's consciousness, what was a sporadic act of turning toward God becomes the very climate of the soul.

III

It will be in order to suggest certain simple aids to this end. One of these is the practice of silence, or quiet. As a child I was accustomed to spend many hours alone in my rowboat, fishing along the river, when there was no sound save the lapping of the waves against the boat. There were times when it seemed as if the earth and the river and the sky and I were one beat of the same pulse. It was a time of watching and waiting for what I did not know – yet I always knew. There would come a moment when beyond the single pulse beat there was a sense of Presence which seemed always to speak to me. My response to the sense of Presence always had the quality of personal communion. There was no voice. There was no image. There was no vision. There was God.

Many years after, I was invited to speak at a Friends First Day Meeting in Pennsylvania. I decided to put aside my usual procedures of preparation for an address and expose myself completely and utterly to the time of "centering down" in the Quaker meeting.[38] I felt that if I were able to share profoundly in that clarifying, centering process the word to be spoken would be clear and sure. I was accustomed to quiet and silence in private but not as part of a collective experience, and I entered into it with some trepidation. After a while all the outer edges of my mind and spirit began to move toward the center. As a matter of fact, the movement seemed to me to be actually fluid and flowing. After some time, I am not sure precisely when, the sense of the movement of my spirit disappeared and a great living stillness engulfed me. And then a strange thing happened. There came into my mind, as if on a screen, first a single word and then more words, until there was in my mind's eye an entire sentence from the Sermon on the Mount. The curious thing was that, familiar as I was with the passage, one part of my mind waited for each word to appear as the sentence built, while another part knew what the sentence was going to say. When it was all there, with avidity my mind seized upon it. I began thinking about it as the text of what I would say. When I was ready to speak, I placed my hands on the railing in front of me and was about to stand, when from behind came the voice of a lady quoting that passage. When she finished, all through the meeting individuals spoke to this theme, and I began to wonder whether I would have a chance to say anything, knowing I had traveled nine hundred miles to do it. At length I had my opportunity to speak.

Silence is of many kinds. There is a silence which is the prelude to prayer – the moment of hush and ingathering. There is a silence that tends to quiet the soundless words that fall from the tongue and to calm the noises of the mind and spirit. Every person who is concerned about the discipline of prayer must find the ministry of silence in accordance with his particular needs. Certain mechanical devices are helpful. We must seek a physical place of withdrawal, a place of retreat, if this is possible. It may be achieved merely by closing the door as a signal that one wishes to be alone; it may be by remaining in bed for a spell after everyone else is up and about; it may be by taking a walk or by extending a walk beyond the initial requirement or demand; it may be by withdrawing one's participation in conversation, even though one has to remain in the midst of company.

Once the physical silencing has been achieved, then the real work must begin. The calming of the mind as an effort to exclude distraction is a complex necessity. The soundless voices take the form of thoughts that distract. One of the most helpful things to do is to read or recall some stilling passage or thing – words that place before the mind a picture or a feeling tone that quiets or subdues and settles. The Psalms are very helpful here. "The Lord is my shepherd, I shall not want." Or, "Lord, Thou hast been our dwelling place in all generations." Or, "Lord, Thou hast searched me and known me." There are many. One may find helpful the literature of devotion aside from the Bible; sometimes a great poem of remembered radiance or a picture which speaks peace to the spirit at a time of great upheaval. Often there is a person whose life gives forth a quality of tranquility as one who has come through troubled seas into a place of calm and confidence.

> He understood what it is that we are trying to work out.
> He was very old, and from the secret swing of planets
> To the secret decencies in human hearts, he understood.
> I used to watch him watering his lawn, scattering the food for the woodpecker,
> Sweeping the crossing before his house. It was not that there was light
> About him, visible to the eye, as in the old paintings.
> Rather, an influence came from him in little breaths.
> When we were with him we became other.
> He saw us all as if we were that which we dreamed ourselves.
> He saw the town already clothed on for its Tomorrow,
> He saw the world, beating like a heart, beating like a heart.
> "How may I, too, know?" I wanted to cry to him. Instead
> I only said: "And how is it with you?" But he answered
> Both questions by the look in his eyes. For he had come to quietness.
> He had come to the place where sun and moon meet
> And where the spaces of the heavens open their doors.
> He was understanding and love and the silence.
> He was the voice of these, as he fed the woodpecker.[39]

For many Christians the contemplation of Jesus Christ is the most helpful aid. I know a man who always, at this point in his preparations, selects some incident in which Jesus is expressing his love for someone. He moves into identification, sometimes with the Master himself, sometimes with the object of the Master's love.

It may be that some problem is so central in thought and concern that it pushes everything else aside. If this happens to be the case, it should not cause undue distress as regards the business at hand. The problem itself may clear away everything else and in a sense perform an important task. This is one of the real services that an overriding problem may render the life of the spirit. It clears the decks for action. If such be the situation, then the individual can attack the problem itself as something that deadens the hunger; thus that which threatens is included in the process itself. If the problem is considered in the light of what it does to the hunger for God, this alone will put it into a different context and a new perspective. It will no longer be regarded merely as something that annoys, frustrates, or discourages, but rather as something that stands squarely in the way, blocking the pathway to God. Under such circumstances fresh insight is apt to come, and even if there is no immediate solution one is now in a position to challenge the integrity of the problem by raising his sights – looking at it from the other side, from the point of view of what it obscures.

Once the interference that drowns out the hunger has been stilled or removed, real communion between man and God can begin. Slowly the hunger begins to stir until it moves inside the individual's self-consciousness, and the sense of the very Presence of God becomes manifest. The words that are uttered, if there be words, may be halting and poor; they may have to do with some deep and searching need of which the individual now becomes acutely aware; it may be a sin that had become so much a part of the landscape of the soul that the soul itself has the feeling of corruption – but this may not last long. On the other hand, it may be a rather swift outpouring of a concern, because here is the moment of complete understanding and the freedom it inspires.

Several years ago I was talking with a very old lady about prayer, and particularly her own experience in prayer. She told me a story from her own most recent past. In her little Congregational church in a small New England community there was an extended crisis over the minister. The congregation felt he should leave because his usefulness was over. He prayed about the matter and as a result was convinced that, all evidence to the contrary notwithstanding, he should remain at his post. My friend said that she decided to take the matter directly to God in her prayer time. I quote her.

> I gave myself plenty of time. I went into a thorough review of the highlights of the sixty years I have been a member of the church right up to the present situa-

tion. I talked it through very carefully. It was so good to talk freely and to know that the feelings and the thoughts behind the words were being understood. When I finished I said, "Now Father, these are the facts as best I can state them. Take them and do the best you can. I have no suggestions to make."

A fresh meaning flooded the words "Thy Will be done."

The experience of communion may elicit an expression of concern for someone whose need is great or for whom one has compelling love. Such a person may be ill, or in trouble, or in deep quandary before the exacting demands of fateful decision. To bring him and his need clearly to mind, or into complete focus, and expose him tenderly to the scrutiny and love of God through our own thought is to pray for him. At such a moment questions as to the efficacy of intercessory prayer becomes merely academic.[40] I share my concern with God and leave the rest to Him. Does such a sharing do any good? Does it make a difference? The conviction of the praying person is that it does some good, that it does make a difference. Can you prove it, he may be asked. In what does proof of such a thing consist? The question of the effectiveness of intercessory prayer does not belong in the experience of the man who prays for his friend – it is his care that is poured out when he is most conscious of being cared for himself. When the hunger for God becomes articulate in a man so that it is one with his initial experience of God, it is the most natural thing in the world to share whatever his concerns may be. A man prays for loved ones because he has to, not merely because his prayer may accomplish something beyond this.

There is no attempt here to deal with the problems and issues that center in a discussion of what is called intercessory prayer. With reference to these I permit myself one comment only. The man who shares his concern for others with God in prayer does two things at the same time. He exposes the need of the other person to his total life and resources, making it possible for new insights of helpfulness and creativity to emerge in him. In other words he sees more clearly how to relate himself to the other person's need. In the second place, he may quicken the spirit of his friend to a sudden upsurging of the hunger for God, with the result that he is in the way of help from the vast creative energies of God. How this is done we may speculate but never explain. That it happens again and again in the religious experience of the race is a part of the data of the prayer experience itself.

Communion may be an overflowing of utter praise, adoration, and celebration. The sense of awe becomes trumpet-tongued, and the sheer joy of the beauty of holiness overwhelms the mind and enlivens all the emotions with a kindling of spiritual fervor. It is at such a moment that one feels he was created to praise God and to enjoy Him forever.

The communion may be an overflowing of thanksgiving. Here I do not mean an order of thanks for services rendered or for good received. Here is no perfunctory grace before meals, when a person chooses to mumble gratitude either out of habit, or superstition, or because of spiritual breeding of a high order. No, I do not mean this sort of thing, but rather the overflowing of the heart as an act of grace toward God. The overflow is not merely because of what has taken place in life or in the world or because of all the manifestations of benevolence that have covered a life. Something far more profound is at work. It is akin to adoration; it is the sheer joy in thanksgiving that God is God and the soul is privileged and blessed with the overwhelming consciousness of this. It is the kind of thanksgiving that sings itself to the Lord because He is God. This praiseful thanksgiving overshadows any bill of particulars, even though many particular things crowd into mind. We can get some notion of what is meant here when, under some circumstances, we encounter a person who, for what seems to be a swirling temporary moment, enjoys us – not what we say or what we are doing or what we represent, but who reaches into the core of our being and touches us purely. How such moments must rejoice the heart of God! I agree most heartily with Rufus Jones when he says that prayer at its best is when the soul enjoys God and prays out of sheer love of Him.

There is one remaining crucial element that must be taken into account in the experience of communion. I refer here specifically to the sense of sin, of unworthiness, that often takes on a dramatic character in the experience with God. Here I am not thinking primarily of human nature and man's general frailty, but more precisely of those awarenesses of having denied the hunger and, in the denial, having done violence to the integrity of the soul and to the sense of goodness and righteousness which became manifest along our journey. This goes deeper than the guilt one feels for going counter to a convention. That may be included, but I refer now specifically to the residue that remains as a man's own deep, personal, and private sense of sin and guilt. Sin has to be absorbed and the guilt washed from the spirit. How this is done we do not know. There are Christians who experience the redeeming love of Christ, which sets them free of guilt because they believe that in some miraculous way He takes their guilt upon Him and absorbs in His Body and Spirit the virus of their sins. For those who believe, the offering of Christ is made to God on their behalf, and in Christ's name they pass from darkness into light.

For many others this whole experience involves something more than can be managed with the mind. There is a strange necessity in the human spirit that a man deal with his sin before God. This necessity is honored in prayer when the deed is laid bare and the guilt acknowledged. I do not know how it happens or quite how to describe it, but I do know that again and again man has come away from prayer freed of his guilt, and with his sin forgiven; he then has a sense of being totally understood, completely dealt with, thoroughly experienced, and utterly healed. This is not to suggest that after the experience a man is always through with his sin. No, but now a solvent is at work on it which dissolves it, and the virus begins to be checked in its breeding place.

The experience of prayer, as I have been describing it, can be nurtured and cultivated. It can create a climate in which a man's life moves and functions. Indeed, it may become a way of living for the individual. It is ever possible that the time may come when a man carries such an atmosphere around with him and gives its quality to all that he does and communicates its spirit to all who cross his path. This was the most remarkable impact of the life of the Master upon those whom he encountered. It was this that stilled the ragings of the madman, that called little children to Him, that made sinners know that their sins were forgiven. His whole countenance glowed with the glory of the Father. And the secret? "A great while before day, he withdrew to a solitary place and prayed, *as was his custom.*"

Section Two

RELIGIOUS EXPERIENCE AND ETHICAL LIFE

Meditation | *Freedom Is a Discipline*

THERE IS A MEDLEY of confusion as to the meaning of personal freedom. For some it means to function without limitations at any point, to be able to do what one wants to do and without hindrance. This is the fantasy of many minds, particularly those that are young. For others, personal freedom is to be let alone, to be protected against any force that may move into the life with a swift and decisive imperative. For still others, it means to be limited in one's power over others only by one's own strength, energy, and perseverance.

The meaning of personal freedom is found in none of these. They lack the precious ingredient, the core of discipline and inner structure without which personal freedom is a delusion. At the very center personal freedom is a discipline of the mind and of the emotions. The mind must be centered upon a goal, a purpose, a plan. Of all possible goals, purposes, plans, a single one is lifted above the others and held as one's chosen direction. Then the individual knows when he is lost, when he has missed the way. There emerges a principle of orderedness which becomes a guide for behavior and action. Under such circumstances, goals may be changed deliberately and the sense of random, pointless living is removed.

Such a principle of orderedness provides a channel for one's emotions and drive. Energy is no longer dissipated but it is used to supply dynamic for the pursuit of the end. Here we come upon the most interesting aspect of personal freedom – the living of one's life with confidence that transcends discouragement and despair. This means that one does not have to depend upon the favorable circumstance, the fortuitous "break," the applause, approval, and felicitation of friends, important as these are. The secret is the quiet inner purpose and the release of vitality with which it inspires the act. Achieving the goal is not measured by some external standard, though such must not be completely ignored. Rather, it is measured in terms of loyalty to the purpose and the freedom which it inspires.

"Seek ye first the rule of God," the Master says. And after that? The key that one needs for one's peace is in the heart. There can be no personal freedom where there is not an initial personal surrender.[41]

CS | *Concerning the Search* (1971)

In 1971, Thurman published The Search for Common Ground, *his formal treatise on the theological foundation of community in human life.*[42] *Thurman often referred to this book as his "lifelong working paper," for it represented the philosophical culmination of his own "search" as expressed in his life and work. In the following chapter, which opens the book, Thurman provides the most comprehensive definition of community of his entire corpus. As he makes clear, community – along with the ethical forms that ultimately prevail in community – is grounded in the discernable moral order of the universe, itself evidence of the Creator's intent.*

> An old man with a double-bit axe
> Is caretaker at the Gore place. The cattle, except a few wild horns, died in that
>   fire; the horses
> Graze high up the dark hill; nobody ever comes to the infamous house; the pain,
>   the hate and the love
> Have left no ghost. Old men and gray hawks need solitude,
> Here it is deep and wide.

> "Winter and summer," the old man says, "rain and the drought;
> Peace creeps out of war, war out of peace; the stars rise and they set; the clouds go
>   north

And again they go south. – Why does God hunt in circles? Has he lost something?
Is it possible – himself?
In the darkness between the stars did he lose himself and become godless, and
seeks – himself?

"Does God exist? – No doubt of that," the old man says. "The cells of my old camel
of a body,
Because they feel each other and are fitted together – through nerves and blood
feel each other – all the little animals
Are the one man: there is not an atom in all the universes
But feels every other atom; gravitation, electromagnetism, light, heat, and the
other
Flamings, the nerves in the night's black flesh, flow them together; the stars, the
winds and the people: one energy,
One existence, one music, one organism, one life, one God: star-fire and rock-
strength, the sea's cold flow
And man's dark soul."

"Not a tribal nor an anthropoid God.
Not a ridiculous projection of human fears, needs, dreams, justice and love-lust."

"A conscious God? – The question has no importance. But I am conscious: where
else
Did this consciousness come from? Nobody that I know of ever poured grain from
an empty sack.
And who, I would say, but God, and a conscious one,
Ended the chief war-makers with their war, so humorously, such accurate timing,
and such
Appropriate ends? . . ."   *– Robinson Jeffers*[43]

THERE IS SOMETHING SO PRIVATE AND PERSONAL about an act of thought
that the individual may very easily seem to be a private island on a boundless human sea. To experience one's self is to enter into a solitary world
that is one's unique possession and that can never be completely and utterly shared. Here is the paradox. A man is always threatened in his very
ground by a sense of isolation, by feeling himself cut off from his fellows.

Yet he can never separate himself from his fellows, for mutual interdependence is characteristic of all of life.

The need to care for and the need to be cared for is another expression of the same basic idea. It is unnecessary to resort to moral or religious authority for a mandate or for an injunction. Such needs are organic, whatever may be their psychological or spiritual derivatives. Therefore, whenever the individual is cut off from the private and personal nourishment from other individuals or from particular individuals, the result is a wasting away, a starvation, a failure of life to be sustained and nourished. Studies show that some fifty years ago, when an effort was made to track down the cause of the death of more than half of the children who died during the first year of life, it was found to be due to a disease known as *marasmus*. This disease was also known as infantile atrophy or devility, coming from the Greek word *marasmós*, meaning "wasting away." The discovery was made that such babies were not neglected as far as their physical care, cleanliness, and the like were concerned. Rather, what was lacking was the free and easy access of the child to the psychic nourishment made possible through mother love. Perhaps it is largely for this reason that hospitals today keep the infant for as short a period as possible. When the real mother is not available, mother-love substitutes are provided. I have heard of an instance in which a mother's heartbeat was put on a tape and the sound amplified through the public address system in a hospital nursery for the benefit of all the babies.

The human spirit cannot abide the enforced loneliness of isolation. We literally feed on each other; where this nourishment is not available, the human spirit and the human body—both—sicken and die. It is not an overstatement that the purpose of all of the arrangements and conventions that make up the formal and informal agreements under which men live in society is to nourish one another *with* one another. The safeguards by which individuals or groups of men establish the boundaries of intimate and collective belonging are meant ultimately to guarantee self-nourishment. All of these are but social expressions of the underlying experience of life with itself. Life feeds on life; life is nourished by life. It is life's experience with itself that establishes the ground for the dogma that life is eternal.

To seek nourishment is a built-in urge, an ingredient of life in its sim-

plest or most complex manifestations. The creative push that expresses itself in this way is the manner by which life realizes itself. The descriptive
term that characterizes such behavior is "actualizing potential." Wherever
life is observed this is its primary activity or business. In this sense all life
is engaged in goal-seeking.

The degree to which the potential in any expression of life is actualized
marks the extent to which such an expression of life experiences wholeness, integration, community. The clue to community can be found in the
inner creative activity of living substances. The more highly developed
the organism, the more pronounced seems to be the manifestation of the
clue. Cells and organisms always show certain characteristics of direction, persistence, and adaptability in their efforts to realize themselves, to
round themselves out, to fulfill themselves, to become, to ripen in integration – in fine, to experience community. The more highly developed the
organism, the more plainly manifest are these characteristics.

It seems reasonable to say, then, that the "intent" of creation is that life
lives by constantly seeking to realize itself in established forms, patterns,
and units. Expressed in this way, it must not be thought that life is static,
something that is set, fixed, determined. The key word to remember always is *potential*: that which has not yet come to pass but which is always
coming to pass. It is only the potential, the undisclosed, the unfinished
that has a future. I find it difficult to think of life apart from the notion of
potential; indeed, they seem synonymous. To be sure, life is not finished
yet; creation is still going on, not only in the spinning of new worlds, sys-
tems, nebulae, and galaxies in the infinitude of space, not only in the invisible world where chemical elements are born and nourished to support
conglomerates of matter yet to appear at some far-off moment in time, but
also in the human body, which is still evolving, in the human mind, which
so slowly loosens its corporal bonds, and in the human spirit, which forever drives to know the truth of itself and of its fellows.

In human society, the experience of community, or realized potential,
is rooted in life itself because the intuitive human urge for community reflects a characteristic of all life. In the total panorama of the external world
of nature, there seems to be a pattern of structural dependability and continuity, or what may be called an inner logic, that manifests itself in forms,

organizational schemes, and in a wide variety of time-space arrangements. The most striking pattern of all is that there seems to be affinity between the human mind and all external forms, a fact that makes an understanding of the world possible for the mind.

The religious basis for such an interpretation of community is the affirmation, which to me is categorical, that the Mind of God realizes Itself in *time,* and that there are observable patterns or sequences in all creation. Thus God is thought of as Creator. From this point of view, all time-space manifestations of substance – in short, all things, even existence itself – are regarded as the Mind of God coming to *Itself* in time and space. This is evident in history and in nature. Existence itself is construed as divine activity. There seems to be a principle of rationality in all existence, and the significance of this can be found in the order of life. True, what seems to be a principle of rationality as expressed in observable order in life may be a limitation of mind itself. Yet it is this assumption of inherent logic in the functioning of the mind that makes comprehension of the external world possible.

I recognize the fact that in using the formal name Creator, I am using anthropomorphic terminology. I do this quite deliberately, because I find it quite impossible to think of action – and this is implicit in the term – as an abstraction. While it is true that when the mind is concerned with something as vast as existence itself, any kind of limitation is paradoxical, if not contradictory; nevertheless, the mind as a thinking entity can only make sense of this complexity by using symbols that can stand for ideas and fields of comprehension. Behind the "thisness and thatness" of experience and observation one has to sense something more. Whatever term is used to express this dimension (also a limiting word) simply extends the boundary; it does not get rid of it. One may use the term *ground* or *infinitude,* or, to borrow a phrase from Northrup, "the undifferentiated aesthetic continuum"; or Eckhart's *nameless nothing* or *Godhead* as he distinguishes it from God; or a contemporary theologian's term, "God above God." All these phrases are an attempt to escape the dilemma of pure existence that, to the mind, is meaningless.

The man who seeks community within his own spirit, who searches for it in his experiences with the literal facts of the external world, who makes this his formal intent as he seeks to bring order out of the chaos of his collective life, is not going against life but will be sustained and supported by life. And for the world of modern man this is crucial. In the conflicts between man and man, between group and group, between nation and nation, the loneliness of the seeker for community is sometimes unendurable. The radical tension between good and evil, as man sees it and feels it, does not have the last word about the meaning of life and the nature of existence. There is a spirit in man and in the world working always against the thing that destroys and lays waste. Always he must know that the contradictions of life are not final or ultimate; he must distinguish between failure and a many-sided awareness so that he will not mistake conformity for harmony, uniformity for synthesis. He will know that for all men to be alike is the death of life in man, and yet perceive the harmony that transcends all diversities and in which diversity finds its richness and significance.

The order in creation and the orderly disorder that seem to characterize what is regarded as random activity in certain aspects of the world external to man, the concepts in the mind that are derivatives of man's experience with his senses, and those other concepts that seem to take their form from the boundless ebb and flow of the imageless tides that wash the shores of the human mind and spirit – all these express an authentic creativity that is Mind at work, and man is an essential part of the order. What is observed as a structure of orderliness or dependability in any and all expressions of life, from the simplest forms to the most complex, is seen most dramatically in the ability of man to create, to conceptualize, to plan, to function purposefully, and to implement in time and space what is idea or thought to the mind. From within the narrow circle of man's mind there can be no thought or action that is not involved in some form of intent – intent as a form of volition, focused or unfocused, deliberate or unconscious. In man's experience with life, within him at all levels and about him in varied manifestations in time-space intervals, he is a part of the world of facts and meaning, suggesting creative intent. It seems reasonable, then, to assume that wherever life is found, evidence of creative intent must also exist in that which is being experienced, reacted to, observed, or studied. One such sign, and the most crucial one, is the way life seeks always to realize itself in wholeness, harmony, and integration within the potential that characterizes the particular expression of life. The most natural question that comes to mind, therefore, whenever men reflect upon or try to rationalize their experiences of life is: How did life get started? What was the beginning of it all?

                                           ∞ | *Excerpt from*
"Mysticism and Social Change" (1939)

The troubling relationship between mysticism and ethics is long-standing in Western Christian traditions. [44] Interpretive questions about the intelligible relevance of mystical union to historical and social existence are always central. [45] Thurman addressed these issues in four lectures presented at the Eden Theological Seminary in 1939, the latter two of which are published here. His primary concern is with the mystic's ethical responsibility to achieve in the commonplace what is experienced as "union" with Divine Presence. Although the experience of union is intensely personal and private, for Thurman it always includes an ethical demand which brings the mystic face-to-face with the society in which he or she functions. Consequently, the mystic discovers that he or she must be responsive not only to the personal demands of the moral life, but to the human needs by which one's life is surrounded. The mystic must therefore be engaged in disciplines and practices that allow for the eradication of all barriers, personal and social, that prevent the realization of the vision of God.

Mysticism and Ethics

MANY THINKERS ARE OF THE OPINION that mysticism makes no contribution to ethical theory in general and social ethical theory in particular. Bertrand Russell says, "What is in all cases ethically characteristic of mysticism is absence of indignation or protest, *acceptance* with *joy,* disbelief in the ultimate truth of the division into two hostile camps, the good and the bad. This attitude is a direct outcome of the nature of the mystical experience; with its sense of unity is associated a feeling of infinite peace."[46] What this point of view and similar ones overlook is the fact of the reality of evil and sin as the mystic discovers it first in his own spirit and then in the world of men. The life of the mystic is worked out in the world of men and things. There *is* an element of the solitariness in his experience. Perhaps it is the solitariness of life that makes it move with such ruggedness. All life is one and yet life seems to move in such intimate circles of awful individuality. The power of life is in its aloneness but this is a paradox of paradoxes. There are thresholds before which all men stop and only God may tread and even He in disguise. Each soul must learn, so the mystic thinks, to stand up in its own right and live. How blissful to lean on another, to seek a sense of the everlasting arm expressed in the presence of a friend. We walk a part of the way together but on the upper reaches of life each path takes itself away to the heights alone. Ultimately, I am alone, so vastly alone that in my aloneness is all the life of the universe. In such moments of profound awareness, I seem to be all that there is in the world and all that there is seems to be I. It seems to be true then that in the mystic's moments of highest spiritual experience (of manifestations) all divisions, all tensions are resolved—only the vision, the experience itself seems to be the real but this is not for long. He knows that he cannot escape the fundamental problem of ethics as it works itself out in his time-space relationships, namely, what is the true end of man and how may that end influence the conduct of his life.

The goal of the mystic, therefore, is to know God in a comprehensive sense; for God is grasped by the whole self or the whole self is laid hold upon by God—the vision of God is realized inclusively. To illustrate precisely what I mean, let me quote an extract from the life of Tolstoy. It is the same quotation used in this connection by Dr. Hocking: "When I saw the head separate from the body and how they both thumped into the box at the moment, I understood, not with my mind, but with my whole being, that no theory of the reasonableness of any present progress can justify this deed; and that though everybody from the creation of the world, on whatever theory had held it to be necessary, I knew it to be unnecessary and bad."[47]

The mystic experiences unity, not identity, but it is a unity that penetrates through all the levels of consciousness and fills him with a sense of the Other. He uses symbolism to help him keep alive this sense of presence. He discovers, however, that it is not possible to keep the consciousness of the presence of God alive at a high point in his experience over long time intervals. The most natural thing for him to do is try to recall by memory what has been experienced. But this, too, fades away even though it leaves a deposit in his personality. The glow that was cast on all of life is apt to be dimmed as he becomes more and more involved in the many. He comes upon the fact that deep within the structure of his own personality and life are the things which obscure and blot out his vision. In other words, the struggle with impulses, with inner divisions, unworthy desires, purely self-regarding tactics including the whole world of egocentric manifestations, all these are regarded by him as an indispensable part of the defect of his vision.

Discipline of some sort becomes necessary and inevitable. The details of his life among the many must be brought into line with the fullness of his vision. The disciplines have tended to center around the struggles of the flesh. Much of the psychopathology of mysticism has to do with this phase of it. To give only one instance of extreme practices, we may refer to Suso's early life as reported by Principal Hughes. From his 18th year on for twenty-two years, he sought to break his wild spirit and his pampered body by a series of painful practices. For the first ten years he shut himself up in absolute seclusion in his cloister. For a long time he wore a hair shirt and an iron chain, later a hair undershirt with nails, which pierced his flesh at every motion and whenever he lay down. In order not to be able to avoid the bites of vermin (for he did not bathe during the twenty-two years), he put his hands in slings during the night. He bore a cross, a span long with thirty nails and seven needles bound upon his bare back; every day he lay down upon it or threw himself upon it. For a long time a door was his bed. The pains of cold, hunger, thirst and the bloody flagellation he inflicted upon himself for so long a time and with such severity that he came near dying.[48] Reference need only be made to the far reaching significance of this tendency in the very warp and woof of monasticism. The fundamental point, however, is that in asceticism and its discipline is a recognition of the reality of evil and the profound conviction that it can be overcome. No one who studies the disciplinary practices of heroic Christian mysticism can hold as tenable the theory that mysticism regards evil merely as illusion. In the extreme forms of asceticism there is that which is profoundly revolting and sadistic but there is the bold recognition of the fact that nothing not even one's physical well-being and life is quite worthy of obscuring the vision of God. In my opinion this insight represents religion at its best and it lifts the moral dignity of the life of man to a high and holy level.

Suppose we approach the problem from another angle? From the earliest moments of conscious life there is a tendency toward a developing self-consciousness or differentiation and uniqueness within the stream of consciousness itself. The babe usually discovers its separateness from others – from its mother, for instance, who stops feeding him sometimes even as he wishes her to continue. In some strange way separateness and divisibility dawn in his mind as a way of thinking about the world. He is beginning to locate himself in a series of other-than-self relationships. He discovers that he cannot control completely the other-than-self's to which he must adjust himself and by which he is surrounded. Various techniques of adjustment and control are developed, such as crying, laughing at the right moment, etc. It must be a great moment in the life of a baby when, acting reflectively upon his experience, he discovers for the first time that often it is the crying baby that gets rocked. Then a moment comes when he can hold his own bottle so as to release the mother or the nurse. From his point of view, that is not the purpose of the act. It is a primary act of self-extension and is the beginning of a social process of cooperation purely in self-interest, that is implied in all of the humanitarian impulses that later as an adult may develop in him.

Another day comes. It is the greatest and most prophetic moment in the life of the child. Struggling along, held almost horizontal to the floor by nature and by his own undeveloped self-consciousness, he staggers unsteadily to an upright position on his feet – miracle of miracles, there he is, suspended between the ceiling and the floor with his little feet touching, he stands alone. His act says: *I did it.* In that moment of deepest awareness his knees give way and the floor rises up to meet him. But always with his environment the struggle goes on apace – the struggle to achieve individuality, to discover a practical reinforcement of the self so he can act as an individual, as a person, as a unit, as a whole.

He carries his struggle for selfhood into his relationships with the world of nature and with the social order. It is the way of growth. The story is essentially the same for all human beings. It is a unity that is developed and perhaps brought into being by the vicissitudes of life and experience. The ground of personal morality and ethics is in this struggle. Things become immoral that defeat this achieving individuality. To be sure it is a morality on the lower level waiting for a higher touch, a higher synthesis.

What is true of human life in general and of the developing of self-consciousness of man in particular, is also true of the mystic in worship. In his act of worship the mystic achieves a transcending unity. His self-centeredness is resolved in a higher synthesis. God possesses him. Something new enters the picture, it is a new value judgment. Now things are not ethical or unethical merely because they aid or take away from his achieving individuality but because they are now viewed as ways that lead to the mount of vision or away from the mount of vision. The meaning of life is for him summarized in the vision of the good which he has thoroughly experienced. The vision makes mandatory that he *be* good so as to stand ever in immediate candidacy for the reception of God.

This is a most radical experience. It involves a judgment of the will with reference to the ends which one has sought in living and achieving the self. The judgement of God stands now where the judgment of the self stood before. Things are no longer merely ethical or unethical, they are sinful or righteous – a religious quality has appeared in morality. Now the moment that the religious quality appears, the stage is set for withdrawal from social intercourse and in a sense a withdrawal of the self from nature. Hence the struggle with the flesh – in short, asceticism.

But this is only one aspect of the logic of the result. As a result of his vision, the former tensions are not resolved in function. He has to go through the whole process of the achieving of individuality with God as the new center of reference. It requires a very stern exercise of the will because a new orientation has taken place. In a sense he is becoming a new creature, a qualitative urgency is at the focal point of his consciousness. I venture to say that every new synthesis of the individual around a fresh goal on whatever level of experience it may take place, is but an implied reference to the ultimate goal of human life, namely, to know God, in some exhaustive and completely thoroughgoing sense. When Commodore Perry suggests that for twelve years he was ill at ease until he planted the stars and stripes over the North Pole; when a music critic says of Roland Hayes that he sings because he must sing; when a news reporter suggests that Walter Hampden had to stop playing in a contemporary drama to play the role of Shylock in order to keep a contract with his soul; when the Apostle Paul says, "woe is me if I preach not the Gospel" or when he exclaims to Agrippa, "I was not disobedient to the heavenly vision"; or when Jesus says, "the spirit of the Lord is upon me, for He has anointed me to preach the Gospel to the poor, to open the eyes of the blind, to unstop the ears of the deaf, to release the captive, to announce the accepted year of the Lord" – all these fundamentally are in the same frame of reference.[49]

It is this inner equilibrium that must be maintained at all costs so that the person will stand ever in immediate candidacy for the direct visitation of God. This is the heart of the meaning of discipline in the religion of the mystic. – All the negative things are present in the discipline, yes, this cannot be denied; the highly abnormal aberrations of mind are present, oftentimes, to be sure. But there is something more, there is strength, power released in the life of man here, a kind of concomitant overflowing of creative energies which demand that he be *true* himself by the highest. This he seeks to do through discipline with unrelenting austerity; he must bring himself, his will, his feelings, his very thoughts and impulses under the synthesizing scrutiny of God. All else is trivial and in a sense irrelevant. The greatest mystic-ascetics in the Christian tradition have turned the whole stream of Christian thought and achievement into new and powerful channels of practical living.

The flesh does fight against the spirit. In Jesus Christ as symbol, temporary or permanent, the Christian mystic sees the meaning of the triumph of the spirit over the body; the transcending and triumphant power of God over the most relentless pressure and persistence of things that divide and destroy. To know Him in the fellowship of His suffering seemed to the Christian mystic the key to his victory. In this the mystic proves himself a man of rarest insight and power. In this insight the mystic anticipates the needs of all men. We want deliverance from things which divide, which bind and render us impotent and purposeless. We want to find a controlling purpose for our living and for our lives. With relentlessness and fever we seek always to find meaning, in some ultimate sense, for our lives so that we may be able to live with dignity and courage in our world. This the mystic achieves by what to him is an experience of an absolute good and his ethical task is to retain that good in the *"for instances"* of experience.

What Professor Hocking has called the principle of alternation is in the very structure of all experience. The mystic discovers this in a most extraordinary fashion. He is a man – he is a part and parcel of all the world of nature – he has warring impulses within and participates in strife without. He sees that the world of things and men does not conform to the unity which he has experienced in his vision. Was his vision false? Was his experience genuine or was it merely an illusion? He finds that the two worlds must in some sense be one because he participates actively in both at the same moment but he is convinced that the meaning of the below is in the above.

With such a conviction, ascetism no longer means withdrawal from men but rather it means a steady insistence that one's human relations conform more and more to the transparency of one's inner graces, one's inner equilibrium in which is his consciousness of the active presence of God. Humanity is viewed as a unit within which are particular individuals all of which must be yielded to the control of God. This calls for the highest possible ethical demands for one's own conduct, for one's outgoing relation. Often it leads one to cut right across all social forms, all social behavior patterns, all conventions. There is a profound element of anarchy in all spiritually motivated behavior. The temptations to pride, arrogance, self-righteousness, are ever present but the risk has to be run and the only safeguard is the recurring vision in the acts of worship themselves. And insistently the significance of the acts of worship must be tested by the degree to which they remain living channels for the direct release of God into the life of the worshipper. When they become institutionalized they are apt to become dead so the mystic seems always to be the foe of institutional religion. He is very sensitive to the crystallizing of acts of worship into dead forms. It is profoundly true that he does not stand in need of the institution or the institutional forms as such. Even in Catholicism any careful reading of the testimony of the mystics convinces one that the church has no real friend in the mystic.

In addition to the scrutiny of the mystic's personal relations as far as what he will do or will not do in a given situation, there is a whole question of the quality of service the mystic must render to his fellowmen.

Canon Kirk has a most illuminating discussion on this point in his *Vision of God*.[50] He insists that the concept of service has two profoundly different elements in it – one is the service of humility, and the other is the service of patronage. Only the former is Christian. It is his opinion that only worship guarantees to service the quality of humility that makes it really Christian – really good. There is no gratuitous quality when it springs from patronage. It is the attitude of condescension, of arrogance, the "holier than thou" manifestation much of which I have experienced in missions and observed on the mission field. It says, I am better than you, poor devil, I am really a very different order of being and out of my plenty, out of my advantage over you, I deign to come to your rescue. You ought to be grateful to me. In fact your gratitude must have in it a certain abjectness in order that my own position and ego may be rendered even more immune to attacks of unity.

Humility cannot be acquired that way. It comes only when a man looks at himself, what he is, in the quiet but penetrating glow of his vision of God. Without this he cannot maintain the necessary increment of humility at the very center of his good deeds. He has been loved by God, he has received the blessing of the presence of God as an act of grace and he must salute the good that there is in the other by the quality of humility present in his deeds for the other. It was in speaking of Jesus that Simkhovitch says, "Humility can never be humiliated."[51] If that quality is present, then to have one's deeds gratefully received, to be thanked, even to be appreciated is beside the point. If what is done is applauded or not applauded, if it

is known by others or unknown to others, it is irrelevant. If one is persecuted by the very individual whom one serves, that, too is beside the
point. It is only in the presence of God, in the moment when one is caught
up in an all-embracing unity that this new way of seeing one's self in one's
relations is achieved. Kirk says, "Disinterested service is the only service
that is serviceable."[52]

The concept of service as a means of acquiring merit has never been
without its witnesses. The highest mystics insist that the essence of right
acting is that it should be performed without regard to merit, to reward or
punishment. Only the rare spirit achieves this as a rule of life but it is to be
noted that whenever men love each other, action for the beloved takes on
this quality of disinterestedness. The implications of behavior of this kind
derived from the mystic's insight has far-reaching and revolutionary significance for social change.

Mysticism and Social Change

I come now to the last and, in some ways, the most fundamentally crucial
lecture of the series. We shall begin with the proposition with which we
closed our last lecture. The basic ethical significance of mysticism is individualistic; this cannot be successfully refuted but it has also been
pointed out that even in the moment of vision there is a sense of community—a unity not only with God but a unity with all of life, particularly
with human life. It is in the moment of vision that the mystic discovers
that (his) "private values are undergirded and determined by a structure
which far transcends the limits of one's individual self." The good which is
given him must somehow be achieved in a framework of experiences native to his own life which his life "for instances" in a rich variety of details.
The ascetic impulse having as its purpose individual purification and living brings the realistic mystic face to face with the society in which he
functions as a person. He discovers that he is a person and a personality
in a profound sense can only be achieved in a milieu of human relations.
Personality is something more than mere individuality—it is a fulfillment
of the logic of individuality in community.

Rufus Jones uses the term, *affirmation mystics,* to apply to those who are concerned with working out in a social frame of reference the realism of their mystic experience. He says that the mystic is always more than any finite task declares, and "yet he accepts this task because he has discovered that only through the finite is the Infinite to be found."[53] Now the mystic is compelled to deal with social relations for two reasons. First, because much of the limitations and corruption of his own life of which he seeks to rid himself through discipline and rigorism is due to the fact of his belonging to a community of men and interests which foster the very things he discovers beclouding his vision. In the second place, in his effort to achieve the good, he finds that he must be responsive to human needs by which his life is surrounded. We shall discuss each of these in its order.

1. Isaiah saw the Lord – when he was dropped back into the stream of his conscious life he saw himself to be a man of unclean lips dwelling among people of unclean lips. The two facts are not different facts, they are essentially the same fact. It is basic to the Christian tradition that social sin and personal sin are bound up together in an inexorable relationship so that it is literally true that no man can expect to have his soul saved alone. The affirmation mystic is driven then, in the very nature of the case, in the very interests of the fulfillment of his mystical vision to a grave concern in the state of the soul of other men. The crudest and barest individualistic ethic, realistically considered would guarantee this. Many a monastic ascetic, fleeing from the world to the wilderness discovered that in the barren wastes of his own solitariness were present all the things from which he had fled. What lesson is more clearly evident than this in the temptation story of Jesus, the basic issues inherent in the political framework of the Roman Empire, the problems of a suppressed minority, all these and many others were with Him. In the lonely night watches they were among the other wild beasts from the world of nature which kept the vigil with the Son of Man. It is not only the socialist but also the affirmation mystic or the man seeking the fullness of the vision of God who must say truly, "While there is a lower class, I am in it. While there is a criminal element, I am of it. While there is a man in jail, I am not free."[54] The distinction between personal selfishness and social selfishness, between personal religion and social religion which we are wont to make, must forever remain artificial and unrealistic.

The mystic, under obligation to achieve the good which in some profound sense is given in the moment of vision and which he already possesses, is concerned about the sins of human life. He discovers that they fall roughly into two general classifications – those that are in some sense personal and private because they concern certain manifestations of the ego, that are unrestrained, undisciplined, chaotic – what is ordinarily thought of as the sins of the flesh. His first move, therefore, is to conquer these, to reduce them to a manageable unit, to bring them under the central domination of a will that is committed to ends of purity and holiness. His second concern must be with those that spring from the collective, unrestraint of his fellows, the social chaos which results from dominant forms of economic and political organization. The personal question, what makes it difficult and well nigh impossible for me as a person to achieve the good in my own life leads inevitably to the question, what makes it so difficult for my society to achieve the good? He may limit the questions to those aspects of his society that are united on the basis of a common goal inspired by a collective vision of God such as a church or order but the problem fundamentally remains the same. For even if it is achieved in a selective group this group bears a fundamental relationship with all others and their achievement stands ever under attack until it is universal.

He sees that the root of many of his own difficulties is located in the fact of his own personal economic insecurity. He must earn a living, under conditions that are not responsive to his master concern, namely, the achieving of the good in his life. It is the merest romanticism to assume that because God is the Creator of human life and human nature and the world of nature that He is also in control of the network of social relationships by which men are bound to each other in ways other than a common ground of being. The freedom of the will of man is always the instrument that is apt to make for chaos in the social relations of men. The problems of human relations can never be solved merely by the radical transformation of individuals in society. Therefore, there are certain basic fears that never leave the mystic, fears that are rooted for instance in the threat of insecurity and all that goes with it. He cannot achieve the good even in his simplest relations with his fellows because of the difficulties involved in establishing a basis of trust between him and them that will not victimize him in his effort to maintain himself in the world. This is true because each man is an actual threat or may easily become an actual threat to his security. The tendency is to let the ethical insight of love remain transcendent in his relationships but never imminent in them. The risk of annihilation is too great. Now the Catholic mystic who identified himself with some order in the church short-circuited this whole problem on the economic side because the church guaranteed to him his economic needs and released him from direct responsibility for them. It simply put the whole problem one or two steps back in the process but did not solve it. We shall have occasion to refer to the bearing of this fact on service a little later in our discussion.

Or again when he tries to achieve the good in his political relations he is brought sharp up against the fact that these relationships are characterized by methods of control in the State which give the advantage to one class as over against another class – that justice is robbed of its moral quality and is merely a state of equilibrium which represents a truce between the exploiters and exploited with the weight of the decision always on the side of privilege and power. The problems seem so hopeless that there is ever present the temptation to flee from the world and attempt to settle the problem of achieving the good along lines true to the very nature of asceticism.

2. The mystic is forced to deal with social relations in the second place because in his effort to achieve the good he finds that he must be responsive to human need by which he is surrounded, particularly the kind of human need in which the sufferers are victims of circumstances over which, as individuals, they have no control, circumstances that are not responsive to the exercise of an individual will however good and however perfect. This brings up for discussion once again the question of service. May I remind you of Kirk's quotation that "Disinterested service is the only service that is serviceable." Now, precisely what is disinterested service? In an appendix to *The Vision of God*, Canon Kirk has a most illuminating analysis of the concept. He defines selfishness "as a lack of due regard for the well-being of others," and "unselfishness . . . is the payment of due regard to the well-being of others." It would seem to me that disinterested

service is a kind of service that has no narrow ulterior motive at work, a kind of service in which the person served is not a means to some end in which he does not share and participate directly. There are at least two levels of disinterestedness – one, in which the individual is free from exploiting the need of others for purely narrow interest or gratification. An American novelist of the last century put it this way, "No man may say I have smiled on him in order to use him or call him my friend that I may make him do for me the work of a servant."[55] There is a second level of service, in which the individual is interested in relieving human need because he sees it as in some definite sense crowding out of the life of others the possibility of developing those qualities of interior graces that will bring him into immediate candidacy for the vision of God. It is in this latter sense that we come upon the mandatory raison d'etre of the affirmation mystic's interest in social change and in social action. He is not interested in social action because of any particular political or economic theory; he is not interested in social action primarily from the point of view of humanitarianism or humanism – as important as these emphases are, but he is interested in social action because society as he knows it to be ensnares the human spirit in a maze of particulars so that the One cannot be sensed nor the good realized. He is not deluded into thinking that once men are freed from carking care, from anxiety due to poverty or riches, from misery due to greed and exploitation, they will automatically be in immediate candidacy for the perfectionism of the spirit. He sees, however, that with these situations relieved there is available a psychological climate in which men may ascend the mount of vision with freedom and abandonment. This can only be done when individuals become persons; they cannot become persons in a society in which the majority of mankind is involved in a life and death struggle for bare security. In this struggle a comparatively small number have arisen above the line of bare security and have established themselves in such a strong position of control of the total economic life of man that they may be regarded as the very custodians of the lifeline of the masses of their fellows. They have possessions of the means of production and are in a position to control for their own interests and the perpetuation of their kind the natural resources that are the main bases of supply for the masses of the people, all of this without a sense responsibility to the people. In the absence of this responsibility to the people there is very little hope that the individuals who make up the rank and file of mankind can become persons. Social power in society as we know it is inevitable. The problem is to place dynamic and effective inner moral and external social checks upon the centers of social power. This can only be done by broadening the basis of social responsibility on the part of social control until it includes all of the individuals in society and by injecting a sense of high morality in the persons who emerge as a result of the radical alteration in the structure of social relationships which is involved. The guaranty of the basic economic needs of the persons will be located in the collective will of the body politic and with reference to the struggle for bread the imperialistic will of persons can be relaxed. When this happens the insight of the mystic as to the ultimate meaning of human life will have practical relevancy without seeming to be unrealistic, romantic or sentimental.

Between the present order of society and that order of society which we have described is a perilous way but it is a way in which the affirmation mystic must chart his course. What then is his course of action? Let me gather up the threads of my position to this point: the affirmation mystic interprets the meaning of man's life in terms of an experienced unity with God in a conscious sense. "To know that our being has been taken up and made an organic part of His very self, because He wills and because we will it, is the end of true mysticism." What he experiences he is under obligation to achieve in experience. In his effort to achieve this in experience he is brought face to face with evil in his own life and in the lives of others and the reflection of this evil in the relationships by which he is bound to his fellows and his fellows are bound to him. He cannot escape the responsibility of working out the good in a manifold of inner and outer relations. He knows that he cannot escape in mere asceticism even as he recognizes its merits he must embrace the social whole and seek to achieve empirically the good which has possessed him in his moment of profoundest insight. In his effort to do this, he constantly checks his action by his insight. It keeps his insight true and his action valid.

Now we are prepared to point out certain things with reference to the way he charts his course. First, he must bring his own spirit, those stubborn and recalcitrant aspects of it, under the domination of the God whom he has known in his mystical union. This, alone, is often the quest of a lifetime. His inmost desires must be checked by his new will. In this he does not ever struggle alone, God is his strength. In the second place, he must be as charitable toward the weaknesses of others as he is toward the weaknesses of himself for he knows through bitter experience that much has flown from his own life into the lives of others that was unworthy and that it is mandatory that he look with understanding compassion upon others as that which is unworthy flows from them to him. Further, his inner purity demands that he must not condemn in society what he does not condemn himself. These considerations belong primarily in the realm of personal piety. There can be no substitute for personal piety for he cannot be a liar to himself. In the third place, he sees that he shares consciously or unconsciously in the collective guilt of his age, of his society, of his race, and his problem is how to work out an atonement for this guilt in ways that would be redemptive and not make this action the goal of life. The obvious thing for him to attempt is some form of moral appeal to his fellows that will make them acutely aware of the nature of sin and to bring them to judgment. If he is dealing with persons who share with him in some collective manner, a conscious sense of the ultimate meaning of human life, his basis of appeal is comparatively simple. It remains to point out to them in a wide variety of ways how their collective action vitiates the possibility of achieving the good in experience. In the absence of such unanimity on the part of the controllers of society his problem is to bring such persons to a mount of vision in which they themselves stand in immediate candidacy to be laid hold on by God. Activity of this sort is apt to be futile for reasons that are obvious. Therefore, the affirmation mystic has to deal with them in the areas of their activities. Preaching to such persons, in my opinion, is apt to be a waste of effort and is a blind alley. Some method must be achieved by which the sufferers in the situation can act so as to shock the oppressor into a state of upheaval and insecurity. This is possible only when the oppressed individuals can become persons in a social classification and a basis of equality can accordingly be established between them and the oppressor. It is for this reason that I do not see any substitute for the emergence of a conscious sense of community among the masses of men which will provide a dignity and a worthfulness characteristic of persons on the basis of which equality between them and the oppressor can be established. The moment this is done the ground is prepared for pointing up to them the ultimate significance of life. It is in moral and spiritual leadership of this quality that the affirmation mystic comes into his own. Resistance to any efforts pointing toward community among the masses is the inevitable reaction of the controllers of society. By threats, coercion, overt violence, depending upon the desperateness of the situation, they will seek to hold the masses in a state of depersonalized individualism and because they dominate the political life of the society the State will be called upon to sanction the measures that are taken. The final question then is, can the affirmation mystic give his approval to coercion? The logic of his ethical insight says "no," for he understands that violence hardens the egocentric will of men and gives to unrestrained self-regarding impulses the widest possible range with the nullification of all inhibiting moral sanctions and impulses.

He, therefore, refuses to reach the conclusion that violent coercion is the ultimate means by which a community of men can be achieved in which individuals may emerge as persons standing in immediate candidacy for the vision of God. At long last it may be true that life is its own restraint, that the seeds of destruction are inherent in the nature of evil and what one individual grasps as the ultimate end of life is somehow even now being worked out through long weary stages in the revelation of God in the progress of history. It is this faith and this confidence that makes the affirmation mystic see that working and waiting are two separate activities of the human spirit but he who works for the new day in that act waits for its coming which can be achieved by God and God, alone.

ᘓ | *Religion in a Time of Crisis* (1943)

With most of the world plunged in war, Thurman gave the commencement address on July 7, 1943 at the Garrett Biblical Institute in Evanston, Illinois.[56] *In language remarkably similar to that of his contemporary, H. Richard Niebuhr,*[57] *Thurman interprets the national crisis created by war within the divine context. He concludes that while the war may rivet all our attention on the private and social ends of individuals and nations, ultimately nothing less than the discernment of the will and purposes of God are at stake. For him, the crisis provides the ground for a vibrant public faith that uplifts the inherent dignity of human life. Therefore, the war demands a prophetic ministry which works toward a just society in which the least and the powerless find succor and support. It was the "peculiar genius" of Fellowship Church, Thurman reflected on this period in later years, "to provide a more profound and permanent basis of unity for the human spirit than is summoned simply by the threat of an external enemy."*[58]

CURIOUS INDEED IS THE FACT that at a time of crisis men must be constantly reminded that the crisis does not mark the end of all things. It is of the nature of crisis so to dominate the horizon of men's thoughts that everything that is not directly related to the crisis situation seems irrelevant and without significance. At such times men seem to accept the con-

124

traditions of experience as being in themselves ultimate. The crisis throws everything out of proportion, out of balance and the balance seems always superficially to be on the side of disaster, on the side of negation. At such moments right is seen as being "on the scaffold" and wrong as being "on the throne" – the human spirit is apt to cry all men have bowed their knees "to Baal and I, I only am left."[59] If the contradictions of experience are ultimate, then the conflict between right and wrong, good and evil, order and chaos can never be resolved and human life is caught eternally in the agonizing grip of a grim and eternal struggle between these two forces. But such a dualism has never been able to satisfy the deepest searchings of the mind and the heart of man. The human spirit at long last is not willing to accept the contradiction of life as being ultimate. There continues ever a margin on the side of the good – yes, the ultimate destiny of man is good – this affirmation becomes the ground of optimism and inspiration in the bitterest crisis when the times are "out of joint," when men have lost their reason and sitting in the "sepulchers of gloom watch their dreams go silently to dust." It is the peculiar task of the preacher to recognize this deep urge within man and to call it to bear witness at all times, but particularly at such a moment as is our own, now that the whole round world is rolling in darkness.

If the ultimate destiny of man is good then he must find *in the present* a way of life that is worth living – he must maintain a faith that can be honestly and intelligently held – he must work for the kind of world in which even the weakest may find refuge and refreshment – in which the smoking flax will not be quenched; nor the bruised reed crushed.

A Way of Life That Is Worth Living

We are all of us in quest of a way of life that is worth living. We want to feel that we are engaged in a total enterprise that is meaningful. There must be a sense of something at stake in the day's experience. If this is not true for us then life grows dingy on our sleeve and days are but days and nights are but treacherous interludes before the monotonous round begins anew. It is for this reason that war, despite its terror, wreckage, and stark tragedy, makes so great an appeal to men, women, and even children. It is not be-

cause there is no memory of what war has cost the human race, it is not because men are deceived into thinking that war is a lark, a holiday – men
know that war is a cruel, evil, nasty business. But when war comes, something is at last at stake in the day's living.

Witness our own land at this moment. It is only for war that we permit
all the details of our lives to be shifted, thrown out of normal balance, re-
adjusted. Something is at stake. The ordinary individual now counts in a
strange new way. His country cares about what he does – all secondary
and tertiary citizens become citizens, first class. It becomes critically important what everybody does. No one is exempt. Everybody and everything counts. Something is in the air – things are happening, the deadly
monotony of ordinary living is blasted out of the doldrums. Something is
at stake! A new kind of civic character appears sired by new and awful responsibilities. My country needs me – I fly to the rescue. It is one of the
most tragic commentaries on modern life that only in times of war is there
seen to be something at stake that is so vitally dependent upon even the
common man.

It is your peculiar task as preachers, my young friends, to call attention
again and again to the fact that something more than one's country is at
stake every day, every moment of every day. God is at stake. God is at stake
in everything that every man does. There is a sharp and pointed urgency
in the living of every day. Each man, be he high or low, rich or poor, learned
or unlearned, sick or well, every man lives directly under the Divine Scrutiny. There is no escape from God.

> He sees all I do
> He hears all I say
> My Lord's writing all the time.[60]

Stripped bare of all pretense, of all shadowy seemings, God sees man *mi-
nutely*. Before Him all motives are clear for what they are, purposes stand
naked before His gaze – there is no desire of the heart or stirring of the
mind that escapes Him.

This truth must be proclaimed, clearly and unequivocally so that even
the most humble person will know that he must live each day in the con-

sciousness of the awareness of the all-encompassing mind of God. What I do, what you do, then is important. How I live is never merely my business. This is the meaning of that ancient truth of religion that men are children of God. This truth remains before, during, and after the crisis and is the logical corollary of the affirmation that the ultimate destiny of man is good.

A Faith That Can Be Honestly and Intelligently Held

In the second place you must declare a faith that can be honestly and intelligently held. Every man must make each day an act of faith toward himself. He must do this again and again. It is important to observe that only on the rarest occasions does a man relax his hold upon himself. As a rule he clings to himself as his basis for moving meaningfully out upon the world. Despite all the things that I know about myself, I cling to myself. I am not as good as my mother or my daughter thinks I am; I am not as bad as some other persons think I am, yet I refuse to give myself up. I cling to myself with an abiding enthusiasm; again and again I make an act of faith toward myself.

This act of faith towards myself arises out of a deeper fount of values that sustains and guarantees me. It is but a manifestation of a profound grounding in God the source of life. Someone long ago whose name I no longer recall expressed it – the statement "know thyself" has been taken more mystically from the statement, "thou hast seen thy brother, thou has seen thy God."

I must make also an act of faith towards my fellowmen even though my fellowmen may be at the moment my national enemy. So much that is not good has flown from me toward my fellowmen that I have learned to look with compassion on much that flows from my fellowman to me. As preachers we must declare this truth. Religion insists upon this as the only antidote against developing a great hatred of men, particularly at a time of war. We must see clearly the function of teaching hate of fellowmen at such a time.

Hate is a powerful force. For weak people who are trapped and encircled by an enemy who has at his completest disposal all the powers of destruction it is easy to turn to hate as the last spasmodic convulsion of the human spirit before it goes down to destruction. I know from the inside the meaning of that. But for the strong, for the powerful, hate serves still another purpose. It becomes the cloak of moral justification for the doing of deeds which under normal circumstances would leave the individual or nation covered with shame and inner spiritual confusion. During times of war we teach men to hate the enemy because if we did not do this, it would be impossible for self-respecting persons to do the things to the enemy that the exigencies of war require. Let us not be mistaken. We must declare the truth that God requires of men that they make again and again an act of faith toward their fellowmen, toward all their fellowmen – black, white, brown, yellow – *all* their fellowmen. If this is not done, any discussion even of love is an empty echo among the barren hills of a desolate experience. Under such circumstances prayer for the kingdom of God is addressed to an empty sky and a deserted heaven.

A Social Order in Which Even the Weakest
May Find Refuge and Refreshment

If men are to find a way of life that is worth living and make an act of faith toward themselves and their fellowmen, then it follows that they must work for a society in which the smoking flax will not be quenched, nor the bruised reed crushed. Long ago it was Eugene Debs who said:

> While there is a lower class I am in it
> While there is a criminal element I am of it
> While there is a man in jail I am not free.[61]

For better or for worse we are tied together in the world. I can never be what I ought to be until you are what you ought to be. The present global war is a tragic illustration of the modern version of this truth. Some years ago there was an invasion of Manchukuo[62] – then some months later Mussolini, drunk with the dream of Empire, moved into Ethiopia – then Hitler, began swimming across Europe in seas of blood tying laurels on his brow with other people's lives and other people's heart strings – and now the whole round world is one battle ground where "ignorant armies clash by night." We are all children of God and our destiny is a common destiny – and no one of us can go his way alone.

It matters not how far before him the turtle extends his two front feet; he cannot move his body until he brings up his hind legs. Into one of the larger welfare agencies in an Eastern city a man came to make formal request for an increase in his allowance. The justification was very simple – because of rapidly failing eyesight he could no longer see how to select the most edible portions from certain garbage pails out of which he had been securing his food for sometime. Persons with better eyesight were eliminating him from competition. He needed more funds so as to purchase his food in the open market. This in the year 1942.

One important lesson at least we are learning from the records of the Selective Service Boards. Illiteracy and disease are the double scourge of our manpower. It is Illinois' business that schools are poor in Mississippi, or that economic conditions are so wretched for the masses of the people that often simple precautions as to health and diet are not possible. If men cannot vote in Georgia the voters in every other state in the Union are threatened with disenfranchisement. We are one. If India cannot be given her freedom under the Atlantic Charter,[63] then freedom of men everywhere can be throttled and side-stepped if the time is not ripe or has become over-ripe.

Rufus Jones told me in a conversation that the one thing he wanted to do when the war was over was to send 3 million "biddies"[64] to Europe by airplane so as to provide chickens for those who must build their countryside anew.

We must proclaim the truth that all life is one and that we are all of us tied together. Therefore it is mandatory that we work for a society in which the least person can find refuge and refreshment. This even on behalf of our own fulfillment.

As prophets and priests of the most High God it is your divine assignment to announce that man lives his days under the persistent scrutiny of God – that God is at stake in man's day. How men treat each other, what they do to the environment in which little children must grow and develop, how they earn their living – all things in the making of which they play a significant part stand bare before the eyes of God. You must live and proclaim a faith that will make men affirm themselves and their fellowmen as children of God. You must lay your lives on the altar of social change so that wherever you are there the Kingdom of God is at hand!

∞ | Jesus – An Interpretation (1949)

Against the backdrop of fractured American race relations in the late forties and the moral indifference of most Christian churches to this and other pressing social concerns, Thurman published what became his most famous book, Jesus and the Disinherited.[65] *Martin Luther King, Jr. purportedly carried a copy of Thurman's book in his briefcase during the peak of the Civil Rights movement. The first chapter, reprinted here, examines the life of the historical Jesus, drawing implicit parallels between the context of the "Master's" life as a member of the outcast Jewish minority without the rights of Roman citizenship, and those of black people in the segregated society of mid-twentieth-century America. Throughout his career Thurman argued that Jesus is best viewed not as a religious object of devotion and worship, but as a religious subject in quest of moral community and spiritual dignity. According to Thurman, when Jesus is viewed as a religious object, the grounds are laid for a principle of exclusiveness. Because the figure of Jesus has been so closely identified with the arrogant domination of traditional Western Christianity, his worship too easily becomes a tool of divisiveness and impedes interreligious fellowship. Instead, the "Jesus idea" should represent the essence of authentic fellowship and serve as the basis for the creation of community among Christians and others committed to the religious life. Thurman's aim in this essay is to present Jesus as an exemplar of a religiously inspired public ethic that takes seriously the plight of the disinherited.*

To some God and Jesus may appeal in a way other than to us: some may come to
faith in God and to love, without a conscious attachment to Jesus. Both Nature
and good men besides Jesus may lead us to God. They who seek God with all
their hearts must, however, some day on their way meet Jesus.[66]

MANY AND VARIED ARE THE INTERPRETATIONS dealing with the teachings and the life of Jesus of Nazareth. But few of these interpretations deal
with what the teachings and the life of Jesus have to say to those who
stand, at a moment in human history, with their backs against the wall.

To those who need profound succor and strength to enable them to live
in the present with dignity and creativity, Christianity often has been ster-
ile and of little avail. The conventional Christian word is muffled, confused, and vague. Too often the price exacted by society for security and
respectability is that the Christian movement in its formal expression
must be on the side of the strong against the weak. This is a matter of tremendous significance, for it reveals to what extent a religion that was born
of a people acquainted with persecution and suffering has become the
cornerstone of a civilization and of nations whose very position in modern
life has too often been secured by a ruthless use of power applied to weak
and defenseless peoples.

It is not a singular thing to hear a sermon that defines what should be
the attitude of the Christian toward people who are less fortunate than
himself. Again and again our missionary appeal is on the basis of the
Christian responsibility to the needy, the ignorant, and the so-called back-
ward peoples of the earth. There is a certain grandeur and nobility in administering to another's need out of one's fullness and plenty. One could
be selfish, using his possessions – material or spiritual – for strictly private
or personal ends. It is certainly to the glory of Christianity that it has been
most insistent on the point of responsibility to others whose only claim
upon one is the height and depth of their need. This impulse at the heart
of Christianity is the human *will to share* with others what one has found
meaningful to oneself elevated to the height of a moral imperative. But
there is a lurking danger in this very emphasis. It is exceedingly difficult
to hold oneself free from a certain contempt for those whose predicament
makes moral appeal for defense and succor. It is the sin of pride and arro-

gance that has tended to vitiate the missionary impulse and to make of it an instrument of self-righteousness on the one hand and racial superiority on the other.

That is one reason why, again and again, there is no basic relationship between the simple practice of brotherhood in the commonplace relations of life and the ethical pretensions of our faith. It has long been a matter of serious moment that for decades we have studied the various peoples of the world and those who live as our neighbors as objects of missionary endeavor and enterprise without being at all willing to treat them either as brothers or as human beings. I say this without rancor, because it is not an issue in which vicious human beings are involved. But it is one of the subtle perils of a religion which calls attention – to the point of overemphasis, sometimes – to one's obligation to administer to human need.

I can count on the fingers of one hand the number of times that I have heard a sermon on the meaning of religion, of Christianity, to the man who stands with his back against the wall. It is urgent that my meaning be crystal clear. The masses of men live with their backs constantly against the wall. They are the poor, the disinherited, the dispossessed. What does our religion say to them? The issue is not what it counsels them to do for others whose need may be greater, but what religion offers to meet their own needs. The search for an answer to this question is perhaps the most important religious quest of modern life.

In the fall of 1935 I was serving as chairman of a delegation sent on a pilgrimage of friendship from the students of America to the students of India, Burma, and Ceylon. It was at a meeting in Ceylon that the whole crucial issue was pointed up to me in a way that I can never forget. At the close of a talk before the Law College, University of Colombo, on civil disabilities under states' rights in the United States, I was invited by the principal to have coffee.

We drank our coffee in silence. After the service had been removed, he said to me, "What are you doing over here? I know what the newspapers say about a pilgrimage of friendship and the rest, but that is not my question. What are *you* doing over here? This is what I mean.

"More than three hundred years ago your forefathers were taken from the western coast of Africa as slaves. The people who dealt in the slave traffic were Christians. One of your famous Christian hymn writers, Sir John Newton, made his money from the sale of slaves to the New World. He is the man who wrote 'How Sweet the Name of Jesus Sounds' and 'Amazing Grace' – there may be others, but these are the only ones I know. The name of one of the famous British slave vessels was 'Jesus.'

"The men who bought the slaves were Christians. Christian ministers, quoting the Christian apostle Paul, gave the sanction of religion to the system of slavery. Some seventy years or more ago you were freed by a man who was not a professing Christian, but was rather the spearhead of certain political, social, and economic forces, the significance of which he himself did not understand. During all the period since then you have lived in a Christian nation in which you are segregated, lynched, and burned. Even in the church, I understand, there is segregation. One of my students who went to your country sent me a clipping telling about a Christian church in which the regular Sunday worship was interrupted so that many could join in a mob against one of your fellows. When he had been caught and done to death, they came back to resume their worship of their Christian God.

"I am a Hindu. I do not understand. Here you are in my country, standing deep within the Christian faith and tradition. I do not wish to seem rude to you. But, sir, I think you are a traitor to all the darker peoples of the earth. I am wondering what you, an intelligent man, can say in defense of your position."

Our subsequent conversation lasted for more than five hours. The clue to my own discussion with this probing, honest, sympathetic Hindu is found in my interpretation of the meaning of the religion of Jesus. It is a privilege, after so long a time, to set down what seems to me to be an essentially creative and prognostic interpretation of Jesus as religious subject rather than religious object. It is necessary to examine the religion of Jesus against the background of his own age and people, and to inquire into the content of his teaching with reference to the disinherited and the underprivileged.

We begin with the simple historical fact that Jesus was a Jew. The miracle of the Jewish people is almost as breathtaking as the miracle of Jesus. Is there something unique, some special increment of vitality in the

womb of the people out of whose loins he came, that made of him a logical
flowering of a long development of racial experience, ethical in quality
and Godlike in tone? It is impossible for Jesus to be understood outside of
the sense of community which Israel held with God. This does not take
anything away from him; rather does it heighten the challenge which his
life presents, for such reflection reveals him as the product of the constant
working of the creative mind of God upon the life, thought, and character
of a race of men. Here is one who was so conditioned and organized within
himself that he became a perfect instrument for the embodiment of a set
of ideals – ideals of such dramatic potency that they were capable of
changing the calendar, rechanneling the thought of the world, and placing
a new sense of the rhythm of life in a weary, nerve-snapped civilization.

How different might have been the story of the last two thousand years
on this planet grown old from suffering if the link between Jesus and Israel had never been severed! What might have happened if Jesus, so perfect a flower from the brooding spirit of God in the soul of Israel, had been
permitted to remain where his roots would have been fed by the distilled
elements accumulated from Israel's wrestling with God! The thought is
staggering. The Christian Church has tended to overlook its Judaic
origins, but the fact is that Jesus of Nazareth was a Jew of Palestine when
he went about his Father's business, announcing the acceptable year of
the Lord.

Of course it may be argued that the fact that Jesus was a Jew is merely
coincidental, that God could have expressed himself as easily and effectively in a Roman. True, but the fact is he did not. And it is with that fact
that we must deal.

The second important fact for our consideration is that Jesus was a
poor Jew. There is recorded in Luke the account of the dedication of Jesus
at the temple: "And when the days of her purification according to the law
of Moses were accomplished, they brought him . . . to the Lord; (as it is
written in the law of the Lord, Every male that openeth the womb shall be
called holy to the Lord) and to offer a sacrifice according to that which is
said in the law of the Lord, A pair of turtledoves, or two young pigeons."
When we examine the regulation in Leviticus, an interesting fact is revealed: "And when the days of her purifying are fulfilled, for a son, . . . she

shall bring a lamb of the first year for a burnt offering, and a young pigeon, or a turtledove, for a sin offering . . . And if she be not able to bring a lamb, then she shall bring two turtles, or two young pigeons; the one for a burnt offering and the other for a sin offering." It is clear from the text that the mother of Jesus was one whose means were not sufficient for a lamb, and who was compelled, therefore, to use doves or young pigeons.

The economic predicament with which he was identified in birth placed him initially with the great mass of men on the earth. The masses of the people are poor. If we dare take the position that in Jesus there was at work some radical destiny, it would be safe to say that in his poverty he was more truly Son of man than he would have been if the incident of family or birth had made him a rich son of Israel. It is not a point to be labored, for again and again men have transcended circumstance of birth and training; but it is an observation not without merit.

The third fact is that Jesus was a member of a minority group in the midst of a larger dominant and controlling group. In 63 B.C. Palestine fell into the hands of the Romans. After this date the gruesome details of loss of status were etched, line by line, in the sensitive soul of Israel, dramatized ever by an increasing desecration of the Holy Land. To be sure, there was Herod, an Israelite, who ruled from 37 to 4 B.C.; but in some ways he was completely apostate. Taxes of all kinds increased, and out of these funds, extracted from the vitals of the people, temples in honor of Emperor Augustus were built within the boundaries of the holy soil.[67] It was a sad and desolate time for the people. Herod became the symbol of shame and humiliation for all of Israel.

In Galilee a certain revolutionary, whose name was Judas, laid siege to the armory at Sepphoris and, with weapons taken there, tried to re-establish the political glory of Israel. How terrible a moment! The whole city of Sepphoris was regarded as a hostage, and Roman soldiers, aided by the warriors of King Aretas of Arabia, reduced the place to whited ash. In time the city was rebuilt – and perhaps Jesus was one of the carpenters employed from Nazareth, which was a neighboring village.

It is utterly fantastic to assume that Jesus grew to manhood untouched by the surging currents of the common life that made up the climate of Palestine. Not only must he have been aware of them; that he was affected by them is a most natural observation. A word of caution is urgent at this point. To place Jesus against the background of his time is by no means sufficient to explain him. Who can explain a spiritual genius – or any kind of genius, for that matter? The historical setting in which Jesus grew up, the psychological mood and temper of the age and of the House of Israel, the economic and social predicament of Jesus' family – all these are important. But they in themselves are unable to tell us precisely the thing that we most want to know: Why does he differ from many others in the same setting? Any explanation of Jesus in terms of psychology, politics, economics, religion, or the like must inevitably explain his contemporaries as well. It may tell why Jesus was a particular kind of Jew, but not why some other Jews were not Jesus. And that is, after all, the most important question, since the thing which makes him most significant is not the way in which he resembled his fellows but the way in which he differed from all the rest of them. Jesus inherited the same traits as countless other Jews of his time; he grew up in the same society; and yet he was Jesus, and the others were not. Uniqueness always escapes us as we undertake an analysis of character.

On the other hand, these considerations should not blind us to the significance of the environmental factors and the social and religious heritage of Jesus in determining the revolutionary character of some of his insights. One of the clearest and simplest statements of the issues here raised, and their bearing upon the character and teaching of Jesus, is found in Vladimir Simkhovitch's *Toward the Understanding of Jesus*. I am using his essay as the basis for our discussion of the problem, but the applications are mine. Simkhovitch says:

> In the year 6 [A.D.] Judea was annexed to Syria; in the year 70 [A.D.] Jerusalem and its temple were destroyed. Between these two dates Jesus preached and was crucified on Golgotha. During all that time the life of the little nation was a terrific drama; its patriotic emotions were aroused to the highest pitch and then still more inflamed by the identification of national politics with a national religion. Is it reasonable to assume that what was going on before Jesus' eyes was a closed book, that the agonizing problems of his people were a matter of indifference to him, that he had given them no consideration, that he was not taking a definite attitude toward the great and all-absorbing problem of the very people whom he taught?[68]

There is one overmastering problem that the socially and politically disinherited always face: Under what terms is survival possible? In the case of the Jewish people in the Greco-Roman world the problem was even more acute than under ordinary circumstances, because it had to do not only with physical survival in terms of life and limb but also with the actual survival of a culture and a faith. Judaism was a culture, a civilization, and a religion – a total world view in which there was no provision for any form of thoroughgoing dualism. The crucial problem of Judaism was to exist as an isolated, autonomous, cultural, religious, and political unit in the midst of the hostile Hellenic world. If there had been sharp lines distinguishing the culture from the religion, or the religion from political autonomy, a compromise could have been worked out. Because the Jews thought that a basic compromise was possible, they sought political annexation to Syria which would bring them under Roman rule directly and thereby guarantee them, within the framework of Roman policy, religious and cultural autonomy. But this merely aggravated the already tense nationalistic feeling and made a direct, all-out attack against Roman authority inevitable.

In the midst of this psychological climate Jesus began his teaching and his ministry. His words were directed to the House of Israel, a minority within the Greco-Roman world, smarting under the loss of status, freedom, and autonomy, haunted by the dream of the restoration of a lost glory and a former greatness. His message focused on the urgency of a radical change in the inner attitude of the people. He recognized fully that out of the heart are the issues of life and that no external force, however great and overwhelming, can at long last destroy a people if it does not first win the victory of the spirit against them. "To revile because one has been reviled – this is the real evil because it is the evil of the soul itself." Jesus saw this with almighty clarity. Again and again he came back to the inner life of the individual. With increasing insight and startling accuracy he placed his finger on the "inward center" as the crucial arena where the issues would determine the destiny of his people.

When I was a seminary student, I attended one of the great quadrennial conventions of the Student Volunteer Movement.[69] One afternoon some seven hundred of us had a special group meeting, at which a Korean girl was asked to talk to us about her impression of American education. It was an occasion to be remembered. The Korean student was very personable and somewhat diminutive. She came to the edge of the platform and, with what seemed to be obvious emotional strain, she said, "You have asked me to talk with you about my impression of American education. But there is only one thing that a Korean has any right to talk about, and that is freedom from Japan." For about twenty minutes she made an impassioned plea for the freedom of her people, ending her speech with this sentence: "If you see a little American boy and you ask him what he wants, he says, 'I want a penny to put in my bank or to buy a whistle or a piece of candy.' But if you see a little Korean boy and you ask him what he wants, he says, 'I want freedom from Japan.'"[70]

It was this kind of atmosphere that characterized the life of the Jewish community when Jesus was a youth in Palestine. The urgent question was what must be the attitude toward Rome. Was any attitude possible that would be morally tolerable and at the same time preserve a basic self-esteem – without which life could not possibly have any meaning? The question was not academic. It was the most crucial of questions. In essence, Rome was the enemy; Rome symbolized total frustration; Rome was the great barrier to peace of mind. And Rome was everywhere. No Jewish person of the period could deal with the question of his practical life, his vocation, his place in society, until first he had settled deep within himself this critical issue.

This is the position of the disinherited in every age. What must be the attitude toward the rulers, the controllers of political, social, and economic life? This is the question of the Negro in American life. Until he has faced and settled that question, he cannot inform his environment with reference to his own life, whatever may be his preparation or his pretensions.

In the main, there were two alternatives faced by the Jewish minority of which Jesus was a part. Simply stated, these were to resist or not to resist. But each of these alternatives has within it secondary alternatives.

Under the general plan of nonresistance one may take the position of imitation. The aim of such an attitude is to assimilate the culture and the social behavior pattern of the dominant group. It is the profound capitulation to the powerful, because it means the yielding of oneself to that which, deep within, one recognizes as being unworthy. It makes for a strategic loss of self-respect. The aim is to reduce all outer or external signs of difference to zero, so that there shall be no ostensible cause for active violence or opposition. Under some circumstances it may involve a repudiation of one's heritage, one's customs, one's faith. Accurate imitation until the facade of complete assimilation is securely placed and the antagonism of difference dissolved – such is the function of this secondary alternative within the broader alternative of nonresistance. Herod was an excellent example of this solution.

To some extent this was also the attitude of the Sadducees. They represented the "upper" class. From their number came the high priests, and most of the economic security derived from contemporary worship in the temple was their monopoly. They did not represent the masses of the people. Any disturbance of the established order meant upsetting their position. They loved Israel, but they seem to have loved security more. They made their public peace with Rome and went on about the business of living. They were astute enough to see that their own position could be perpetuated if they stood firmly against all revolutionaries and radicals. Such persons would only stir the people to resist the inevitable, and in the end everything would be lost. Their tragedy was in the fact that they idealized the position of the Roman in the world and suffered the moral fate of the Romans by becoming like them. They saw only two roads open before them – become like the Romans or be destroyed by the Romans. They chose the former.

The other alternative in the nonresistance pattern is to reduce contact with the enemy to a minimum. It is the attitude of cultural isolation in the midst of a rejected culture. Cunning the mood may be – one of bitterness and hatred, but also one of deep, calculating fear. To take up active resistance would be foolhardy, for a thousand reasons. The only way out is to keep one's resentment under rigid control and censorship.

The issue raised by this attitude is always present. The opposition to those who work for social change does not come only from those who are the guarantors of the *status quo*. Again and again it has been demonstrated that the lines are held by those whose hold on security is sure only as long as the *status quo* remains intact. The reasons for this are not far to seek. If a man is convinced that he is safe only as long as he uses his power to give others a sense of insecurity, then the measure of their security is in his hands. If security or insecurity is at the mercy of a single individual or group, then control of behavior becomes routine. All imperialism functions in this way. Subject peoples are held under control by this device.

One of the most striking scenes in the movie *Ben Hur* was that in which a Roman legion marches by while hundreds of people stand silently on the roadside. As the last soldier passes, a very dignified, self-possessed Jewish gentleman, with folded arms and eyes smoldering with the utmost contempt, without the slightest shift of his facial muscles spits at the heel of the receding legionary – a consummate touch. Such – in part, at least – was the attitude of the Pharisee. No active resistance against Rome – only a terrible contempt. Obviously such an attitude is a powder keg. One nameless incident may cause to burst into flame the whole gamut of smoldering passion, leaving nothing in its wake but charred corpses, mute reminders of the tragedy of life. Jesus saw this and understood it clearly.

The other major alternative is resistance. It may be argued that even nonresistance is a form of resistance, for it may be regarded as an appositive dimension of resistance. Resistance may be overt action, or it may be merely mental and moral attitudes. For the purposes of our discussion resistance is defined as the physical, overt expression of an inner attitude. Resistance in this sense finds its most dramatic manifestation in force of arms.

Armed resistance is apt to be a tragic last resort in the life of the disinherited. Armed resistance has an appeal because it provides a form of expression, of activity, that releases tension and frees the oppressed from a disintegrating sense of complete impotency and helplessness. "Why can't we do something? Something must be done!" is the recurring cry. By "something" is meant action, direct action, as over against words, subtleties, threats, and innuendoes. It is better to die fighting for freedom than to rot away in one's chains, the argument runs.

> *Before I'd be a slave*
> *I'd be buried in my grave,*
> *And go home to my God*
> *And be free!*[71]

The longer the mood is contemplated, the more insistent the appeal. It is a form of fanaticism, to be sure, but that may not be a vote against it. In all action there is operative a fringe of irrationality. Once the mood is thoroughly established, any council of caution is interpreted as either compromise or cowardice. The fact that the ruler has available to him the power of the state and complete access to all arms is scarcely considered. Out of the deeps of the heart there swells a great and awful assurance that because the cause is just, it cannot fail. Any failure is regarded as temporary and, to the devoted, as a testing of character.

This was the attitude of the Zealots of Jesus' day. There was added appeal in their position because it called forth from the enemy organized determination and power. It is never to be forgotten that one of the ways by which men measure their own significance is to be found in the amount of power and energy other men must use in order to crush them or hold them back. This is at least one explanation of the fact that even a weak and apparently inconsequential movement becomes formidable under the pressure of great persecution. The persecution becomes a vote of confidence, which becomes, in turn, a source of inspiration, power, and validation. The Zealots knew this. Jesus knew this. It is a matter of more than passing significance that he had a Zealot among his little band of followers, indeed among the twelve chosen ones.

In the face of these alternatives Jesus came forth with still another. On this point Simkhovitch makes a profound contribution to the understanding of the psychology of Jesus. He reminds us that Jesus expressed his alternative in a "brief formula – The Kingdom of Heaven is in us." He states further:

> Jesus had to resent deeply the loss of Jewish national independence and the aggression of Rome . . . Natural humiliation was hurting and burning. The balm for that burning humiliation was humility. For humility cannot be humiliated . . . Thus he asked his people to learn from him, "For I am meek and lowly in heart; and ye shall find rest unto your souls. For my yoke is easy, and my burden is light."[72]

It was but natural that such a position would be deeply resented by many of his fellows, who were suffering even as he was. To them it was a complete betrayal to the enemy. It was to them a counsel of acquiescence, if not of despair, full to overflowing with a kind of groveling and stark cowardice. Besides, it seemed like self-deception, like whistling in the dark. All of this would have been quite true if Jesus had stopped there. He did not. He recognized with authentic realism that anyone who permits another to determine the quality of his inner life gives into the hands of the other the keys to his destiny. If a man knows precisely what he can do to you or what epithet he can hurl against you in order to make you lose your temper, your equilibrium, then he can always keep you under subjection. It is a man's reaction to things that determines their ability to exercise power over him. It seems clear that Jesus understood the anatomy of the relationship between his people and the Romans, and he interpreted that relationship against the background of the profoundest ethical insight of his own religious faith as he had found it in the heart of the prophets of Israel.

The solution which Jesus found for himself and for Israel, as they faced the hostility of the Greco-Roman world, becomes the word and the work of redemption for all the cast-down people in every generation and in every age. I mean this quite literally. I do not ignore the theological and metaphysical interpretation of the Christian doctrine of salvation. But the underprivileged everywhere have long since abandoned any hope that this type of salvation deals with the crucial issues by which their days are turned into despair without consolation. The basic fact is that Christianity as it was born in the mind of this Jewish teacher and thinker appears as a technique of survival for the oppressed. That it became, through the intervening years, a religion of the powerful and the dominant, used sometimes as a instrument of oppression, must not tempt us into believing that it was thus in the mind and life of Jesus. "In him was life; and the life was the light of men." Wherever his spirit appears, the oppressed gather fresh courage; for he announced the good news that fear, hypocrisy, and hatred, the three hounds of hell that track the trail of the disinherited, need have no dominion over them.

I belong to a generation that finds very little that is meaningful or intelligent in the teachings of the Church concerning Jesus Christ. It is a generation largely in revolt because of the general impression that Christianity is essentially an other-worldly religion, having as its motto: "Take all the world, but give me Jesus." The desperate opposition to Christianity rests in the fact that it seems, in the last analysis, to be a betrayal of the Negro into the hands of his enemies by focusing his attention upon heaven, forgiveness, love, and the like. It is true that this emphasis is germane to the religion of Jesus, but it has to be put into a context that will show its strength and vitality rather than its weakness and failure. For years it has been a part of my own quest so to understand the religion of Jesus that interest in his way of life could be developed and sustained by intelligent men and women who were at the same time deeply victimized by the Christian Church's betrayal of his faith.[73]

During much of my boyhood I was cared for by my grandmother, who was born a slave and lived until the Civil War on a plantation near Madison, Florida. My regular chore was to do all of the reading for my grandmother—she could neither read nor write. Two or three times a week I read the Bible aloud to her. I was deeply impressed by the fact that she was most particular about the choice of Scripture. For instance, I might read many of the more devotional Psalms, some of Isaiah, the Gospels again and again. But the Pauline epistles, never—except, at long intervals, the thirteenth chapter of First Corinthians. My curiosity knew no bounds, but we did not question her about anything.

When I was older and was half through college, I chanced to be spending a few days at home near the end of summer vacation. With a feeling of great temerity I asked her one day why it was that she would not let me read any of the Pauline letters. What she told me I shall never forget. "During the days of slavery," she said, "the master's minister would occasionally hold services for the slaves. Old man McGhee was so mean that he would not let a Negro minister preach to his slaves. Always the white minister used as his text something from Paul. At least three or four times a year he used as a text: "Slaves, be obedient to them that are your masters . . . as unto Christ." Then he would go on to show how it was God's will that we were slaves and how, if we were good and happy slaves, God would bless us. I promised my Maker that if I ever learned to read and if freedom ever came, I would not read that part of the Bible."

Since that fateful day on the front porch in Florida I have been working on the problem her words presented. A part of the fruits of that search

throw an important light upon the issues with which I am dealing. It cannot be denied that too often the weight of the Christian movement has
been on the side of the strong and the powerful and against the weak and
oppressed – this, despite the gospel. A part of the responsibility seems to
me to rest upon a peculiar twist in the psychology of Paul, whose wide and
universal concern certainly included all men, bond and free.

Let us examine the facts. The apostle Paul was a Jew. He was the first
great creative interpreter of Christianity. His letters are older than the
Gospels themselves. It seems that because he was not one of the original
disciples, he was never quite accepted by them as one able to speak with
authority concerning the Master. This fact hung very heavily upon the
soul of the apostle. He did not ever belong, quite. One of the disciples
could always say, "But of course you do not quite understand, because, you
see, you were not there when . . ."

But the fact remains: Paul was a Jew, even as Jesus was a Jew. By blood,
training, background, and religion he belonged to the Jewish minority,
about whom we have been speaking. But unlike them, for the most part,
he was a free Jew; he was a citizen of Rome. A desert and a sea were placed
between his status in the empire and that of his fellow Jews. A very
searching dilemma was created by this fact. On the one hand, he belonged to the privileged class. He had the freedom of the empire at his disposal. There were certain citizenship rights which he could claim despite
his heritage, faith, and religion. Should he deny himself merely because
he was more fortunate than his fellows? To what extent could he accept
his rights without feeling a deep sense of guilt and betrayal? He was of a
minority but with majority privileges. If a Roman soldier in some prison in
Asia Minor was taking advantage of him, he could make an appeal directly
to Caesar. There was always available to him a protection guaranteed by
the state and respected by the minions of the state. It was like a magic formula always available in emergencies. It is to the credit of the amazing
power of Jesus Christ over the life of Paul that there is only one recorded
instance in which he used his privilege.[74]

It is quite understandable that his sense of security would influence
certain aspects of his philosophy of history. Naturally he would have regard for the state, for the civil magistrate, unlike that of his fellows, who

regarded them as the formal expression of legitimatized intolerance. The
stability of Paul's position in the state was guaranteed by the integrity of
the state. One is not surprised, then, to hear him tell slaves to obey their
masters like Christ, and say all government is ordained of God. (It is not to
meet the argument to say that in a sense everything that is, is permitted of
God, or that government and rulers are sustained by God as a concession
to the frailty of man.) It would be grossly misleading and inaccurate to say
that there are not to be found in the Pauline letters utterances of a deeply
different quality – utterances which reveal how his conception transcended all barriers of race and class and condition. But this other side is
there, always available to those who wish to use the weight of the Christian message to oppress and humiliate their fellows. The point is that this
aspect of Paul's teaching is understandable against the background of his
Roman citizenship. It influenced his philosophy of history and resulted in
a major frustration that has borne bitter fruit in the history of the movement which he, Paul, did so much to project on the conscience of the human race.

Now Jesus was not a Roman citizen. He was not protected by the normal guarantees of citizenship – that quiet sense of security which comes
from knowing that you belong and the general climate of confidence
which it inspires. If a Roman soldier pushed Jesus into a ditch, he could
not appeal to Caesar; he would be just another Jew in the ditch. Standing
always beyond the reach of citizen security, he was perpetually exposed to
all the "arrows of outrageous fortune," and there was only a gratuitous refuge – if any – within the state. What stark insecurity! What a breeder of
complete civil and moral nihilism and psychic anarchy! Unless one actually lives day by day without a sense of security, he cannot understand
what worlds separated Jesus from Paul at this point.

The striking similarity between the social position of Jesus in Palestine
and that of the vast majority of American Negroes is obvious to anyone
who tarries long over the facts. We are dealing here with conditions that
produce essentially the same psychology. There is meant no further com-
parison. It is the similarity of a social climate at the point of a denial of full
citizenship which creates the problem for creative survival. For the most
part, Negroes assume that there are no basic citizenship rights, no funda-

mental protection, guaranteed to them by the state, because their status as citizens has never been clearly defined. There has been for them little protection from the dominant controllers of society and even less protection from the unrestrained elements within their own group.

The result has been a tendency to be their own protectors, to bulwark themselves against careless and deliberate aggression. The Negro has felt, with some justification, that the peace officer of the community provides no defense against the offending or offensive white man; and for an entirely different set of reasons the peace officer gives no protection against the offending Negro. Thus the Negro feels that he must be prepared, at a moment's notice, to protect his own life and take the consequence therefore. Such a predicament has made it natural for some of them to use weapons as a defense and to have recourse to premeditated or precipitate violence.

Living in a climate of deep insecurity, Jesus, faced with so narrow a margin of civil guarantees, had to find some other basis upon which to establish a sense of well-being. He knew that the goals of religion as he understood them could never be worked out within the then-established order. Deep from within that order he projected a dream, the logic of which would give to all the needful security. There would be room for all, and no man would be a threat to his brother. "The kingdom of God is within." "The Spirit of the Lord is upon me, because he hath anointed me to preach the gospel to the poor."

The basic principles of his way of life cut straight through to the despair of his fellows and found it groundless. By inference he says, "You must abandon your fear of each other and fear only God. You must not indulge in any deception and dishonesty, even to save your lives. Your words must be Yea-Nay; anything else is evil. Hatred is destructive to hated and hater alike. Love your enemy, that you may be children of your Father who is in heaven."

CO | *Deception* (1949)

In Jesus and the Disinherited, *Thurman dissects the "anatomy" of violence, whose critical dimensions he identifies as fear, deception, and hatred.*[75] *In his chapter on deception, Thurman argues that for the powerless, deception has its genesis in fear wrought by precipitous and systemic violence. In this respect, deception serves as a technique of survival which cultivates habits and practices which insure minimal harm. Thurman's perspective, however, is that deception practiced over time becomes self-defeating and destructive to others. For Thurman, deception or lying are never viable moral alternatives because they destroy the value structure of the one who deceives and lies. "The penalty of deception," Thurman suggests, "is to become a deception, with all sense of moral discrimination vitiated." He counsels that in all circumstances or situations, truth-telling is the only proper response. Truth-telling underscores the fundamental dignity and worth of human persons and highlights the equality of all people regardless of color, class, status, or social advantage. When the disinherited adhere to the truth, the relationship between the powerful and powerless becomes equalized, whereas deception perpetuates the relationship of inequality. Truth understood in this way has radical social implications for it liberates the individual from any form of external bondage: within the person who internalizes the truth, there is an inner authority which allows him or her to say "no" even at the threat of violence and death. For Thurman, this "sense of option" is the essence of individual freedom and each human being's birthright as a child of God.*

DECEPTION IS PERHAPS THE OLDEST of all the techniques by which the weak have protected themselves against the strong. Through the ages, at all stages of sentient activity, the weak have survived by fooling the strong.

The techniques of deception seem to be a part of the nervous-reflex action of the organism. The cuttlefish, when attacked, will release some of the fluid from his sepia bag, making the water all around him murky; in the midst of the cloudy water he confuses his attacker and makes his escape. Almost any hunter of birds has seen the mother simulate a broken wing so as to attract attention to herself and thereby save the life of her young. As a boy I have seen the shadow of the hawk on the grassy meadow where I lay resting underneath a shade tree. Consider the behavior of the birds a few feet away as they see the shadow. I have seen them take little feet full of dried grass or leaves, turn an easy half somersault, and play dead. The hawk blinks his eyes, thinks he has had an optical illusion, and goes on to find birds that do not know enough to pretend to be dead. We often played a game of hide-and-seek in which the refrain was, "Lay low, slick duck, the hawk's around." Natural selection has finally resulted in giving to various animals neutral colors or blending colors so that they fade into the landscape and thus protect themselves from destruction by deceiving the enemy.

All little children well know this technique. They know that they cannot cope with the parental will on equal terms. Therefore, in order to carry on their own purposes, they work all kinds of simple – and not so simple – schemes for making the parents do the children's will as if it were their own. Until the teacher catches on, it is a favorite device of students. When a particular lesson has not been studied, or there is danger that the teacher will cover territory that extends beyond the day's preparation, some apparently innocent question is asked about the teacher's prejudice, pet interest, or particular concern. Once the teacher is discussing the particular point, there is nothing more to fear; for before he comes to the end of his talk, the bell will ring and all will be saved.

It is an ancient device that a man-dominated social order has forced upon women, even down to latest times. Olive Schreiner spent much of her energy attacking this form of deception by which the moral life of women was bound.[76] Much of the constant agitation for an equal-rights amendment to the Constitution grows out of recognition of the morally degrading aspects of deception and dishonesty that enter into the relationship between men and women.[77]

When the children of Israel were in captivity in Babylon, the prophet Ezekiel could not give words of comfort and guidance by direct and overt statement. If he had, he would not have lasted very long, and the result would have been a great loss to his people and a tightening of the bonds that held them. He would have been executed as a revolutionary in short order and all religious freedom would have been curtailed. What did the prophet do? He resorted to a form of deception. He put words in the mouth of an old king of Tyre that did not come from him at all, but from Nebuchadrezzar. It was Nebuchadrezzar who had said, "I am a God." He used what we would call now "double talk." But the Jews understood, even though the Babylonian "secret service" was helpless because he was not openly talking against the state.

In a certain southern city a blind Negro had been killed by a policeman. Feeling ran very high. The Negroes were not permitted to have any kind of eulogy or sermon at the funeral service. There was fear of rioting. Nevertheless, the funeral was held, with policemen very much in evidence. There was no sermon, but there was a central prayer. In the prayer the minister told God all that he would have said to the people had he not been under very rigid surveillance. The officers could do nothing, for the minister was not addressing the people; he was talking to his God. How tragically sordid! But it is the old, old method by which the weak have survived through the years.

One of the oldest of the Negro spirituals deals quite interestingly with this technique. The setting is very dramatic.

The slave had often heard his master's minister talk about heaven, the final abode of the righteous. Naturally the master regarded himself as fitting into the category. On the other hand, the slave knew that he too was going to heaven. He reasoned, "There must be two heavens – no, this cannot be true, because there is only one God. God cannot possibly be divided in this way. I have it! I am having my hell now. When I die, I shall have my heaven. The master's having his heaven now. When he dies, he will have his hell." The next day, chopping cotton beneath the torrid skies, the slave said to his mate:

> *I got shoes,*
> *You got shoes,*
> *All God's children got shoes.*
> *When we get to heaven*
> *We're goin' to put on our shoes*
> *An' shout all over God's heaven,*
> *Heaven! Heaven!*

Then, looking up to the big house where the master lived, he said:

> *Everybody talkin' 'bout heaven*
> *Ain't goin' there!*

Instances could be multiplied from all over the world, and from as far back in human history as records have been kept. It is an old, old defense of the weak against the strong. The question of deception is not academic, but profoundly ethical and spiritual, going to the very heart of all human relations. For it raises the issue of honesty, integrity, and the consequences thereof over against duplicity and deception and the attendant consequences. Does the fact that a particular course of action jeopardizes a man's life relieve him of the necessity for following that course of action? Are there circumstances under which the ethical question is irrelevant, beside the point? If so, where does one draw the line? Is there a fine distinction between literal honesty and honesty in spirit and intent? Or is truthtelling largely a matter of timing? Are there times when to tell the truth is to be false to the truth that is in you? These questions and many related ones will not be downed. For the disinherited they have to do with the very heart of survival.

It may be argued that a man who places so high a price upon physical existence and survival that he is willing to perjure his own soul has a false, or at least an inadequate, sense of values. "What shall a man give in exchange for his own soul?" Jesus asks. The physical existence of a man makes of him the custodian, the keeper, of the fragment of life which is his. He lives constantly under the necessity to have life fulfill itself. Should he take chances, even in behalf of the values of a kind other than those which have to do with his physical survival? With reference to the question of deception the disinherited are faced with three basic alternatives.

The first alternative is to accept the apparent fact that, one's situation being what it is, there is no sensible choice offered. The individual is disadvantaged because he is not a member of the "party in power," the dominant, controlling group. His word has no value anyway. In any contest he is defeated before he starts. He cannot meet his opponent on equal terms, because there is no basis of equality that exists between the weak and the strong. The only thing that counts is victory – or any level on which victory can be achieved. There can be no question of honesty in dealing with each other, for there is no sense of community. Such a mood takes for granted a facile insincerity.

The fact is, in any great struggle between groups in which the major control of the situation is on one side, the ethical question tends to become merely academic. The advantaged group assumes that they are going to be fooled, if it is possible; there is no expectation of honesty and sincerity. They know that every conceivable device will be used to render ineffective the advantage which they have inherited in their position as the strong. The pattern of deception by which the weak are deprived of their civic, economic, political, and social rights without its appearing that they are so deprived is a matter of continuous and tragic amazement. The pattern of deception by which the weak circumvent the strong and manage to secure some of their political, economic, and social rights is a matter of continuous degradation. A vast conspiracy of silence covers all these maneuvers as the groups come into contact with each other, and the question of morality is not permitted to invade it.

The tragic consequences of the alternative that there is *no* alternative are not far to seek. In the first place, it tends to destroy whatever sense of ethical values the individual possesses. It is a simple fact of psychology that if a man calls a lie the truth, he tampers dangerously with his value judgments. Jesus called attention to that fact in one of his most revealing utterances. His mother, in an attempt to excuse him from the harsh judgment of his enemies, said that he was a little out of his mind – not terribly crazy, but just a little off-balance. Those who did not like him said that he was all right with regard to his mind, but that he was full of the devil, and that it was by the power of the devil that he was casting out devils. Jesus, hearing the discussion, said that these men did not talk good sense: "A house . . . divided against itself . . . cannot stand." He suggested that if they continued saying that he was casting out devils by the power of the devil – and they knew that such was not the case – they would commit the unpardonable sin. That is to say, if a man continues to call a good thing bad, he will eventually lose his sense of moral distinctions.

Is this always the result? Is it not possible to quarantine a certain kind of deception so that it will not affect the rest of one's life? May not the underprivileged do with deception as it relates to his soul what the human body does with tubercle bacilli?[78] The body seems unable to destroy the bacilli, so nature builds a prison for them, walls them in with a think fibrosis so that their toxin cannot escape from the lungs into the bloodstream. As long as the victim exercises care in the matter of rest, work, and diet, normal activities may be pursued without harm. Is deception a comparable technique of survival, the fibrosis that protects the life from poison in its total outlook or in its other relations? Or, to change the figure, may not deception be regarded under some circumstances as a kind of blind spot that is functional in a limited area of experience? No! Such questions are merely attempts to rationalize one's way out of a critical difficulty.

The penalty of deception is to *become* a deception, with all sense of moral discrimination vitiated. A man who lies habitually becomes a lie, and it is increasingly impossible for him to know when he is lying and when he is not. In other words, the moral mercury of life is reduced to zero. Shakespeare has immortalized this aspect of character in his drama of Macbeth. Macbeth has a high sense of destiny, which is deeply underscored by the testimony of the witches. This is communicated to his wife, who takes it to head and to heart. By a series of liquidations their friends disappear and their enemies multiply, until Macbeth is king and his wife is queen. Together they swim across Scotland in seas of blood, tying lau-

rels on their brows with other people's lives, heartstrings, and hopes. Then
fatal things begin happening to them. Lady Macbeth walks in her sleep,
trying in vain to wash blood from her hands. But the blood is not on her
hands; it is on her soul. Macbeth becomes a victim of terrible visions and
he cries:

> Methought I heard a voice cry "Sleep no more!
> Macbeth does murder sleep!" The innocent sleep.

One day, at the most crucial point in Macbeth's life, an attendant announces to him that Lady Macbeth is dead. His reply reveals, in one agonizing flash, the death of values that has taken place in him:

> She should have died hereafter;
> There would have been a time for such a word.
> To-morrow, and to-morrow, and to-morrow,
> Creeps in this petty pace from day to day
> To the last syllable of recorded time,
> And all of our yesterdays have lighted fools
> The way to dusty death. Out, out brief candle!
> Life's but a walking shadow, a poor player
> That struts and frets his hour upon the stage
> And then is heard no more; it is a tale
> Told by an idiot, full of sound and fury,
> Signifying nothing.

Life is only a tale told by a fool, having no meaning because deception has
wiped out all moral distinctions.

The second alternative is a possible derivation from the first one. The
underprivileged may decide to juggle the various areas of compromise, on
the assumption that the moral quality of compromise operates in an
ascending-descending scale. According to this argument, not all issues
are equal in significance nor in consequence; it may be that some compro-
mises take on the aspect of inevitability because of circumstances over
which the individual has no control. It is true that we are often bound by a

network of social relations that operate upon us without being particularly affected by us. We are all affected by forces, social and natural, that in some measure determine our behavior without our being able to bring to bear upon them our private will, however great or righteous it may be.

All over the world there are millions of people who are condemned by the powerful in their society to live in ghettos. The choice seems to be the ghetto or suicide. But such a conclusion may be hasty and ill-advised; it may be the counsel of the kind of fear we discussed previously, or it may be the decision of cowardice. For all practical purposes there are great numbers of people who have decided to *live,* and to compromise on the matter of place and conditions. Further, we may say that those who have power know that the decision will be to live, and have counted on it. They are prepared to deal ruthlessly with any form of effective protest, because effective protest upsets the *status quo.* Life, then, becomes a grim game of wits, and the stakes are one's physical existence.

The term "compromise" then takes on a very special and highly differentiated meaning. It is less positive than ordinary deception, which may be regarded as deliberate strategy. If the assumption is that survival with some measure of freedom is at stake, then compromise is defined in terms of the actions which involve one's life continuation. It is a matter of behavior patterns. Many obvious interferences with freedom are ignored completely. Many insults are cast aside as of no consequence. One does battle only when not to do battle is to be vanquished without the recognition that comes from doing battle. To the morally sensitive person the whole business is sordid and degrading.

It is safe to say that the common attitude taken toward these deceptions that have to do with survival is that they are amoral. The moral question is never raised. To raise such a question is regarded as sheer stupidity. The behavior involved is in the same category as seeking and getting food or providing shelter for oneself. It belongs in the general classification of simple survival behavior. Obviously this is the reason why it is so difficult to make a moral appeal, either to the dominant group or to the disinherited, in order to bring about a change in the basic relation between them. For better or for worse, according to this aspect of our analysis, there is no point at which mere moral appeal makes sense. Whatever moral sensitiveness to the situation was present at some stage in the life of the individual has long since been atrophied, due to betrayal, suffering, or frustration.

This alternative, then, must be discussed from the point of view of the observer rather than from that of the victim. The rank and file of the oppressed do not formally raise the questions involved in their behavior. Specifically, the applicability of religion is restricted to those areas in which religious considerations commend themselves as being reasonable. A profound piece of surgery has to take place in the very psyche of the disinherited before the great claim of the religion of Jesus can be presented. The great stretches of barren places in the soul must be revitalized, brought to life, before they can be challenged. Tremendous skill and power must be exercised to show to the disinherited the awful results of the role of negative deception into which their lives have been cast. How to do this is perhaps the greatest challenge that the religion of Jesus faces in modern life.

Mere preaching is not enough. What are words, however sacred and powerful, in the presence of the grim facts of the daily struggle to survive? Any attempt to deal with this situation on a basis of values that disregard the struggle for survival appears to be in itself a compromise with life. It is only when people live in an environment in which they are not required to exert supreme effort into just keeping alive that they seem to be able to select ends besides those of mere physical survival. On the subsistence level, values are interpreted in terms of their bearing upon the one major concern for all activity – not being killed. This is really the form that the dilemma takes. It is not solely a question of keeping the body alive; it is rather how not to be killed. *Not to be killed* becomes the great end, and morality takes its meaning from that center. Until that center is shifted, nothing real can be accomplished. It is the uncanny and perhaps unwitting recognition of this fact that causes those in power to keep the disinherited from participation in meaningful social process. For if the disinherited get such a new center as patriotism, for instance – liberty within the framework of a sense of county or nation – then the aim of *not being killed* is swallowed up by a larger and more transcendent goal. Above all else the disinherited must not have any stake in the social order; they must be made to feel that they are alien, that it is a great boon to be allowed to remain alive, not be exterminated. This was the psychology of the Nazis; it grew out of their theory of the state and the place given the Hebrew people in their ideology. Such is also the attitude of the Ku Klux Klan toward Negroes.

Even within the disinherited group itself artificial and exaggerated emphasis upon not being killed tends to cheapen life. That is to say, the fact that the lives of the disinherited are lightly held by the dominant group tends to create the same attitude among them toward each other.

We come now to the third alternative – a complete and devastating sincerity. I have in my possession a copy of a letter from Mahatma Gandhi to Muriel Lester. The letter says in part: "Speak the truth, without fear and without exception, and see everyone whose work is related to your purpose. You are in God's work, so you need not fear man's scorn. If they listen to your requests and grant them, you will be satisfied. If they reject them, then you must make their rejection your strength." The acceptance of this alternative is to be simply, directly truthful, whatever may be the cost in life, limb or security. For the individual who accepts this, there may be quick and speedy judgment with attendant loss. But if the number increases and the movement spreads, the vindication of the truth would follow in the wake. There must always be the confidence that the effect of truthfulness can be realized in the mind of the oppressor as well as the oppressed. There is no substitute for such a faith.

Emphasis upon an unwavering sincerity points up at once the major challenge of Jesus to the disinherited and the power of his most revolutionary appeal. "Let your communication be, Yea, yea; Nay, nay: for whatsoever is more than these cometh of evil." "Ye have heard that it hath been said, An eye for an eye, . . but I say unto you, That ye resist not evil." What does he mean? Does he mean that factors having to do with physical survival are trivial or of no consequence? Is this emphasis merely the counsel of suicide? It seems inescapable that either Jesus was infinitely more realistic than we dare imagine or, taking his words at their face value, he is talking as one who has no understanding of the basic facts of life that touch this central problem. From our analysis of the life of Jesus it seems clear that it was from within the framework of great social pressures upon him and his group that he taught and lived to the very end. It is reasonable to assume, then, that he speaks out of understanding and that his words cannot be lightly disregarded, however devastating they may seem.

It may be argued that the insistence upon complete sincerity has to do only with man's relation to God, not with man's relation to man. To what does such a position lead? Unwavering sincerity says that man should always recognize the fact that he lives always in the presence of God, always under the divine scrutiny, and that there is no really significant living for a man, whatever may be his status, until he has turned and faced the divine scrutiny. Here all men stand stripped to the literal substance of themselves, without disguise, without pretension, without *seeming* whatsoever. No man can fool God. From him nothing is hidden.

> *Thou compassest my path and my lying down,*
> *and art acquainted with all my ways.*
> *For there is not a word in my tongue,*
> *but, lo, O Lord, thou knowest it altogether . . .*
> *Whither shall I go from thy spirit?*
> *or whither shall I flee from thy presence?*
> *If I ascend up into heaven, thou art there:*
> *if I make my bed in hell, behold, thou art there . . .*
> *If I say, Surely the darkness shall cover me;*
> *even the night shall be light about me.*
> *Yea, the darkness hideth not from thee;*
> *but the night shineth as the day:*
> *the darkness and the light are both alike to thee.*

Was it against the background of his heritage and his religious faith in the 139th psalm that Jesus assumed his great ethical imperative? This seems to be conclusively brought out in his treatment of the climax of human history. The Judge is on his throne; the sheep are on the right, the goats on the left. The Judge speaks: "I was [hungry,] and ye gave me no meat. . . . sick, and in prison, and ye visited me not." The climax of human history is interpreted as a time when the inner significance of men's deeds would be revealed to them. But here a new note is introduced. Sincerity in

human relations is equal to, and the same as, sincerity to God. If we accept this explanation as a clue to Jesus' meaning, we come upon the stark
fact that the insistence of Jesus upon genuineness is absolute; man's relation to man and man's relation to God are one relation.

A death blow is struck to hypocrisy. One of the major defense mecha-
nisms of the disinherited is taken away from them. What does Jesus give
them in its place? What does he substitute for hypocrisy? Sincerity. But is
sincerity a mechanism of defense against the strong? The answer is No.
Something more significant takes place. In the presence of an overwhelming sincerity on the part of the disinherited, the dominant themselves are caught with no defense, with the edge taken away from the
sense of prerogative and from the status upon which the impregnability
of their position rests. They are thrown back upon themselves for their
rating. The experience of power has no meaning aside from the other-
than-self reference which sustains it. If the position of ascendancy is not
acknowledged tacitly and actively by those over whom the ascendancy is
exercised, then it falls flat. Hypocrisy on the part of the disinherited in
dealing with the dominant group is a tribute yielded by those who are
weak. But if this attitude is lacking, or is supplanted by a simple sincerity
and genuineness, then it follows that advantage due to the accident of
birth or position is reduced to zero. Instead of relation between the weak
and the strong there is merely a relationship between human beings. A
man is a man, no more, no less. The awareness of this fact marks the supreme moment of human dignity.

⊂⊃ | *Leadership* (1960)

Thurman made the following speech upon being made an honorary member of the Zeta Upsilon chapter (Boston University) of Alpha Phi Omega, a primarily white national college fraternity.[79] *Here Thurman underscores the significance of morally anchored character as the basis for visionary public leadership. Leaders must above all be seekers after truth or, as he put it elsewhere, "high priests of truth." A major problem for public leadership, he argues, is the inevitable conflict of loyalties between duty to office and the moral obligation to self. Responsible leadership, Thurman suggests, begins with critical self-examination, an honest search for the truth about oneself. Self-criticism, for Thurman, is the source for discernment of responsible moral action. Responsibility, however, includes responsibility for both one's actions and reactions.*

. . . The new mother looks down upon her little child's head and whispers in her heart: "Oh, may you seek after truth. If anything I teach you be false, may you throw it from you and pass on to higher and deeper knowledge than I ever had. If you are an artist, may no love of wealth or fame or admiration and no fear of blame or misunderstanding make you ever paint with pen or brush an ideal or a picture of external life otherwise than as you see it; if you become a politician, may no success for your party or yourself or the seeming good of even your nation ever lead you to tamper with reality and play a diplomatic part. In all the

difficulties which will arise in life, fling yourself down on the truth and cling to
that as a drowning man in a stormy sea flings himself on to a plank and clings
to it, knowing that, whether he sink or swim with it, it is the best he has. If you
become a man of thought and learning, oh, never with your left hand be afraid
to pull down what your right has painfully built up through the years of thought
and study, if you see it at last not to be founded on that which is; die poor, un-
loved, unknown, a failure – but shut your eyes to nothing that seems to them
the reality."   – *Olive Schreiner*[80]

One of the most searching demands of leadership is integrity and honesty. The leader must above all else be a seeker after truth. In his private
life of thought and deed he must not violate the ideals which he embraces
in his role as the leader of others. The integrity of the act cannot be separated from the integrity of the person and the word. Therefore, the leader
must seek the truth.

He must seek the truth about himself. The single fact is that he must
accept himself. It is probably true that he is not as brilliant or as able as
someone else seems to be; he may not have the kind of charm that attracts
others to him in the way someone else does; he may not have the advantages of background and family heritage that someone else can claim. He
may lay claim to some of these seeming assets. Nevertheless, he must at
long last say "Yes" to his own basic equipment.

Lincoln says that if you could change the fact of yourself,

> *"You might fetch the wrong jack-knife in the swap.*
> *It's up to you to whittle what you can*
> *With what you've got – and what I am, I am . . ."*[81]

In addition to accepting himself, the leader must be willing to take responsibility for his own actions. This is a most searching demand. It is
very tempting to shift the responsibility for decisions. The leader can say
very easily that he is held captive by the tyranny of his responsibilities. He
must do what the role demands of him and take no personal responsibility
for such actions. This is a real delusion. True it is that there is an etiquette
and sometimes what seems to be a morality of office that leaves little room

for the integrity of the person. But that fact does not provide an alibi for shifting responsibility to the position or office which one holds. It is a *man* who is the chairman, or the president or the leader. As a *man* he is responsible for his actions in his office. Life does not know about status, position, or place, it knows only that the man, the living, breathing man, is a responsible agent however he may function in his roles.

In addition to taking responsibility for his action, the leader must be willing to take responsibility for his *reactions.* Sometimes it does seem that the responsibility for a person's reaction to the events of his life is not his to determine. Again and again we are involved in experiences and events which sweep into our lives without any reference to our own wills. They arise in regions beyond out control. True. But the moment we encounter them, *how* we react to them, *what* we do with them – these matters are our responsibility and concern. It is here that the true character of the person is often revealed. It is for this reason that two people visited by the same circumstances may be seen to react to it in diametrically opposed ways. One may respond with bitterness and hostility, the other with gentleness and grace. The leader is responsible for his reaction to life.

We are living in a time of revolutions, technological and social. Our reaction to these revolutions may be one of fear, panic, and despair. We may in our reaction be stripped of all hope and all confidence not only about the meaning of our own lives but about the significance of the future for mankind. Or we may in our reaction be inspired to a deeper commitment to higher purposes and more meaningful resolves to the end that in us the dreams for mankind that are cherished will be worked at with fresh vigor and new hope. How we react is our responsibility – and from this there is no escape.

The leader must seek the truth about his society. He must be able to assess it properly and clearly. He must know that what he condemns in others he dare not encourage in himself. The ideals which he demands of the political or social life of his times must not be other than the ideal which he cherishes for himself. In so doing he will discover that at long last the only place of refuge for any man in the world is in his own heart.

CO | *Reconciliation (1963)*

In the following chapter, reprinted from Disciplines of the Spirit, Thurman *discusses the role of religion in public life, the place of moral imagination in our relations with others, and the ways that a nonviolent ethic provides the highest means to personal and social transformation.*[82] *The place of reconciliation as an ethical imperative in human relations is essential to understanding Thurman's vision of community. The normative character of community is not an external imposition upon life, according to Thurman, but a disclosure of what life is about as it seeks to realize itself in myriad time-space manifestations. Reconciliation is the spiritual and moral discipline which makes loving and respectful relations between people possible — even in the presence of dramatic cultural differences. Love is synonymous with reconciliation and expresses the "intent" of God. Reconciliation begins within when the individual's inner need to be cared for and understood is met in encounter with God. The experience of reconciliation with God becomes the ground and moral mandate for sharing one's experience in relations with others and in society. For Thurman, whatever impedes the actualization of community either personally or socially must be confronted and transformed into a higher synthesis of love. The way to the reconciliation of society is through redemptive suffering rooted in love or nonviolence. Nonviolence, for Thurman, is more than a technique or tactical maneuver; rather, it is the only means through which a peaceful and just society can be ordered. "Experiences of meaning which people share are more compelling than the barriers that*

separate them," Thurman writes. "If such experiences can be multiplied over a time in-
terval of sufficient duration, then any barrier between men, of whatever kind, can be un-
dermined." For him, this is the central ethical imperative of religion, to love and to be rec-
onciled.

I

THE LITERAL FACT OF THE UNDERLYING UNITY of life seems to be established beyond doubt. It manifests itself in the basic structural patterns of
nature and provides the precious clue to the investigation and interpretation of the external world of man. At any point in time and space one may
come upon the door that opens into the central place where the building
blocks of existence are always being manufactured. True, man has not
been able to decipher all the codes in their highly complex variations, but
he is ever on the scent.

If life has been fashioned out of a fundamental unity and ground, and
if it has developed within such a structure, then it is not to be wondered at
that the interest in and concern for wholeness should be part of the conscious intent of life, more basic than any particular conscious tendency
toward fragmentation. Every expression of life is trying to experience itself. For a form of life to experience itself it must actualize its own unique
potential. In so doing it experiences in miniature the fundamental unity
out of which it comes.

The purpose of this chapter is to explore the meaning of man's elemental grounding in unity for the larger life of his mind and spirit as he relates
to his fellows. Our immediate purpose is to explore the possibilities in
terms of the discipline of reconciliation. It applies not only to ruptured
human relations but also to disharmony within oneself created by inner
conflict. The quality of reconciliation is that of wholeness; it seeks to effect and further harmonious relations in a totally comprehensive climate.

The concern for reconciliation finds expression in the simple human
desire to understand others and to be understood by others. These are the
building blocks of the society of man, the precious ingredients without
which man's life is a nightmare and the future of his life on the planet
doomed. Every man wants to be cared for, to be sustained by the assur-

ance that he shares in the watchful and thoughtful attention of others –
not merely or necessarily others in general but others in particular. He
wants to know that – however vast and impersonal all life about him may
seem, however hard may be the stretch of road on which he is journeying – he is not alone, but the object of another's concern and caring;
wants to know this in an awareness sufficient to hold him against ultimate
fear and panic. It is precisely at this point of awareness that life becomes
personal and the individual a person. Through it he gets some intimation
of what, after all, he finally amounts to, and the way is cleared for him to
experience his own spirit.

The need to be cared for is essential to the furtherance and maintenance of life in health. This is how life is nourished. The simpler the form
of life, the simpler the terms of caring. It does seem to me at times that,
even with the simplest forms of life in plants, a new quality of growth appears if, beyond the care expressed in watering and feeding, an additional
something is added. One year, in addition to watering my flowers and dig-
ging around the roots and so on, two or three times a week I would go into
the garden and look at them, brood over them gently, and on occasion ver-
balize my feelings by talking to them directly. It may have been my imagination, but I am convinced that it made a great difference in the richness
of their growth and bloom.

There is less uncertainty about what happens when this need is honored in animal life. A news item appeared not long ago in a daily paper describing a novel kind of job held by a high school girl in a large general hospital. She was employed as a mouse-petter. Her sole occupation was to
take the white mice out of their cages several times during each day, pet
them, croon over them, and gentle them. It had been discovered that mice
treated in this way responded to various experiments with less tension
and therefore with more relaxation – i.e., more positively – than those that
had not been thus dealt with. The petting touched something deep within
them and their response was both automatic and authentic. Their organism was given a sense of well-being that put them at their ease. This enabled them to hold their own against limited upheaval in their environment without panic. The literature growing out of such experimentation
with animals is increasingly abundant.

It is in human life that the need to be cared for can be most clearly observed, however, because here it can be most clearly felt. There was a lady in my church in San Francisco who felt very poignantly the need to be needed beyond the limits of her family. One day she went with a small group to visit the children's ward in a hospital. She noticed a baby in a crib against the wall. Despite the things that were going on in the ward and the excitement created by a group of English bell-ringers and their tunes, this little child remained lying on his side with his face to the wall. But it was discovered that he was not asleep—his eyes were open in an unseeing stare. The nurse explained that the entire ward was worried because the child responded to nothing. Feeding had to be forced. "Even if he cried all the time, that would be something to work with. But there is nothing. And he is not sick as far as anything clinical can be determined. He will surely die unless something is done." Then the lady decided to try to do something. Every day for several weeks she visited the ward, took the little boy in her arms, talked to him, hummed little melodies and lullabies, and did all the spontaneous things that many years ago she had done with her own son. For a long time there was absolutely no response. One day when she lifted the child into her arms there was a slight movement of the body, and the eyes appeared to be somewhat in focus. This was the beginning. Finally, on a later day, as her voice was heard greeting the nurse when she came into the ward, the child turned over, faced the ward, and tried to raise himself to a sitting position. Things happened rapidly thereafter until he was restored to health.

When the need to be cared for is dishonored, threatened, or undetermined, then the individual cannot experience his own self as a unity and his life may become deeply fragmented and splintered. In its extreme form the disturbance upsets the balance of the mind, and a man gradually loses his sense of identity. When I was a boy I had a graphic experience of the meaning of this. In the corner down at the end of our street, my mother noticed that a large group of people had gathered and others were coming. She sent me down there to see what was going on. As I got to the corner I saw that the center of attraction was the strange behavior of Kenchion Butler, who ran a barbershop. He was describing a large circle around an oak tree. Each time he completed the circle he would strike the tree with a huge cross-tie ax he had in his hands, and call someone's name. He was clearly out of his mind. The sheriff had come to take him away to jail as a preliminary to sending him to the mental hospital – or, as we said at the time, the asylum. The sheriff could not get to him because of the ax in his hand. It was a game of waiting it out.

Then someone thought of Ma Walker, and I was sent for her. She was a most unusual woman in our community, distinguished for two things: her personal care for all kinds of people, and her beautiful rose garden, dedi-cated to God. From her garden came roses for the altar table in the church and for funerals. I went to her house, told her the story, and she came back with me. When she was within earshot of the group she called the name of the man with the tortured mind. There was just a slight hesitation in his step as he located her and the sound of the voice, but he kept walking. Meanwhile, she and I approached; the sheriff took his pistol out of the holster and the crowd moved completely to one side, making way for us. I dropped back when we were at the outer edge of the group. Ma Walker kept on, repeating his name as she stood in his circular path. Then they met, their eyes held, she said simply, "Come, Kenchion, you must go home with me." And he did.

Here was a woman who had the quality of personality that could make the gift of reconciliation to another human being. Sometimes it heals the inner breach by the simple offering. What it does is to introduce harmony into another's life by sensing and honoring the need to be cared for and therefore understood. This is the miracle. One person, standing in his own place, penetrates deeply into the life of another in a manner that makes possible an ingathering within that other life, and thus the wild-ness is gentled out of a personality at war with itself.

The talent of reconciliation may be native to the personality of him who has it – I do not know. But I am confining my thoughts, to begin with, to the inner reconciliation that an individual experiences when he feels that his life is bottomed by another's caring. The roots of such an actively healing disposition may lie in the fact that a person is so profoundly as-sured that he is cared for that his spontaneous attitude toward others car-ries over the spirit of this caring. Indeed, he may be so sensitized to the personality needs of others that his self-giving to them is an expression of the natural flow of his life to others in distress. Or he may be so conscious of the way in which the inner harmony of his life is held by another that he feels ever the urge to seek ways of doing this precise thing in the lives of his fellows. Or, out of the assurance that his experience with God confirms and keeps him whole, despite the intruding disillusionments of life, he expresses his praise of God in sharing this quality with others.

In addition to all this there must be a discipline either to develop the talent or to keep it alive. And in what does such a discipline consist? In the first place, there must be the *intent* itself. The individual must want to do it. A climate must be generated out of which the talent or gift moves forth into the life of another. Such a climate is a matter of growth. It may begin with simple interest in others, a simple identification with them in their need, anguish, or distress. Out of such identification a real searching for ways of approach arises – for keys that will unlock the door to others' lives or for a kind of personal activity in relatedness that may inspire another person to open the door, to turn toward one. In other words, the whole process must be worked at and all personal resources drawn upon to this end. The mood that induces trust has to be developed and projected.

When I took my dog, Kropotkin, to a kennel to be trained, I was very much impressed with the approach of the trainer. I told him what I wanted the dog to learn and why. After listening carefully he said, "I've been working with dogs in training for more than fifteen years. Over this period of time I've developed an over-all attitude toward dogs in general and toward any dog I am to train in particular. Now, any time I see a dog, of whatever kind or condition, at once he is enveloped by a sense of 'dogness' that gathers him to me. I know that my attitude-feeling for him can be trusted. But it takes me from seven to fourteen days of contact to discover if a responding something can come from the dog to me. Once that has happened, the rest is easy and simple. My attitude gentles the dog into trust and confidence. I've had only one real failure in the last five years."

It is essential to the Christian's vocation that attention be given to training in the direction of trust and confidence. Of course, I think such training should enter into every man's vocation, but it is especially binding upon the Christian who undertakes by commitment and intention to follow the teaching of his Master. There is the intent, the desire, the decision – all must become central in the individual's awareness of what he means by himself.

At the Primate Laboratory at the University of Wisconsin, under the direction of Dr. Harry Harlow, some very interesting observations have been made about the behavior of monkeys and what it implies about children. Some of the baby monkeys were given terry-cloth-covered manikins[83] as mother-substitutes. It seems that the comfort of the manikins met all the initial urgencies of feeling of the monkeys while they were growing up. But when they reached the age to find mates and become parents themselves, they failed. What was the reason for this neurotic behavior? Was it due to the fact that the manikins were not real mothers? Perhaps. Another possibility has been explored. The monkeys with the manikins were reared in separate cages where they could hear and see other monkeys but could not mix and play with them. It was discovered that

> . . . regardless of mothering or lack of it, infants who have a chance to play with
> other little monkeys for periods as short as twenty minutes a day become so-
> cially normal monkeys. Even the offspring of the brutal mothers from the mani-
> kin experiment show no serious maladjustment . . . On the other hand, all of
> the monkeys who were cut off from contact with playmates were unable to in-
> teract normally with other monkeys, socially or sexually.

Dr. Harlow states, "Our experiments suggest that the chance to play freely with other children is as important as mothering."[84]

First, then, reconciliation and the harmony that it produces must be experienced by the individual as a normal routine. This is what happens to monkeys and children who experience themselves through experiencing their playmates. Simple techniques and skills emerge which are regarded as the child's direct reaction to his immediate play environment. He learns how to belong and the fearful price of isolation. His general experience with the group becomes a part of his formal intent as a member of the group. Association with others, contacts with fellowship, this is the setting in which recognition of the need to be cared for emerges and may become a part of the working purpose of the individual in defining and de-

termining the quality of his own relationships. He accepts the fact that,
whatever others' behavior toward him may seem to be, or however contradictory the problem, the real issue always is the same – the other person's
need to be cared for must be honored. Behind all his hostility, hate, and
antisocial behavior, the hunger persists – the ache to be cared for, for oneself alone.

> *If I knew you and you knew me,*
> *And each of us could clearly see*
> *By the inner light divine,*
> *The meaning of your life and mine,*
> *I am sure that we would differ less*
> *And clasp our hands in friendliness –*
> *If I knew you and you knew me.*[85]

Let us keep clearly in mind the issue here. The need to be cared for is
fundamental to human life and to psychic and spiritual health and well-
being. When this need is not met, the individual is thrown into conflict,
an inner conflict that can only be resolved when the need is honored. The
conflict expresses itself in many ways, from profound mental disturbance
to the complete projection upon others of the hate and violence the person himself is feeling. The individual experiences the fulfillment of his
need in a diffused way, by living in an atmosphere of acceptance and belonging. It is here that simple techniques of co-operation and adjustment
are developed, which in time become the channels through which the intent to honor this deep need in others is implemented. Unwillingness to
accept ill will, hatred, or violence directed toward oneself from another as
the fundamental intent is the role of the reconciler, the function of reconciliation. "Father, forgive them, for they know not what they do," says Jesus
as he is dying on the cross.

II

One of the forms that reconciliation takes is what is generally known as
nonviolence, that is, a response to a violent act, directed toward oneself in

the first place, in a manner that meets the need of the individual to be cared for, to be understood, rather than the apparent nature of the act itself. The term "violence" usually carries with it the connotation of physical force of some sort. Violence as physical force, when employed directly in face-to-face encounter, may be overwhelming and compelling. It is quick, decisive, and definite. There is a certain limited efficiency in its use. It tends to inspire fear and often makes for temporary capitulation. Its central purpose is to make it possible for one man to impose his will on another. As an instrument of national policy, its purpose is to impose one nation's will on another nation.

There is a very interesting and instructive discussion of violence in Ortega y Gasset's *The Revolt of the Masses*,[86] where it is suggested that violence is always present, in fact or threat, in all human relations. The thing that distinguishes the barbarian from the civilized man is the priority given to the use of it. The civilized man postpones violence until all other methods are exhausted; while the barbarian resorts to it as soon as his will is thwarted.

It is well to remember that the violent act is the desperate act. It is the imperious demand of a person to force another to honor his desire and need to be cared for, to be understood. In this sense the violent act is a plea, a begging to have one's need to belong fulfilled and confirmed. For this reason, to confine the definition of violence to its physical expression is too restricting and limiting. Defenses against physical violence may be built and maintained until the individual is exhausted in death. Terrible as it is, it is not violence in its worst form. No. Violence at its worst may be nonphysical. Love itself may be a form of nonphysical violence. Many years ago I read an article in a magazine called *The World Tomorrow* describing an early experience of Mahatma Gandhi when he was the head of a school for boys. The sense of community between himself and the boys had been ruptured by a lie one of them told. Instead of punishing the boy directly, Gandhi announced that *he* would do penance for this by fasting for twenty-four hours. What was an act of nonviolence as far as the offender was concerned was an act of violence on Gandhi's body. Emotionally, it must have been a devastating experience for the hapless boy and others.

The effect of nonviolence on the offender is apt to be so threatening that the security he feels in the violent act deserts him and he is thrown back upon the naked hunger of his own heart to be cared for, to be understood, to experience himself in harmony with his fellows. When violence is met with violence is met with violence, the citadel of the spirit is not invaded. The most that is accomplished is a limited truce – a standoff – a stalemate. The fact of isolation becomes a way of life. All communication breaks down, and slowly the spirits of men become asphyxiated. For this reason, the only thing that can maintain the mood of violence between men beyond the heat and excitation of direct encounter is hatred. Hate is the great insulator making it possible for one man to deny the existence of another or to *will* his nonexistence. Since the necessity to honor one's need to be cared for cannot be fundamentally denied, the only recourse left to the hater is to will the very nonexistence of the other person. Violence is the act through which such a will is implemented, and hate is its dynamic.

The very act of affirming the nonexistence of another human being is at once, in positive terms, an act of self-affirmation. Hate may become the basis of one's own self-estimate when one is faced with the will to one's own nonexistence. When a man is despised and hated by other men and all around are the instruments of violence working in behalf of such attitudes, then he may find himself resorting to hatred as a means of salvaging a sense of self, however fragmented. Under such circumstances, hate becomes a man's way of saying that he is present. Despite the will to his nonexistence on the part of his environment or persons in it, he affirms himself by affirming the nonexistence of those who so regard him. In the end the human spirit cannot tolerate this. Men are made for each other, and any sustained denial of this elemental fact of life cannot stand.

Thus nonviolence occurs and recurs on the horizon throughout man's life. It is one of the great vehicles of reconciliation because it creates and maintains a climate in which the need to be cared for and understood can be honored and effectively dealt with. The mood of nonviolence is that of reconciliation. It engenders in the individual an attitude that inspires wholeness and integration within. It provides the climate in which the things that are needed for peace, or for one's own peace, may be sensed, disclosed, and developed. It presupposes that the desire to be cared for and to care for others is one with the very essence of all one's meaning and significance. It thus provides a working atmosphere in which this mutual desiring may be normal, reasonable, and accepted.

But nonviolence is not merely a mood or climate, or even an attitude. It is a technique and, in and of itself, a discipline. In the first place, it is a rejection of physical force, a renunciation of the tools of physical violence. These may be renounced because they are not available; such a renunciation has only tactical significance. Here nonviolence may be used effectively by violent men as a practical necessity. In this sense it has the same moral basis as violence. This is one of the ancient weapons of the weak against the strong and is a part of the overall tactic of deception. It is instructive to note that when nonviolence is used in this way in response to external necessity, this may not at all vitiate its creative impact upon those against whom it is used. The importance of this cannot be overemphasized. Because nonviolence is an affirmation of the *existence* of the man of violent deeds, in contradistinction to the fact that violence embodies a will to *nonexistence,* the moral impact which nonviolence carries may potentially realize itself in a given situation by rendering the violent act ineffective and bringing about the profoundest kind of change in attitude. All this may take place in encounter, even though the users of nonviolence are full of violence themselves. This is apt to be true in situations where the tools for physical violence are not available, or because even if used, the chances for their success are poor. It is entirely possible for an individual to use nonviolence with detachment – as an effective weapon and a substitute for weapons of violence – while the mood continues to be violent, a mood that inspires hate, that wills the nonexistence of another.

The logic of hate is to kill. It is to translate the willing of the nonexistence of another into the literal deed of his extermination. Men who war against each other, if they are to be effective in their undertaking, must hate. They must will the nonexistence of each other. Once this happens, all moral responsibility disappears and they are free to do *anything* to them, to perform any act of violence or outrage upon them, without undermining their own sense of worth or value. Nonviolence and nonkilling mean, therefore, essentially the same thing.

In the second place, nonviolence may be a rejection not merely of the *physical* tools of violence – since their use is aimed at the destruction of human life, which is the ultimate denial of the need to be cared for – but also of the *psychological* tools of violence as well. Here we assume that, even if the tools of physical violence were available and could be of tactical significance, their use would be renounced because their purpose is to kill – to make good the will for the nonexistence of another human being. And this is to cut off his chances for the actualizing of his potential sometime in his living future by dealing with him in the present.

But the psychological tools of nonviolence are of another order. Their purpose is to open the door of the heart so that what another is feeling and experiencing can find its way within. They assume that it is possible for a man to get real insight into the meaning of his deeds, attitudes, or way of life as they affect the life of his fellows. A man faced with nonviolence is forced to deal with himself, finally; every way of escape is ultimately cut off. This is why there can be no possible limit as to time or duration of nonviolent acts. Their purpose is not merely to change an odious situation, but, further, to make it urgent for a man to face himself in his action. Finally all must face the same basic question: Is what I am doing an expression of my fundamental intent toward any man when I am most myself? The more persistent nonviolent acts become, the more threatening they are to the person who refuses to deal with the ultimate question.

What then are some of the nonphysical tools of nonviolence? One is the will to refrain from the automatic response to violence: to fight or to flee. I use the word "tool" here advisedly. It is a graphic reconditioning of an ancient behavior pattern on the basis of which the survival of the species has been possible. It is a deliberate training or disciplining of the nervous patterns of the organism to a new kind of response. It places upon them the demand to absorb violence rather than to counteract it in kind. In initiating this procedure or process a person may know naked fear for the first time in life. He is threatened below the threshold of all his inherited defenses, and for a timeless moment is completely vulnerable and exposed. There is rioting in the streets of the soul, and the price of tranquility comes terribly high. Order and reconciliation must be restored within – here the major conquest must be achieved. At such a moment one is not dealing with a perpetrator of violence, a violent man, but with the stark fact of violence itself. This has to be conquered first. Once that has happened the power of the violent man is broken.

This principle is illustrated in a firsthand experience told by an undergraduate student who participated in sit-in demonstrations in one of the southern cities. She was one of several students who made up a team assigned to a particular drugstore to cover the lunch counter. As soon as they entered the store the lunch counter was cleared of all white patrons and closed. After about half an hour had elapsed, she noticed that down at the lower end of the counter the rope had been removed and, rather surreptitiously, white patrons were being permitted to come through and sit for service. Immediately she left her position and went down to the other end where the service was beginning. Just as she started to take a seat, a man who had been standing quietly against the wall sprang forward and ordered her to remove herself. This he did in the name of the law. Quietly she asked him to identify himself, since he was in plain clothes. He opened his coat to reveal his badge of authority. Whereupon the young lady said, "That's not a ———— County badge; you have no jurisdiction here." Nonplussed, the officer seized her by the wrist, his fingers biting into her flesh, and pushed her up against the wall, holding her there. What follows now are her words as nearly as I can recall.

> It was my very first direct encounter with real violence. All the possibilities of what we were up against had been drilled into us in our training and every conceivable kind of situation had been simulated; but even so, I was not prepared for the stark panic that moved through me. This passed quickly and in its place I felt an intense and angry violence – but something in me held. I looked him in the face until I felt his fear and sensed his own anguish. Then I thought, now quite calmly, how desperate a man must be to behave this way to a defenseless girl. And a strange peace came over me and I knew now that violence could be taken, and that I could take it and triumph over it. I suppose that as long as I live I will be winning and losing this battle with myself.

The spirit of retaliation must be relaxed and overcome. Here again the reconciliation must go on in a man's spirit before he can be at one with the technique of nonviolence he employs as an instrument for social change. The spirit of retaliation is rooted profoundly in the total history of the race. It has an instinctual ground. Some of the latest findings of cultural anthropologists make the point very clearly that man's immediate ancestors were not peaceful root- and fruit-eating primates but predatory, territory-seeking animals. The conflict between the positive and creative inclination toward community and the positive and destructive inclination toward conquest seems to be older than the conscious life of mankind. Both inclinations have to do with survival. There is a quality in the spirit of reconciliation that heals the inner breaches by confirming the need to be cared for, to be held, honored in one's own life and in the lives of others. And this is the work of reconciliation. It begins with a man's own spirit. When he is challenged by the violent act, all kinds of feelings clamor to be heard. They appear singly and in fateful combination: fear in its many masks – of loss of face, loss of self-respect, loss of life; cowardice in all its subtleties – the futility of being a hero, the waste of energy on a situation that can only defeat one's true aim, one's vocational fulfillment; hate with all its self-affirming vitality when all other avenues of support are denied. At such a time a man may twist, turn, juggle and shift his ground, until at last he is face to face with his own sense of ultimate worth. This he puts over against the implication and intent of the violent act. Then, out of some deeper region than the mind, there begins to flow up into his spirit that which gives fresh courage, new strength, and wholeness. I do not understand this. I do not know how the miracle takes place when it does – all that I know is that such triumph is possible to the spirit of man.

Even so one may be mistaken. That is to say, the margin of self-deception is ever in flux. We are not quite sure that things are, in truth, as they seem to be in fact. We are therefore threatened by each new situation because it may reveal the awful magnitude of our previous self-deception. Hence it is most necessary for a man to try to establish some other-than-self reference in support of what seems to be his true state of being. Even as he seeks to do this, he knows that the validity of his inner peace and sense of triumph over the violent act does not depend on anything outside himself. But he must seek to establish it.

This brings our discussion at once to the primary function of nonviolence as a tool in the hands of a man of good will – as over against its use by a man of violence, as we saw earlier. The existential question is: How may the nonviolent attitude invade a violent situation and tame the wildness out of it?

It is not my purpose to explore extensively the considerable and growing literature on this subject, but rather to isolate some of the elements at work that can turn violence into a more harmonious situation and common feeling. Violence feeds on fear as its magic source of energy – the fear it engenders in those against whom it is directed. As long as men react to it with fear, their lives can be controlled by those in whose hands the instruments of violence rest. It is important in the etiquette of violence that the fear be centered around one's physical life and well-being or that of one's loved ones. By every cunning contrivance and subtlety, emphasis must be placed upon *physical* existence as the supreme good. All the conditioning that has gone into man's survival on the planet is in favor of such an emphasis. Once this is established, the only thing remaining for violence is to threaten to kill. If the highest premium is placed upon life, the fear of its loss or injury enables violence to maintain itself in active control over the lives of others. If there is no fear at this point, then the power of violence is critically undermined.

When there is a face-to-face encounter between nonviolence as a tool in the hands of a nonviolent man and violence as a tool in the hands of a violent man, the human element makes reconciliation a real potential in the situation. Unless the actual status of a human being as such is denied, reconciliation between people always has a chance to be effective. But when this status is denied, a major reappraisal or reassessment must take place *before* the work of reconciliation – which is the logic of nonviolence – can become effective.

Is there anything about the nonviolent act itself that can do this? The moral impact of nonviolence on violent men cannot be denied. There is a strange alchemy and contagion about courage in the face of danger that threatens and imperils. It awakens, first, a kind of admiration which is often apt to develop into subtle identification. In one of Olive Schreiner's books telling of her early experiences as a girl in South Africa, she tells of her reaction to a story about a woman who led African men against a group of armed European soldiers. The soldiers had guns but the Africans had only spears and shields made of hide. But with her inspiration, they marched up the hill under the terrible aegis of her courage until the last man died. Another story had to do with a woman whose husband brought back to his hut a new wife, to the shame and dishonor of his present wife and little child. Next day, early in the morning, the mother took her child to a high hill overlooking a rocky ledge and there, with the child in her arms, jumped to their death. The author writes that the courage of these two women settled for her forever the fact that community between her and the black women transcended all barriers that separated black from white in her South Africa.

Again and again we find that courage does this in the face of violence – it awakens admiration and then identification. Once this has happened, the grounds of reconciliation are established. For meaningful situations of community must be established. Courage is only one of them. Experiences of meaning which people share are more compelling than the barriers that separate them. If such experiences can be multiplied over a time interval of sufficient duration, then any barrier between men, of whatever kind, can be undermined. Thus the way of reconciliation is opened.

The problem is of a slightly different order if the violence is impersonal. One cannot, merely by a personal attitude of nonviolence, effect reconciliation in a violent system. A way has to be found to personalize the system. The fact that a system is violent has to be brought home to those who are largely in control of the power structure of which it is a collective expression. This demands more than the discipline of the nonviolent person. The techniques of nonviolence must be employed. In recent years wide use of such techniques has been so much in evidence that a new group of words has come into the vocabulary – "sit-ins," "walk-ins," "pray-ins," etc., not to speak of the familiar "boycott." It is in connection with these that the individual is apt to meet violence directly – notwithstanding the fact that the technique is aimed at a violent system rather than at violent individuals.

The purpose of his use of nonviolence as a collective device is to awaken conscience and an awareness of the evil of a violent system, and to make available the experience of the collective destiny in which all people in the system are participating. There is always the possibility that the effect of the nonviolent technique will be to solidify and organize the methods of violence used in counteraction. There is nothing unnatural here. Clearly, if the system is altered along the lines of the needs of those who are practicing nonviolence, then a profound change has to take place within the power structure so that *all* may share the fruits of the common life. The resistance to nonviolence discussed here is the last line of defense of those who cannot yet understand or feel that the ancient need to be cared for and understood, and to care for and understand, is asserting itself. And this is, at last, the work of reconciliation. The discipline for all who are involved has the same aim – to find a way to honor what is deepest in one person and to have that person honor what is deepest in the other.

III

The discipline of reconciliation for the religious man cannot be separated from the discipline of religious experience. In religious experience a man has a sense of being touched at his inmost center, at his very core, and this awareness sets in motion the process that makes for his integration, his wholeness. It is as if he saw into himself, beyond all his fragmentation, conflicts, and divisiveness, and recognized his true self. The experience of the prodigal son is underscored in the religious experience of the race – when he came to himself, he came to his father's house and dwelling place. The experience of God reconciles all the warring parts that are ultimately involved in the life of every man as against whatever keeps alive the conflict, and its work is healing and ever redemptive. Therefore there is laid upon the individual the need to keep the way open so that he and his Father may have free and easy access to each other.

Such is the ethical imperative of religious experience. This is not to suggest that religion is the only basis of the ethical imperative, but to state clearly that such an imperative is central to the religious experience. "So if you are offering your gift at the altar, and there remember that your brother has something against you, leave your gift there before the altar and go; first be reconciled to your brother, and then come and offer your gift" (Matt. 5:23–24).

What a man knows as his birthright in his experience before God he must accept and confirm as his necessity in his relations with his fellows. It is in the presence of God that he feels he is being *totally* dealt with, that the words of the Psalmist find a resting place in his own heart: Thou has "not dealt with us according to our sins, nor rewarded us according to our iniquities" (Ps. 103:10). The sins, bitterness, weakness, virtues, loves, and strengths are all gathered and transmuted by His love and His grace, and we become whole in His Presence. This is the miracle of religious experience – the sense of being totally dealt with, completely understood, and utterly cared for. This is what a man seeks with his fellows. This is why the way of reconciliation and the way of love finally are one way.

At the beginning of our discussion reference was made to the fact that the building blocks for the society of man and for the well-being of the individual are the fundamental desire to understand others and to be understood. The crucial sentence is, "Every man wants to be cared for, to be sustained by the assurance of the watchful and thoughtful attention of others." Such is the meaning of love.

Sometimes the radiance of love is so soft and gentle that the individual sees himself with all harsh lines wiped away and all limitations blended with his strengths in so happy a combination that strength seems to be everywhere and weakness is nowhere to be found. This is a part of the magic, the spell of love. Sometimes its radiance kindles old fires that have long since grown cold from the neglect of despair, or new fires are kindled by a hope born full-blown without beginning and without end. Sometimes the same radiance blesses a life with a vision of its possibilites never before dreamed of or sought, stimulating new endeavor and summoning all latent powers to energize the life at its inmost core.

But there are other ways by which love works its perfect work. There is a steady anxiety that surrounds man's experience of love. It may stab the spirit by calling forth a bitter, scathing self-judgment. The heights to which it calls may seem so high that all incentive is lost and the individual is stricken with utter hopelessness and despair. It may throw in relief old and forgotten weaknesses to which one has made the adjustment of acceptance – but which now stir in their place to offer themselves as testimony of one's unworthiness and to challenge the love with their embarrassing reality. At such times one expects love to be dimmed, in the mistaken notion that it is ultimately based upon merit and worth.

Behold the miracle! Love has no awareness of merit or demerit; it has no scale by which its portion may be weighed or measured. It does not seek to balance giving and receiving. Love loves; this is its nature. This does not mean that it is blind, naive, or pretentious, but rather that love holds its object securely in its grasp, calling all that it sees by its true name but surrounding all with a wisdom born both of its passion and its understanding. Here is no traffic in sentimentality, no catering either to weakness or to strength. Instead, there is robust vitality that quickens the roots of personality, creating an unfolding of the self that redefines, reshapes, and makes all things new. Such an experience is so fundamental that an individual knows that what is happening to him can outlast all things without itself being dissipated or lost.

Whence comes this power which seems to be the point of referral for all experience and the essence of all meaning? No created thing, no single unit of life, can be the source of such fullness and completeness. For in the experience itself a man is caught and held by something so much more than he can ever think or be that there is but one word by which its meaning can be encompassed – God. Hence the Psalmist says that as long as the love of God shines on us undimmed, not only may no darkness obscure, but we may find our way to a point in other hearts beyond all weakness and all strength, beyond all that is good or evil. There is nothing outside ourselves – no circumstance, no condition, no vicissitude – that can ultimately separate us from the love of God or of one another. And we pour out our gratitude to God that this is so!

The appearance of love may be used as a technique of social control or for the manipulation of other people while the manipulator himself has no sense of personal involvement. The ethic may become divorced from the spiritual and/or religious commitment out of which it comes, by which it is inspired. In other words, instead of being a moral imperative it can become a moral pretension. The love ethic may become a love dogma or doctrine, to which the mind may make an intellectual adjustment and to which mere mental assent may be given. This is one of the real perils when the ethic becomes incorporated in a system or in the organizational structure of an institution.

The reason for this is not far to seek. Neither a man nor an institution can embrace an ethical imperative without either becoming more and more expressive of it in the common life or developing a kind of increasing enmity to it. Here is the essential challenge of the modern world to the Christian Church.

What then is the nature of the discipline that love provides? In the first place, it is something that I must quite deliberately *want* to do. For many of us this is the first great roadblock. In our relations with each other there is often so much that alienates, that is distasteful; there seems to be every ground for refraining from the kind of concern that love demands. It is curious how we feel the other person must demonstrate a worthiness that commends itself to us before we are willing to *want* to move in outflow, in the self-giving that love demands. We want to be accepted just as we are, but at the same time we want the other person to *win* the right to our acceptance of him. This is an important part of the sin of pride. There must be genuine repentance for such an attitude. Forgiveness for this sin is the work of the grace of God in the human heart. A man seeks it before God and becomes aware of forgiveness only when, in his attitude toward his fellows, he comes to want to make available to them the consciousness of what God shares with him. God enables him to *want* to love. This is one of the reasons why I cannot separate the discipline of love from the discipline of religious experience.

In the second place, I must find the opening or openings through which my love can flow into the life of the other, and at the same time locate in myself openings through which his love can flow into me. Most often this involves an increased understanding of the other person. This is arrived at by a disciplined use of the imagination. We are accustomed to thinking of imagination as a useful tool in the hands of the artist as he reproduces in varied forms what he sees beyond the rim of fact that circles him round. There are times when it is regarded merely as a delightful, whimsical trait of the "childish mind." Our judgment trembles on the edge of condescension, pity, or even ridicule when imagination is confused with fancy in reports of the inner workings of the mind of the "simpleton" or "fool." But we recognize and applaud the bold, audacious leap of the mind of the scientist when it soars far out beyond what is known to fix a beachhead on distant, unexplored shores. But the imagination shows its greatest powers as the *angelos* of God in the miracle it creates when one man, standing on his own ground, is able while there to put himself in another man's place. To send his imagination forth to establish a point of focus in another man's spirit, and from that vantage point so to blend with the other's landscape that what he sees and feels is authentic – this is the great adventure in human relations. Yet this is not enough. The imagination must report its findings accurately, without regard for all previous prejudgments and private or collective fears. And even this is not enough. There must be both a spontaneous and a deliberate response to such knowledge which will result in the sharing of resources at their deepest level.

Very glibly we are apt to use such words as "sympathy," "compassion," "sitting where they sit," but in experience it is genuinely to be rocked to one's foundations. We resist making room for considerations that will bend us out of the path of preoccupation with ourselves, our needs, our problems. We corrupt our imagination when we give it range over only our own affairs. Here we experience the magnification of our own wills, the distortion of our own problems, and the enlargement of the areas of our misery. The activity of which we deprive our imagination in the work of understanding others turns in upon ourselves with disaster and sometimes terror.

The willingness to be to another human being what is needed at the time the need is most urgent and most acutely felt – this is to participate in a precise act of redemption. This is to stand for one intimate moment *in loco dei* in the life of another – that is, to make available to another what has already been given us. We are not the other person; we are ourselves. All that he is experiencing we can never know – but we can make accurate soundings which, properly read, will enable us to be to him what we could never be without such awareness. To the degree to which our imagination becomes the *angelos* of God, we ourselves may become His *instruments.* As the apostle says in the Phillips translation: "My prayer for you is that you may have still more love – a love that is full of knowledge and wise insight. I want you to be able always to recognize the highest and best, and to live sincere and blameless lives until the day of Jesus Christ" (Phil. 1:9–10).

In the third place, there must be a sense of leisure out of which we relate to others. The sense of it is far more important than the fact of leisure itself. Somehow it must be conveyed to the other person that our effort to respond to his need to be cared for is one with our concern to be cared for ourselves. Despite the pressures under which we live, it is entirely possible to develop a sense of leisure as the climate in which we function. We cannot be in a hurry in matters of the heart. The human spirit has to be explored gently and with unhurried tenderness. Very often this demands a reconditioning of our nervous responses to life, a profound alteration in the tempo of our behavior pattern. Whatever we learn of leisure in the discipline of silence, in meditation and prayer, bears rich, ripe fruit in preparing the way for love. Failure at this point can be one of unrelieved frustration. At first, for most of us, skill in tarrying with another has to be cultivated and worked at by dint of much self-discipline. At first it may seem mechanical, artificial, or studied, but this kind of clumsiness will not remain if we persist. How indescribably wonderful and healing it is to encounter another human being who listens not only to our words, but manages, somehow, to listen to *us*. Everyone needs this and everyone needs to give it, as well – thus we come full circle in love.

If all this is true, then it is clear that any structure of society, any arrangement under which human beings live, that does not provide maximum opportunities for free-flowing circulation among one another, works against social and individual health. Any attitudes, private or group, which prohibit people from coming into "across-the-board" contact with each other work against the implementation of the love ethic. So considered, segregation, prescriptions of separation, are a disease of the human spirit and the body politic. It does not matter how meaningful the tight circle of isolated security may be, in which individuals or groups move. The very existence of such circles, whether regarded as a necessity of religious faith, political ideology, or social purity, precludes the possibility of the experience of love as a part of the necessity of man's life.

The experience of love is either a necessity or a luxury. If it be a luxury, it is expendable; if it be a necessity, then to deny it is to perish. So simple is the reality, and so terrifying. Ultimately there is only one place of refuge on this planet for any man – that is in another man's heart. To love is to make of one's heart a swinging door.

∞ | *Martin Luther King, Jr.* (1968)

The relationship between Thurman and Martin Luther King, Jr., has been examined by
a number of scholars.[87] *King did not mention Thurman's influence in any of his formal*
writings, but in his extemporaneous preaching he clearly appropriated ideas and entire
statements from Thurman's works.[88] *Thurman, with characteristic modesty, always*
spoke of his relationship with the younger visionary in personal and endearing terms,
though he never claimed to have had direct influence on King's intellectual formation.
Both thinkers drew heavily from the traditions of protestant liberalism, personal ideal-
ism, and the black church experience in America. Thurman's major contribution seems
to have been that of a counselor to the young civil rights leader, a ministry provided to
many in the modern Civil Rights movement. In the following selection, delivered over
radio station KSFO in San Francisco on the evening of King's assassination, Thurman
speaks to the ideal of community and the hope for a transformed American society sym-
bolized in the life and witness of the fallen prophet.

MARTIN LUTHER KING, JR., is dead. This is the simple and utter fact. A few
brief hours ago his voice could be heard in the land. From the ends of the
earth, from the heart of our cities, from the firesides of the humble and the

mighty, from the cells of a thousand prisons, from the deep central place in the soul of America the cry of anguish can be heard.

There are no words with which to eulogize this man. Martin Luther King was the living epitome of a way of life that rejected physical violence as the life style of a morally responsible people. His assassination reveals the cleft deep in the psyche of the American people, the profound ambivalence and ambiguity of our way of life. Something deep within us rejects non-violent direct action as a dependable procedure for effecting social change. And yet, against this rejection something always struggles, pushing, pushing, always pushing with another imperative, another demand. It was King's fact that gave to this rejection flesh and blood, courage and vision, hope and enthusiasm. For indeed, in him the informed conscience of the country became articulate. And tonight what many of us are feeling is that we all of us must be that conscience wherever we are living, functioning, and behaving.

Perhaps his greatest contribution to our times and to the creative process of American society is not to be found in his amazing charismatic power over masses of people, nor is it to be found in his peculiar and challenging courage with its power to transform the fear-ridden black men and women with a strange new valor, nor is it to be found in the gauntlet which he threw down to challenge the inequities and brutalities of a not quite human people – but rather in something else. Always he spoke from within the context of his religious experience, giving voice to an ethical insight which sprang out of his profound brooding over the meaning of his Judeo-Christian heritage. And this indeed is his great contribution to our times. He was able to put at the center of his own personal religious experience a searching ethical awareness. Thus organized religion as we know it in our society found itself with its back against the wall. To condemn him, to reject him, was to reject the ethical insight of the faith it proclaimed. And this was new. Racial prejudice, segregation, discrimination were not regarded by him as merely un-American, undemocratic, but as mortal sin against God. For those who are religious it awakens guilt; for those who are merely superstitious it inspires fear. And it was this fear that pulled the trigger of the assassin's gun that took his life.

Tonight there is a vast temptation to strike out in pain, horror, and anger; riding just under the surface are all the pent up furies, the accumulation of a generation of cruelty and brutality. A way must be found to honor our feelings without dishonoring him whose sudden and meaningless end has called them forth. May we harness the energy of our bitterness and make it available to the unfinished work which Martin has left behind. It may be, it just may be that what he was unable to bring to pass in his life can be achieved by the act of his dying. For this there is eloquent precedence in human history. He was killed in one sense because mankind is not human yet. May he live because all of us in America are closer to becoming human than we ever were before.

I express my deep compassion for his wife, his children and his mother, father and brother. May we all remember that the time and the place of a man's life on the earth are the time and the place of his body, but the memory of his life is as vast, as creative, and as redemptive as his gifts, his times, and the passionate commitment of all his powers can make it.

Our words are ended – and for a long, waiting moment, the rest is silence.

Section Three

"COMMUNITY AND THE WILL OF GOD"

Mᴇᴅɪᴛᴀᴛɪᴏɴ | *Friends Whom I Knew Not*

Thou hast made known to me friends whom I knew not
Thou has brought the distant near and made a brother of the stranger.

ᴛʜᴇ ꜱᴛʀᴇɴɢᴛʜ ᴏꜰ ᴛʜᴇ ᴘᴇʀꜱᴏɴᴀʟ ʟɪꜰᴇ is often found in the depth and intensity of its isolation. The fight for selfhood is unending. There is the
ever-present need to stand alone, unsupported and unchallenged. To be
sure of one's self, to be counted for one's self *as* one's self, is to experience
aliveness in its most exciting dimension. If there is a job of work to be done
that is impossible, if there is a need to be met that is limitless, if there is a
word to be said that can never be said, the spirit of the whole man is mus-
tered and in the exhaustive effort he finds *himself* in the solitariness of
strength renewed and courage regained. Below the surface of all the activity and functioning in which life engages us, there is a level of disen-
gagement when the individual is a private actor on a lonely stage. It is here
that things are seen without their outer garbs – the seedlings of desires
take quiet root, the bitter waters and the sweet springs find their beginnings, the tiny stirrings that become the raging tempests are seen to
shimmer in the semi-darkness – this "the region," "the place," "the clime"

where man is the lonely solitary guest in the vast empty house of the world.

But this is not all of a man's life, this is not the full and solid picture. The strands of life cannot be so divided that each can be traced to a separate source. There is no mine, there is no thine. When there is that which I would claim as my very own, a second look, a subtle strangeness, something, announces that there can never be anything that is my very own. Always moving in upon a man's life is the friend whose existence he did not know, whose coming and going is not his to determine. The journeyings take many forms – sometimes it is in the vista that opens before his mind because of lines written long before in an age he did not know; sometimes it is in a simple encounter along the way when before his eyes the unknown stranger becomes the sharer of tidings that could be borne only by a friend. Sometimes a deep racial memory throws into focus an ancient wisdom that steadies the hand and stabilizes the heart. Always moving in upon a man's life is the friend whose existence he did not know, whose coming and going is not his to determine. At last, a man's life is his very own *and* a man's life is never his, alone.[89]

CO | *The Task of the Negro Ministry (1928)*

In this essay Thurman develops an earlier article on religion and black youth to suggest
an agenda for ministry to the wider African-American community as it grappled with the
complexities of modernity.[90] *Thurman speaks with the force of the New Negro intellec-*
tuals whose mission was to reconstruct the intellectual coherence of African-American
spiritual, cultural, and political practices. Here he contrasts the rise of materialism in
post-war black culture with the traditional African-American integration of religion and
life. In particular, Thurman warns that imitation of wealthy, urban white churches –
with their centralized organization and managerial efficiency, their construction of
monumental church buildings, and their dependence on wealthy parishioners – threat-
ened to compromise the spiritual and moral grounding provided by the historic black
church. At the same time, he cautions black ministers against allowing apocalypticism
and anti-intellectualism to overshadow their responsibility to preserve the ethical core of
African-American Christianity. In Thurman's view, black ministers must become "stu-
dents" of modern life so as to subject mass consumer culture and the reign of science to
religious and ethical interpretation for their economically diverse, morally disoriented,
geographically displaced congregations.

IN A RECENT ARTICLE ON "Higher Education and Religion" appearing in
the *Home Mission College Review*[91] I suggested that in order for the

claims of religion to be made effectively to our developing youth, four characteristic attitudes must obtain:

1. We must refuse to be caught in the current demand for things and must find our security in the reality of God and the spiritual tasks to which He has set our hands.
2. We must put a vast faith in the contagion in the Spirit of Jesus rather than in the building of organizations to perpetuate his Spirit.
3. We must seek to demolish the artificial barrier between religion and life.
4. We must not allow any phase of human knowledge to lie outside our province, but must provide a creative synthesis, in the light of which all the facts of science or whatnot may be viewed.

In this paper I shall use these four suggestions as the basic outline for my discussion of an aspect of the present task of the Negro ministry.

I

We must refuse to be caught in the present demand for things and must find our security in the reality of God and the spiritual tasks to which He has set our hands.

Negroes are poor. Despite the phenomenal increase in houses and land during the last decade or two; despite the relatively large amount of economic power that has come under their control – Negroes are poor. They are a part of a social system in which the dominant group is represented by vast economic power and the social security it brings. To counsel a minority group, such as Negroes represent in this country, to put greater confidence in values than in material possessions, per se, is to seem to urge the development of a kind of defense mechanism which may be the result of a mere protective philosophy. Further, it seems to play into the hands of many crafty persons who are ready to take advantage of the unsuspecting by securing for themselves more than a gentleman's share of this world's goods.

As a result of a period of extended crisis, Negroes have discovered that a rare spiritual beauty and insight are much more possible if the thing that gives meaning to one's life is not grounded in economic power. The slave worked for his master but he did not carry the burden or responsibility for economic survival. Once deprived of rancor (a superhuman feat in itself under the circumstances) his soul was free to grow with utter abandonment of the cotton which he hoed. There developed a simple disregard for possessions in terms of what they could bring as security. The tyranny of things did not entrap the vast majority of these people.

The problem became greatly complicated when the slave became an economic competitor. He was swindled and cheated because he had developed no mentality for making his interest in economic goods so keen that the possession of them would give him security. To this day the adjustment has not been adequately made. In a desperate attempt to make the adjustment there is an almighty danger of overemphasis.

It is at this point that the task of the Negro minister becomes very clear. He must interpret the deadening effect upon American life of the growing dependence upon things and what they may accomplish. He must lay bare the awful truth that where the highest premium is put upon the possession of things, human life is relatively cheapened. And where life is cheap, ideals languish and the souls of men slowly die.

> "Shall I ask my God Sunday by Sunday to brood across the land and bind all its children's hearts in a close knit fellowship; – yet when I see its people betrayed, and their jaw-bone broken by a strike from the hand of gold; when I see freedom passing from us, and the whole land being grasped by the golden claw, so that the generations after us shall be born without freedom, to labor for men who have grasped all, shall I hold my peace?"[92]

II

We must put a vast faith in the contagion in the Spirit of Jesus rather than in the building of organizations to perpetuate his Spirit.

A member of a certain Foreign Mission Board was asked by a friend of mine why his board refused to send Negroes out as missionaries. He said that Negroes knew very little about technique of organization and the risk involved would be too great. Sometimes men who dispense millions of dollars in the interest of the Kingdom of God are very easily deceived as to the relation between the dollars and the machinery for spending them and the spirit of Jesus and its propagation.

The idea of large-scale production with its attendant economic advantages, due to centralization and the like, is having its bearing upon the institutional religious life of America.[93] There seems to be a growing passion for building temples and towering structures which call for bigger and better organizations – which in turn call for more dynamic energy to keep them "efficient." They almost always represent great spiritual waste. Negro churches seem inclined to follow the lead of white churches in the form of expansion. I heard a man say one day, "People always build their temples to their dead Gods."[94]

As this expansion becomes characteristic there is more dependence upon those in a community whose incomes make substantial giving possible. This may easily mean that the gifts of a person who makes $5.00 a week, let us say, will become less and less significant. Then what? For the most part, Negro churches in America have been built by the pennies, nickels, and dimes of simple toilers. For this reason, if for no other, there is a sense of possession which they feel for the church which is unique. As an old lady said to a passerby as she stood weeping because her church was being burned: "I wouldn't mind it, son, but that's blood money that's being burned. These old hands have rubbed to the quick to get money to put on that altar."

The danger may be remote but the task of the Negro minister is clear. It expresses itself in a very interesting paradox. A dynamic idea cannot continue to persist unless it is housed in some form of organization. In order for it to become intelligible it must be couched in current concepts and the like. The disciples of Jesus were not long in discovering this fact. (It has always impressed me that Jesus did not seem to make the same discovery unless we think of his disciples as a form of organization. They had more of a fellowship.) It is also true that just as a dynamic idea is conserved in some form of organization, it is also destroyed by the very organization that preserved it. Hence the paradox: The power that makes it breaks it.

The minister must encourage the development of systematic procedure in the institutional religious life but it must be clear to him and he must make it clear to his people that the Spirit of Jesus grows by contagion and not by organization. One life aglow with the Spirit of Jesus is far more efficacious than a dozen organizational attempts to salvage society. In the final analysis a man's life is changed by contact with another life.

Dr. Albert Parker Fitch sums it up rather adequately: "The clergy are not businessmen. They are of a different order, and their primary office is not to be organizers. Men are not to be made good by machinery."[95]

III

We must seek to demolish the artificial barrier between religion and life.

Christianity in America has tended in its more practical bearing to be more theological than ethical. Mark you, I emphasize this as the tendency. This has been most noticeable in areas of conflict. It is often safer, as Rauschenbusch[96] points out somewhere, to be eloquent about the immortality of the soul than about the ethical demand that the soul makes for a living wage. It may be a very strengthening exercise to be concerned about the Trinity and the Apostle's Creed but a precise theological statement of what is involved in these may make no ethical demands upon him who states it.

As the wife of the minister in *Trooper Peter Halket* says, "If it is necessary for you to attack someone, why don't you attack the Jews for killing Christ, or Herod, or Pontius Pilate; why don't you leave alone the men who are in power today?"

And the minister replied: "Oh, my wife, those Jews and Herod, and Pontius Pilate are long dead. If I should preach of them now would it help them? Would it save one living thing from their clutches? The past is dead, it lives only for us to learn from. The present, the present only, is ours to work in, and the future is ours to create."[97]

Christianity in Negro churches has little to do with dogmatic controversy. Life has been too realistic for that. This intense realism has caused their soul to recoil into an overemphasis upon the other world. The emphasis has been more speculative than ethical. This has been offset somewhat by the fact that the conditions upon which the joy of the future has been meted out are ethical in their inferences. The net results on American life from the two groups of Christians has been well nigh identical. The ethical has gone a-begging in both instances. But not quite. The fact that the overemphasis on the other world on the part of the Negro Church sprang out of a situation of extended crisis has given to it a sense of reality which may not be found in a form of Christianity which has overemphasized the theological. The Negro minister must read, though through tears, the story of the spiritual strivings of his people. He would not underestimate the value and the validity of a quiet confidence in the other world, but with marked insight he will help his people to see that there is no clear-cut cleavage between this world and the other world – that life and religion may not be separated without disaster to both. He must assert continually the ethical demands of the religion of Jesus upon those who would walk the earth by the light in the sky.

IV

We must not allow any phase of human knowledge to lie outside of our province, but must provide a creative synthesis, in the light of which all the facts of science or what not may be viewed.

There are more Negro young people in school today than ever before. More books and magazines and newspapers are being read than ever before. The facts and the pseudo-facts which are the burden of modern science are becoming increasingly intelligent to the man in the street. The Dayton Trial did more to popularize the theory of evolution than tomes of manuscripts revealing careful scientific research could have ever done. Men everywhere are asking questions.[98]

There is the development and the increasing perfection of the radio. Thousands of homes have brought to them through the air all kinds of lectures, sermons, etc. A new world is being opened up even to those who cannot read. Vast stirrings of inquiry which are faint now will be most articulate presently.

Add to all of this the general suspicion that "the letter killeth"[99] and the Negro minister is caught between the demand for preparation and the fear which many feel for what exhaustive preparation may do for one's spiritual insight.

The audience to which the Negro minister preaches is becoming more and more complex. He is called upon to give some word of hope to people who live and suffer in a hostile environment; to be a steadying influence to the business and professional men who are finding life to consist largely of a series of points of ethical confusion; to throw a gleam of light upon dark areas where men and women, high school and college boys and girls wander aimlessly because of bewilderment created for them by much reading and study.

The young people are a part of the present reaction against certain conventional standards of morality. They have questions about sex which their elders cannot or will not answer. The questions must be met.[100] He who helps them there will gain their confidence and will be privileged to share in their spiritual rebirth, if he will.

The meaning of all these things is clear. The Negro minister must find how to interpret life in terms of a creative expansive idealism. Therefore, he must be a student. For instance, he must know what the problem of evolution is and must be prepared to think clear through it with the anxious ones who share their doubts with him. He must be aware of the findings in all the major fields of human knowledge and interpret their meaning in terms of the Kingdom of God.

He must be a thinker. He must sense the dilemmas which his people face in American life and must offer intelligent spiritual and practical guidance to them. To his eye must be clear the thin line between cowardice and fear and dynamic redemptive love. He must judge the ethical significance of the religion of Jesus in the light of the Zulu proverb: "Full belly child says to empty belly child, be of good cheer."

He must be God-conscious. This will keep him close to life and will serve also as a valuational consciousness which will reveal the meaning of all the facts of experience. It will be to him a creative synthesis in the light of which all the facts of science or what not may be viewed.

∞ | *What We May Learn from India (1936)*

Thurman's trip to the Indian subcontinent from September 1935 through April 1936 was crucial to his own commitment to the Christian faith.[101] *It provided him with concrete instances in an international setting to come to terms with the church's poor record with regard to other religions. It also gave him an opportunity to experiment further with his developing sense of the power of religious experience to create human community among diverse races, ethnicities, and cultures. When first approached with the proposal to lead the delegation of African Americans on a "pilgrimage of friendship" to India,*[102] *Thurman was reluctant to assume a representative role on behalf of a racially-segregated American Christianity. He agreed only when assured of the freedom to interpret his faith according to his own experience. The result of his independent assessment is summarized in this early version of Thurman's formal report of the delegation's trip—which was much longer, less candid, and left incomplete until 1938. In this precursor to the formal report, probably drafted during the delegation's return voyage, Thurman offers his fresh, first-hand account of the pilgrimage and a scathing indictment of Western imperialism. The segregated structure of Western Christianity in India, especially as practiced through its missionary activities, offered strong evidence for Mahatma Gandhi's statement to Thurman that "The greatest enemy to Jesus in India is Christianity." Thurman also provides a comparative analysis of race and caste functions in religious hierarchies in both India and United States and concludes that Western Christianity has historically provided the religious and moral foundations for imperialism.*

Part One: Christianity in India

I HAVE BEEN ASSIGNED A TOPIC "What We May Learn From India." I shall discuss the subject under two general headings – some aspects of the central problem of Christianity in India and the problem of colored prejudice. I shall point out certain similarities and differences as they apply to our situation in America. According to the tradition, Christianity through the Syrian Church has been in India since the first century. Whether it is a fact that the church was started by St. Thomas near the close of one A.D. or not, it is well authenticated that the Syrian Church has had a continuous life since the sixth century. The locale of the Syrian Church for the most part is in Travancore and the Malabar area across the ghats on the southwestern coast. The history of the Church has not been impressive for it has concerned itself with its own internal development and has given very little, if any, consideration to questions of expansion among the non-Christian religions. It has taken on some of the customs of its Hindu neighbors such as the recognition of caste and the like. However, I must add that the most independent and forward-looking group of Christians to be found in India are those who are a part of its fellowship. They have more independence and, in my opinion, more fundamental self-regard than the other Christian communities of India. The only Christian college supported outright by Indian funds is the Syrian Christian College at Alway. The staff and its program are largely indigenous.

Western Christianity came into India by way of the Portuguese who established their hierarchy throughout their sphere of influence. The spearhead of this movement was St. Francis Xavier.[103] Under the mission of propaganda in the seventeenth century the papacy began its large and influential work in the country. Between 1911 and 1923 the Roman Catholic population of India increased by more than three hundred thirty-two thousand; while the Protestants' increase over the same period was five hundred forty-seven thousand. Protestant Christianity came into India about 1813. Protestantism represents many things other than a united front. Let us look at the picture: among the Baptists, there are English, Canadian, and American Baptists; the Methodists include the English Wesleyan, the Free Methodist of America, and the Methodist Episcopal Church; the Lutherans include the United Lutheran of America, the Church of Sweden, the Basel Church, the Leipsig Mission, the Missouri

Evangelical Mission, and the Danish Society; there are the Disciples of Christ, the Seventh Day Adventists, the Mennonites: among the Congregationalists the American and the British, the Scandinavian, Swedish, Free Church of Finland, and the London Missionary Society; among the Presbyterians the Irish Presbyterian, the United Presbyterian of America, the American Presbyterian, the United Church of Canada, the Canadian Presbyterian, the Welsh Calvinistic Methodist, and in addition to all these the Salvation Army, a few sects of the Holy Rollers, the Church of Scotland, the Anglican Church and the YM and YWCA – all Protestants. Each one of these groups has its own tenets, doctrinal differences, policies, et cetera. They are united in three important particulars: first, they are all Western and white; second, they all claim loyalty to Christ; third, they all definitely, or ostensibly endorse and cooperate with British rule. Inasmuch as sixty-eight out of every hundred Indians are Hindu, the dominant culture of the land is Hindu. Since the vast Mogul Empire in the North, there has been a sharp cultural and religious conflict between the Moslem and the Hindu.[104] Hinduism is a religion, a culture, and a civilization. Its genius is ordinarily a synthesizing one. In the vast palace of the Hindu faith there are yet many unoccupied rooms. To all and any new faith Hinduism says "your room is ready, come in, make yourself at home." Christianity, therefore, has been compelled, even if it could have acted otherwise, to project itself as a culture, a civilization, and a religion, for the genius of Christianity tends to be exclusive. The result is that it has not been possible for Christianity to extricate itself from the western civilization whose culture patterns it has taken over in the whole process of becoming at home in the West. When the Indian embraces Christianity, he therefore takes over the religion and its framework. He changes his name from an Indian Hindu name to a Christian name. Now precisely what is a Christian name? Obviously the name the missionary bears or a name taken "whole cloth" from the Christian Bible; hence, there are many Mr. Adames, Mr. Tituses, Mr. Moseses, et cetera. His children are likewise named. When he marries he uses the Christian ceremony. He gives his wife a Christian wedding ring and takes her on a Christian honeymoon. His break with Hindu culture is well nigh complete.

When he begins to make his religion at home in the country, he finds

that all of his old culture patterns are Hindu and that if his religion becomes indigenous he must make use of certain forms, social and cultural,
which according to his profession of faith are anathema to him. So that
one finds the Indian Christian today singing Western hymns, wearing
Western clothes and inclined to think of the God of the Christian religion
in terms of the ideology of the dominant controlling European of his
country. The missionary faces a very peculiar dilemma. He comes into
the country as a product of Western civilization and such culture as he has
been able to absorb. He propagates a faith which to him is personal and ultimate. It is a faith, however, built upon certain definite assumptions relative to the established order of which he is a part. If he is a Britisher it is a
faith that is built upon the assumption of empire. I shall return to this in
the second half of my discussion. If he is any other kind of European, including the American, it is a faith that is built upon the assumption of the
ultimate supremacy of his religion, his civilization, and his race. The missionary cannot ever escape the damaging fact that the conqueror of the
people to whom he is going is not only like him as to race, but is also a
Christian. Over and over again I encountered the comment: "But you see,
Mr. Thurman, our conquerors are Europeans and are Christians." Therefore, the missionary is driven to limit his message by the fact of his race
and his kinship in faith with the conqueror.

There are two reasons why the form that Christianity has taken in India tends to be highly theological and orthodox. First, when a particular
religion is making converts in the midst of very old religions and cultures,
it is necessary for it to establish its position as rapidly as possible by defining its terms and especially its categories in contrast to the definitions and
the categories of the faiths by which it is surrounded. The converts must
be given formulae that are easily manipulated so as to defend their position on the shortest possible notice. The psychological climate of the converts is charged with antagonism and attacks, very often, and the bullets
of his faith must always be available; hence, the tremendous emphasis
upon concrete definition. This tendency makes for over simplicity, con-
servatism and "cock-suredness." Now the second thing that has made for
the strict and rigid policy of evangelism of the enterprise is that there is no
danger to imperialism if the religionist confines his emphasis primarily to

the relationship of the individual human soul to God. Almost everywhere I encountered what amounted to fear, practically, of the social emphasis of Christianity. To be sure, I found many people who were feeding the hungry, administering to the sick, et cetera, but very little fundamental attack was being made on the established order lest the missionaries themselves should become persona non grata to the government. Stanley Jones told me how much anxiety he spent in contemplating possible consequences of the effect of his book *Jesus and the Underprivileged* on the friendly relationship that existed between him and the British government.[105] Two other rather subsidiary but somewhat important factors should be mentioned in this connection. One is the Western supporters of the missionary enterprise must be assured that souls are being saved. There can be no substitute for this. Second, among certain branches of Hinduism a much more comprehensive social service and humanitarian program is being found than the social service program along narrow orthodox Christian lines. Finally, Western Christianity has brought with it its class distinctions which have largely vitiated it in the West. The missionary and the representative of Western Christianity in India has succeeded in bringing home to the Indian one impressive fact, that is, that he is infinitely superior and more worthful than the Indian. Over and over again I found myself saying however kind and benevolent an autocrat is, he is still an autocrat. I visited a church in Jaffna at which twenty years ago there were two pulpits. One high and lifted up; the other on the ground floor. From the elevated pulpit the missionary and the missionary alone or some other European preached; while from the pulpit on the floor the Indian national was permitted to preach. It was the boast of a Roman Catholic priest, the head of a college, that unlike Protestantism the Roman Catholic Church recognized no class distinction in its clergy as between Indian and European. In my opinion, one of the most hopeful signs in evidence in the ranks of official Christianity is the work toward the union of the Protestant Church in India. I do not see how the Church, which at the moment represents a great vested interest in the country and which must continue its support of British rule, can expect to bring to Indians in any formal sense an interpretation of the Christian religion which springs out of the heart of Jesus of Nazareth, a member of an underprivileged, disinherited group in the Greco-Roman world. Here and there are glorious illustrations of individuals who have transcended to some degree the limitation of cultures and civilizations and have exemplified a quality of life, timeless and all embracing. But they are rare and are not to be included in the same group with the official upholders of the established order. I close this section of my discussion with the rather striking words of Mahatma Gandhi to me: "The greatest enemy that the religion of Jesus has in India is Christianity in India."

Part Two: Colored Prejudice

The second day after we arrived in Ceylon a rather brilliant barrister at the close of a lecture before a law society invited me downstairs for coffee. When we were seated we were joined by two other friends, the door was closed, the coffee served and drunk and, then, he opened up as follows: "What are you doing here?" I said, "What do you mean?" He said, "Precisely that. I note what this pamphlet says that your mission is but what are you doing over here?" He said, "More than four hundred years ago your African forebears were taken from the Western coast of Africa by slave traders who were Christians; in fact, not only was the name of one of the English slave vessels *Jesus,* but one of your very celebrated Christian hymn writers was a dealer in the slave traffic. You were sold in America to other Christians. You were held in slavery three hundred years by Christians. You were freed a little more than seventy years ago by a man who, himself, was not a Christian but who was a spearhead of certain political, economic and social forces the full significance of which he, himself, did not quite understand. And for seventy years you have been lynched and burned and discriminated against by Christians; in fact, I read one incident of a Christian church service that was dismissed in order that the members may go join a mob and after the lynching came back to church and now," said he, "here you are over here as a Christian and I think, Sir, you are a traitor to all of the darker peoples of the earth. And I wondered what you, an intelligent man, would have to say for yourself." We discussed this matter for more than three hours.

The question of color prejudice in India for the purposes of our discussion is confined to the relationship that obtains between three groups of people in India—the European, the Anglo-Indian, and the Indian. With the exception of a group of some sixty-five Negroes from the West Indies, with an occasional African who has the status of European, all of the Europeans are white. The Anglo-Indians are those whose parentage is mixed. The first impetus given to the establishing of such a group is located in the extramarital relationships that obtain between the British tommy and the Indian lady. It seems to be a part of established British imperialism to recognize any adulterated expressions of British blood by giving the offspring a special status which is midway between the top and the bottom. This status perpetuated into an economic class. In South Africa there are Europeans at the top, the colored race in the middle—those of mixed blood—and the African at the bottom. The same thing obtains in India. The Anglo-Indian is not only a separate class socially but is also a separate class economically, for they have been given for many years the exclusive privilege to perform all of the services in connection with the railroad and the telegraph. The Anglo-Indian is much prouder of his Scottish grandmother than he is of his Indian father or Indian mother. The tension, therefore, that exists between the Anglo-Indian and the Indian National is very marked. The Anglo-Indian feeling that he is much better than the Indian and is trying always to get away from him while he is reaching up to be considered a European and his European half-brother is always trying to get away from him. It is only in recent years that the Indian and the Anglo-Indian are beginning to see that the fate of one is the fate of all.

I remember one night traveling through enroute to Calcutta from the Musilapatam and being compelled to spend most of the night at the Bezwaba Junction; an Indian Student Secretary was traveling with us part of the way. In the railway station at the Junction there are rooms in which one may spend the night that are divided one-half for Europeans and one-half for Indians; because the Indian was a part of our party we wanted him to spend the night with us. The Indian attendant refused to permit this saying to the Indian "you know you have no business in the European section." It reminded me a great deal of the "land of the free and the home of the brave." The Britisher is very sure of one thing and that is that he is a

brilliant illustration of the favoritism of Divine Providence. All of his religion, ethics, and morality move out from the assumption of empire.
Granted the prerogatives of empire the Britisher is a just white man when
he is dealing with lesser breeds without the law. As far as my own personal
experience is concerned in India I found the Britisher courteous, often
generous, sometimes benevolent, always superior. It remained for a great
American religious leader from Kentucky who has recently been made
a bishop of India by the Methodist Church to give what was meant to
be the only real snub during the sixteen thousand miles of travel in the
country.[106]

Christianity is powerless to make any inroads on the question of color
and race prejudice in India because of the way it has made its peace with
color and race prejudice in the West. In America our civilization is too
young and there have been so many extenuating circumstances in our past
and present situation to make the kind of careful deliberate classification
among Negroes that the British have made both in India and South Africa. It may be instructive to examine the background of the situation in
this country for a moment. During the days of slavery there were many
children of mixed parentage born on the plantation. The master favored
his offspring and sometimes their mother by making of them household or
yard slaves rather than field hands. They enjoyed certain protecting privileges which were denied their cruder more African half-brothers in the
fields. Among the slaves themselves there grew up a distinction between
the house slaves, who for the most part were mulattoes, and the field
slaves. Another interesting fact that belongs in the picture is that only
about four hundred thousand of the four or five million white people that
lived in the South during these years were slaveowners. The others were
divided into two classes that were unfortunately referred to as "crackers"
and "poor white trash." Those who were dubbed "crackers" were a kind of
middle-class businessmen. They ran the stores and things of that sort.
The "poor white people" lived often in the hills and on very poor land from
which they were forced to wrest an exceedingly precarious livelihood.
They naturally looked upon the presence of the slaves as the cause rather
than the occasion for their insecurity, for they reasoned that if the slave
had not been present in the society they would have tilled the rich soil and

would have been the artisans and craftsmen and their economic security would have by that fact been guaranteed. So for nearly ten generations they looked upon the slave with eyes that smouldered with bitterness and hatred.

When the Civil War was fought the economic life of the South was largely destroyed and the flower of that culture lay prostrate on a hundred battlefields. After military rule of the Union army had been withdrawn the people who came into power were these traditional enemies of the slaves, often lacking in culture and refinement even more than the slaves who had through many generations lived under the shadow of aristocracy. So determined were they in their taking over the economic, political and social life of the South to seek revenge upon these slaves and so difficult and precarious were the times, that they did not think about dividing the slaves among themselves by giving prior consideration and preferential treatment to the mulattoes; the net result was that all of the slaves were grouped as a unit. This, in my opinion, from the point of view of white supremacy and control in America was the master blunder in strategy. It did not take very long after Reconstruction had gotten under way for the whole color feeling dating back to slavery time to disintegrate in Negro life, so that today it is more rare than common to find a family of mulatto Negroes who feel that they are superior to their black half-brothers.

The important thing to notice is that as our civilization grows older and our culture ripens it is beginning to be a practice among many policy-making white Americans to make a separate class of mulattoes giving them preferential treatment as to jobs and positions so that in the next one hundred years we may have in America the same sort of thing that obtains wherever the Britisher goes among darker peoples. A friend of mine was telling me the other day about a certain man who had written a paper showing that only one black Negro had ever received a Ph.D. from an American University. Of course, this is not true. It is rather a common experience among certain agencies that find jobs for Negroes that if a darker Negro and a mulatto Negro both apply the preference is given to the mulatto Negro. It is a rather general feeling among certain Negro intellectuals that many of the choice executive positions that are dispensed by people who are professionally interested in Negroes are reserved almost

exclusively for those who are mulatto and the end is not yet. To conclude –
I was deeply impressed by the fact that the European, (and the American
is included here), has spread the rumor wherever he has gone that the race
that is at the bottom of all the other races in culture, intelligence, integrity
of character is the Negro. Imagine reading in the *Delhi-Statesman* a long
article about Joe Louis, an article written by an Englishman in which he
talked a great deal about Joe Louis as boxer, about the amazing amount of
money he has made in a year and a half and to find that he ends this sup-
posedly critical appraisal with this choice bit of information; to wit: "Joe
Louis eats five pounds of meat, one chicken and a container of ice cream
at each meal and typical of his race he wears gaudy color shirts, gaudy
color suits and light yellow shoes."[107] As I consider the Indian as he faces
the question of color prejudice in his own land and compare him with the
American Negro as he faces color prejudice in this land, the following
things stand out in bold relief: 1. The Indian is the victim of color prejudice at the hands of a white conqueror who is expressing himself in a land
which he has stolen. 2. He is a victim of a prejudice which is mixed with
fundamental differences in religion and culture. 3. The Indian has no political ideal in an imperialistic regime on which he may bring the Britisher
or European to the bar of moral judgment. With reference to the American Negro, we find the following: 1. He, along with the American white
man, is a foreigner in a land stolen from the American Indian. They are
both, the American Negro and the American white man, trying to become a nation on foreign soil. 2. The political ideal of America is in favor
of practices that are democratic in their genius and before which undemocratic practices can be condemned as antithetical and immoral. 3. Both
the American Negro and the white man are definitely committed to the
same Christian ideal of brotherliness in the light of which unbrotherly
practices can be properly classified as sinful and unchristian. May I add a
personal word in closing: there seems to me to be one important difference between the brutality and the inhumaneness of the Britisher in
lands which he has conquered and the American white man. The brutality of the Britisher seems to me to be deliberate, mature, reflective; while
the brutality of the American strikes me as being adolescent and imma-
ture. The thing that fills me with complete despair is that as I consider the

future in the light of what seems to me to be a crystallization of American mores and folkways in this particular is that he is rapidly becoming mature and reflective in his brutality. The moment that brutality becomes mature and reflective it becomes moral and righteous.

⟨⟩ | The Will to Segregation (1943)

For all the reasons discussed in this article, African Americans experienced World War II
as the most intensive period of formal civic engagement since black citizenship was rec-
ognized with the passage of the Fourteenth Amendment in 1867.[108] The crisis also
brought Thurman to the peak of his powers. Published in the official organ of the Fellow-
ship of Reconciliation soon after he had decided to pursue the dream of an interracial
church, "The Will to Segregation" is Thurman's most synthetic, brief account of why and
how racial segregation must be overcome. For Thurman, the "cult of segregation" threat-
ens to ravage the sound judgment of blacks and whites alike, thus undermining civic
character along with democracy itself. The transformation of the "will" to segregate, he
argues, would have to take root culturally in the religious foundations provided in
churches, as well as in the individual hearts of those committed to democratic social ac-
tivism.

ANY DISCUSSION OF THE RELATIONSHIP between Negro and white people
in the year 1943 must examine certain important developments that exercise wide influence in this area.

The first and most important single fact is the war. Under ordinary circumstances the Negro is at most a citizen, second class. He pays taxes on

property, participates in the franchise in some sections, and holds a few offices of public trust, but for the most part normal life for him is two or three steps removed from what may be regarded as normal life for other members of the community. At a time of national peril, much of this situation is altered. Even the least citizen begins to count in terms of specific assignments that are deemed essential for survival. Thus war has caused the average Negro to become aware of counting civically in a new way: he is encouraged to buy bonds and defense stamps, he participates in the leadership program, his manpower comes under the selected judgment of the National Selective Service Act, he is involved in Civilian Defense in many of its manifestations, he is taking special training courses for carrying increasing responsibility in defense industry and the farms, he is in the armed forces.[109]

Civic character is possible only where men are permitted to carry civic responsibility. With this new sense of civic responsibility, a new kind of civic character is beginning to appear. This new character, although occasioned by the war, makes for the development of a more careful regard for the future not only of democracy but also the particular future of the Negro in labor, professions, politics, etc. In a sense it is like the coming of age when the first full bloom of manhood possesses the mind and the body. It is unfortunate that it took a global war with its concomitant effect upon our national life to give the Negro a fresh sense of significance and power.

The second significant development stems from the fact that it is no longer possible merely to define national aspirations in terms of "making the world safe for democracy"; it is necessary now to talk concretely in terms of the four freedoms, adding footnotes to make them more definitive and less general than they would appear on the surface. The Axis nations have made clear their goals in terms of a thorough-going fascism, and have thus defined their political, social and economic philosophy. The United Nations must be just as concrete and specific.[110] Mere slogans are completely meaningless. High ranking government spokesmen in public utterances are defining democracy in language that the simplest man can understand.

Meanwhile, the diseases in the body politic become much more acute in the minds of less privileged persons such as Negroes. As these diseases are exposed to the searching diagnosis of the meaning of democracy, the gulf between the dream as uttered and the idea as practiced is wide, abysmal, and deep. *The measure of the frustration of Negroes is in direct proportion to the degree to which the meaning of democracy is made clear and definitive.* We behold then the spectacle of the Negro with a new civic character growing out of a new sense of civic and social responsibility, yet caught in the grip of a deeper frustration and restlessness than he has ever known.

In the third place, the fact that we were attacked by Japan has aggravated greatly the tension between the races. I am not suggesting that the war between Japan and the United States is a race war, but certainly many people have thought of it in terms of a non-white race "daring" to attack a white race.[111] This has given excellent justification for the expression of the prejudices against non-white peoples just under the surface of the American consciousness. There has been a relaxation of mutual regard and respect between the races in many walks of life where these previously existed. This has made for definite reactions on the part of Negroes, often reactions in kind with increasing bitterness, intolerance, hatred.

And in the fourth place, the attitudes described above have been met by an increasing determination and grimness on the part of white Americans. It seems perfectly clear to them that Negroes everywhere are getting out of their place. The argument runs like this: "Negroes do not know what to do with their new sense of significance. They are flippant, arrogant, bigoted, overbearing. Therefore, they must be curbed, held in check so that when the war is over they may drop quickly back into their prewar secondary citizen status." With this kind of situation facing the two groups in America, what can be done?

The "Will to Segregation"

The most fundamentally important thing that must be done is to relax the "will to segregation" that through the years has become the American technique for the control of the Negro minority. This "will to segregation" has taken the form of policy in business, in the church, in the state, in the school, in living zones. Let us examine this "will to segregate."

It is important to realize that segregation can exist only between peoples who are relatively weak and relatively strong, respectively. The strong may separate themselves in certain ways from the weak, but because the initiative remains in their hands they are ever at liberty to shuttle back and forth between the proscribed areas. The weak can only be segregated because, lacking the initiative, they cannot move at will between the proscribed areas. A simple case in point may be observed on any Southern train carrying day coaches. Members of the train crew, who are white, often sit in the section of the coach designated for Negroes. They may sit, by custom, in either section. The train porter, who is a Negro, may sit only in the Negro coach. White passengers move at will from one section to the other, but the passengers in the Jim Crow car sometimes experience difficulty even in passing through the other coaches en route to the diner. Waiters in the diner must always use the toilet facilities in the Jim Crow coach, while white members of the train crew may use either facilities.

The psychological effect of segregation on both groups is the critical issue. For segregation dramatizes a stigma, and becomes a badge of inferiority. A group segregated systematically over many generations experiences a decisive undermining of self-respect. For the sensitive, it means a constant, persistent resentment that is apt so to disease the personality that mental health is critically attacked. It is easy to say that the sensitive should resist segregation without including in their resistance the persons who are directly responsible for the laws and the social patterns that uphold them, but there are many who regard such a position as mere romanticism.

For the less sensitive there is ever the possibility of the acceptance of segregation, with its concomitant conscious admission of inferiority, of humiliation, of despair. Men who are despised, or who are treated systematically as if they were despised, are apt eventually to despise themselves. There is a sense in which society is a mirror through which individuals and groups see themselves reflected. It requires the veriest kind of vigilance and wide awareness to resist the temptation to accept the judgment of society upon one's group. Society sets the mode or the frame of reference that is apt to determine judgment. It is in an effort to overcome this that minority groups seem inclined to develop tendencies toward chauvinism, racism and other manifestations of the "cult of segregation."

More than all of this there is at least one great fear growing out of segregation: the fear of violence. The fear of physical violence is characteristic
of most human beings and other animals, but among the segregated the
fear takes on a heightened significance because they are so circumscribed
by society that exposure to direct violence is ever present and there are no
particular types of behavior that may guarantee immunity. The basic fact
is that when human beings are segregated they provide a "tethered goat"
on whose innocent and unsuspecting head vengeance may be poured for
deeds infinitely removed from anything for which they may have responsibility. The ghetto and the Negro section are always present and into them
may be dumped releases from frustration and from social and economic
blunders, and revenge for private wrongs that originate in a world into
which the victims are not even permitted to enter. *To the extent to which
this is true the mere fact of being alive provides a specific liability over and
above the normal fate of the average man!*

This fear of violence is not traceable merely to the fear of death. To accommodate oneself to the fact of death is one of the basic elements in a
normal adjustment of life. Everyone knows that for him death is inevitable; "one by one the duties end; one by one the lights go out." But the fear
of violence is a part of the fear that man has of dying out of his bed; dying
under circumstances that degrade and debase; dying like a dog in an alley,
or a rat in a gutter. Death by accident, or as a result of some freakish act of
nature has some of the elements of horror that are present here, but such
deaths have in them something that is clean, unconscious, whole. But to
be killed by other men without benefit of purpose or great cause is to die
ignobly and in shame. The last thread of dignity and worthfulness is
stripped from personality and death under such circumstances is sordid,
nasty, ghoulish.

The result of this fear makes for a definite alteration in the behavior
pattern. Very early the tendency is to make the body commit to memory
the ways of behavior that may reduce the exposure to immediate violence.
This explains in large part why there is so little organized resistance
against segregation. Each new generation of children is psychologically

and socially conditioned in an effort to reduce the exposure to spasmodic, irresponsible, systematic and calculating sadistic impulses. The injury to personality is far greater than can be adequately grasped even by the most sensitive. To be denied freedom of movement, freedom of participation in the common life, is to have the ground of personality value seriously shaken. When in moments of national crises the segregated are granted temporary citizenship, one of the first acts is to attack segregation. This is a sound instinct of self-preservation and it provides the opening for all people of good will to give concrete expression to their commitments.

The effect of segregation on the part of the white group is just as deadly. It gives them a false sense of superiority. What is in essence a superiority of advantage becomes rationalized into superiority based upon logical, physical and spiritual difference. It is impossible for a white child to grow up in an atmosphere in which normal impulses of friendliness must be constantly short-circuited so as to apply only to his own kind, without there dawning upon him that the fact of this difference in attitude is not due to a difference in superior essence. The mind becomes a seed-bed of all kinds of fears and superstitions with reference to Negroes, and if there is nothing in the environment at home or abroad to counteract these fears they become facts on the basis of which the life is planned and years are fulfilled. *All emphasis on brotherhood or love inherent in the Christian religion is doomed to recognize these "fear facts" as extenuating circumstances in which love and brotherhood are not supposed to be effective.*

Therefore, unless the "will to segregate" is relaxed there can be no sound basis of hope for the fulfillment of the dream of democracy in this life of ours.

The Church's Task

For the church this means a radical internal reorganization of policy and of structural change. I am realistic enough to know that this cannot be done overnight. My contention is that if the "will to segregate" is relaxed in the church then the resources of mind and spirit and power that are already in the church can begin working formally and informally on the radical changes that are necessary if the church is to become Christian. This of course, may not mean that there will be no congregations that are all Negro, or that are all white, but freedom of choice, which is basically a sense of alternatives, will be available to any persons without regard to the faithful perpetuation of the pattern of segregation upon which the Christian church in America is constructed.

How dare we undertake to teach reverence to children when we ourselves do not believe in reverence for life in general or life in particular as a valid concept in our kind of world? Shall we teach lies to children? How dare we proclaim sincerity and genuineness as essential qualities for healthy living if in our innermost selves we do not have confidence in the survival values of such ideals of living? Can we teach trust when we are bound by a vast network of impersonal social relations which create the kind of climate in which trust cannot possibly thrive? Or can we teach trust even as we confess how little of trust we have in each other, in our cause and in our God? I wonder. What do we mean when we teach the brotherhood of man, when over and over again we give the sanction of our religion and the weight of our practice to those subtle anti-christian practices expressed in segregated churches and even in segregated graveyards! Can we expect more of the state, of the body politic, of industry than we expect of the church? How can we teach love from behind the great high walls of separateness?

A Man's Task

But more personally, what must a man do who wishes to work effectively on this problem within the framework of Christian ethics?

In the first place I must see to it that what I condemn in society, I do not permit to grow and flower in me. The will to discriminate against other men must be rooted out of the springs of my own action.

But even if my heart is pure, my motives above reproach and my personal action unequivocal and positive, this is not enough. I must share the guilt of my age, my society, and my race. Therefore, I must exhaust all possible means that do not conflict with my ends for bringing about the kind of society in which it is possible for men to live in large groups without external limitations, to experience the good life. This means that for my second action I must put my creative mind to work in the devising of techniques, personal and group, for the achievement of these ends.

High among these techniques are those that belong in the general classification of moral suasion, attempts to make individual and social conscience articulate with reference to a specific sin. Moral suasion has only one serious limitation: the amount of moral atrophy that has taken place in the mind and character of the persons who are to be aroused. I must be patient. I must keep working and persuading and appealing on the assumption, of course, that all men are the children of God – the good and the bad. This means that the Christian will brood over the hearts of men as the living instrument of the spirit of God until there is a stirring of consciousness both of sin and of sonship in their hearts.

The third type of personal action is even more difficult because a conflict of loyalties makes the decision of positive Christian action in a given situation very difficult to determine. There may be a conflict between my loyalty to the ideal brotherhood viewed with reference to the weak, and my kinship with them. The strong are my brothers as truly as the weak are my brothers. I am apt to be caught between the recognition of fundamental kinship with the strong, and the desperation of the weak. Or the conflict may arise from a completely ethical demand of my religion that I wash my hands of the doers of iniquity and leave them to go on their recklessly destructive way, feeling that there are some types of struggle in which even God does not demand that I participate. I may say this type of action is not for me and to all the pull of the needy who are on the receiving end of the violence of the wicked I may turn a deaf ear – if I can.

But I may decide that I cannot wait for the thing to work itself out. There is too much agony, too much hunger, too much poverty and misery everywhere, too many flagrant denials of kinship and brotherhood all along the line. Something concrete must be done now. To wait for moral pressure to work its perfect work may be too late.

What do I do then? I may resort to the exercise of some form of shock, by organizing a boycott, or widespread non-cooperation, or the like. The function of these techniques is to tear men free from their alignments to the evil way, to free them so that they may be given an immediate sense of acute insecurity and out of the depths of their insecurity be forced to see their kinship with the weak and the insecure. Men do not voluntarily relinquish their hold on their place. It is not until something becomes movable in the situation that men are spiritually prepared to apply Christian idealism to un-ideal and un-christian situations. Examples of these techniques are being developed by FOR groups and others in different parts of the world even now.[112]

Action of this kind requires great discipline of mind, emotions and body to the end that forces may not be released that will do complete violence both to one's ideals and one's purpose. All must be done with the full consciousness of the Divine Scrutiny.

∞ | The Fellowship Church of All Peoples (1945)

The establishment of Fellowship Church, founded in 1943, was truly an historic under-taking.[113] *Thurman became copastor in 1944, and later the pastoral leader of the multiracial, intercultural church. As he argues in this article which originally appeared in the journal* Common Ground, *the challenge of modern democracy lies in the courage and conviction of a dedicated, inclusive fellowship where the experiences of community are more compelling than the concepts, habit patterns, prejudices, and beliefs that divide. Here Thurman outlines Fellowship Church's programs in its earliest years. Although he does not discuss the church's equally ground-breaking worship services, which included liturgical dance, music from a variety of cultural traditions, and meditation periods, the piece provides something of the flavor and excitement of the church's efforts to forge interracial community among its members.*

SAN FRANCISCO is a "thousand cities within a city." There are rich international units from all over the earth nestled in the midst of its hills. In a very real sense it is the crossroads of the world and particularly of the Pacific Basin with which the destiny of America will be increasingly involved. No better spot could have been selected for a bold experiment in the genius of democratic living within the framework of religious faith.

220

The Fellowship Church of All Peoples in San Francisco was originally projected as a neighborhood venture in interracial religious fellowship. The plan for its organization and development was proposed a little more than a year ago by Dr. Alfred G. Fisk, Professor of Philosophy at San Francisco State College. The church as such came into being the second Sunday in December 1943, and its first name was the Neighborhood Church.[114] Support for the venture was given by the Presbyterian Church, U.S.A., in whose fellowship Dr. Fisk is an active clergyman.

The idea of an interracial church has been part of the thinking of many groups in this country, and it is a dream which has haunted me for ten years. The first contemporary effort toward establishing such a church was made in Philadelphia in 1936, when an interracial committee of the American Friends Service Committee[115] launched a Fellowship Church there. It held monthly meetings during the winter months, at alternating Negro and white churches. All those sharing responsibilities for the particular service were taken from the Negro and white groups. Usually Negro and white local pastors took the worship and the responsibility of presiding. The guest preacher was either Negro or white. The idea was not to establish a regular church in the community but rather to give a genuine testimony in the field of group relations. From Philadelphia, the idea has spread to other cities in the East.

The original idea of the Fellowship Church in San Francisco was different at one major point from the eastern movement: it was projected as a permanent full-time church located in a building, with a Negro and a white clergyman serving as co-pastors. Dr. Fisk has been the white co-pastor since the beginning. I came West in July of 1944 to join him.[116] The plan for a Neighborhood Church was somewhat broadened and the name Fellowship Church of All Peoples established instead. The Church is a creative experiment in interracial and intercultural communion, deriving its inspiration from a spiritual interpretation of the meaning of life and the dignity of man. In faith and genius it is specifically Christian. Its membership commitment recognizes and undertakes to implement the conviction that the God of life and the God of religion are one and the same and that the normal relationship between men, therefore, is one of fellowship, understanding, and confidence rather than distrust, prejudice, and strife.

The membership is open to any person willing to accept the commitment, to participate in its program, and to share in its responsibilities.

There are four kinds of membership: those who join bringing with them a letter from some other church, those who have never been a part of a church fellowship before, those who wish to be associated in this venture while maintaining their membership in their own church, and those living out of the city who wish to become national affiliates.[117]

We think it important that an experiment of this kind should take place within the framework of historical Protestantism rather than as a movement outside the stream of the church. In this sense it may be regarded as a direct challenge to the policy of separatism and segregation in which all the historical Protestant denominations are involved.

The Fellowship Church is dedicated to seeking the answer to several crucial questions for Christianity and democracy. First, is it possible to establish islands of community or fellowship in a sea of religious and social strife, with any hope of their resolving the strife? Second, is it possible for an authentic interracial and intercultural church to develop – a church that will not be largely dominated by one particular group with some other group on the fringes? Third, is it possible for a Negro and white minister to share the leadership of such a church on the basis of their respective gifts rather than on the basis of their group affiliations? In other words, in any given venture of this sort will the Negroes tend to gravitate toward the Negro pastor for leadership and counsel, and white people gravitate toward the white pastor for these same services? Fourth, how fundamental, and of what kind, will be the opposition to the development of the idea in practice, both from ecclesiastical interests and other interests of the community? What steps will be taken to neutralize its effect and to defeat its purpose? The work of the Church is too new yet for any conclusions to be valid. I can only indicate the kind of things we have been doing.

For about eight weeks during the summer of 1944, the Church conducted a Fellowship Camp. The program of participation was built around "adventures in friendship." Our purpose was to deepen the interest of the children in other nationalities and races, and feed this interest with authentic factual materials calculated to give them personal experience in appreciating some of the art, music, folkways, and group contributions of other cultures. The peoples studied included the American Indian, and Mexican, Filipino, Russian, Negro, Japanese, Jewish, and Chinese Americans. As far as our skills permitted, songs, stories, handicrafts, and worship materials were built entirely around the peoples studied. There were exhibits of large photographs of scenery and persons, posters, costumes, dolls in native dress. Once, during the period each particular group was studied, a flesh-and-blood member of that group visited the camp and talked intimately with the children about his cultural heritage. The most creative result of the weeks was the production of a series of watercolor drawings using as subjects those things the children had learned about the people. In the drawing class one day, several little Mexican, Anglo-Saxon, and Negro boys were looking at a large poster of Russian children. Presently one said, "There's a boy who looks like me." This remark was followed by the same expression from each boy present despite the fact that all the children in the picture were Russian.

There were occasional excursions to various parts of the city of special interest from the point of view of intercultural emphasis. For many of the children the far-famed Chinatown of San Francisco was visited for the first time. They were most excited to see the Chinese Post Office and Telephone Exchange. It was good also to see Bufano's statue of Sun Yat Sen, who they had been told was a figure like the American George Washington.[118]

Another of our activities is a series of monthly Fellowship Dinners extending through the winter. The November dinner, first in the series, was designed primarily to point up the fellowship within the Church itself. Persons from three racial groups, in the preparations for the dinner, became much better acquainted as individuals. The after-dinner program that night featured a distinguished Chinese American soloist. The December dinner was in honor of the Filipino American community, with the program provided by the Filipino Community Church, whose members came as special guests. The pièce de résistance of the meal was Filipino, and there was authentic music by gifted musicians and an illuminating lecture by a Filipino woman on the life of women in the Philippines. The Monday night adult craft group of the Church had prepared the decorations, which gave those attending some feel of life in the Islands them-

selves. The January dinner had as its special point of emphasis the home-
coming of the Japanese Americans to San Francisco, with those who had
returned by that time guests of honor.[119] The dinners are conceived as a
psychological attack on the barriers that tend to separate Americans from
each other.

A new development in religious experience has been the monthly Twilight Hours, projected as a means for inspiring group worship through art
appreciation. Thus far, music, poetry, and drama have been employed.
The Christmas Twilight Hour presented a series of Living Madonna
Types in tableaux. The representatives included persons of American Indian, Anglo-Saxon, Negro, Filipino, Mexican, Korean, Chinese, Russian,
Italian, Armenian, and Japanese American extraction. Light for each
scene was focused on the particular "Madonna face," draped in "native"
materials, in most instances using authentic headpieces representing the
cultural backgrounds. Appropriate music created an international atmosphere. The result was not only beautiful but made for awareness that the
Madonna conception is universal, as wide as the family of man.

The development of such an intercultural-interracial fellowship program is still only in process. We are experimenting with standing commit-
tees to give each person in the membership opportunity to express himself at those points which will give him fullest and most satisfactory
participation. A reading room is being established in which there will be
available the significant journals of opinion and other publications issued
by various cultural and racial groups in the country. The national membership includes service men who are located all over the world, many
persons from academic circles, churchmen, and several persons carrying
major responsibilities in government.

It is too early to evaluate the significance of the venture. If in every
community in the United States an experiment such as ours could be undertaken, the Church itself would once again set in motion those spiritual
processes which gave to it its original impetus and power. The ideal may
develop in various ways that are indigenous to the community in which it
is unfolded. To those of us who have dreamed of it for years, it represents
an authentic growing edge of far-reaching social change in making possible communities of friendly men in a world grown gray with suffering and
hate.

∞ | *The Commitment (1943; 1945)*

When Fellowship Church was established in 1943, Thurman and Alfred Fisk developed a statement of commitment to the church's principles to which all members were asked to subscribe.[120] Over the following two years, the statement was modified to reflect the cultural and religious multiplicity of the church's growing membership. Fellowship Church began with less than fifty members from various denominational, ethnic, and cultural backgrounds, primarily Caucasian, African American, and Asian American. Before Thurman resigned in 1953, the congregation had grown to over 200 resident members and over 1,000 members-at-large. "You will note that the purpose of the restatement," *stated the letter accompanying the new Commitment, "is to strengthen the basic ideas and not to alter their fundamental character and import." Some members, however, felt that the second statement's exclusion of reference to Jesus altered the original's meaning very much indeed. Nonetheless, the additions made to the original affirmation reveal the broader, ecumenical character of Thurman's theological and social perspective, especially as they relate to his view of Jesus and the ethical witness of the church.*

1943

I DESIRE TO HAVE A PART in the unfolding of the ideal of Christian Fellowship through the union of men and women of varying national, cultural and racial heritage, in church communion.

In this commitment I am pledged to the growing understanding of all men as sons of God and seek after a vital interpretation of the highest manifestation of God – Jesus Christ – in all my relationships.

I desire the strength of corporate worship with the imperative of personal dedication which will be found through membership in the Fellowship Church of San Francisco.

1945

I affirm my need for a growing understanding of all men as sons of God, and I seek after a vital experience of God as revealed in Jesus of Nazareth and other great religious spirits whose fellowship with God was the foundation of their fellowship with men.

I desire to share in the spiritual growth and ethical awareness of men and women of varied national, cultural, racial, and creedal heritage united in a religious fellowship.

I desire the strength of corporate worship through membership in The Church For the Fellowship of All Peoples, with the imperative of personal dedication to the working out of God's purpose here and in all places.

∞ | *The Responsibility*
of the Professional Person to Society (1957)

The professionalization of the American middle classes – that is, the creation of a "white-collar," educated, primarily urban work force – had been under way since the late nineteenth century.[121] *But American victory during World War II along with the technological demands of the cold war, created an even greater need for "brain workers," who now tended to congregate in the growing suburbs. Americans became more self-consciously and ambivalently aware of "the organization man" and the scientific "expert," than ever before, and many argued that there was a peculiar absence of community loyalty in the world they inhabited. In this article, based on his keynote address to the 1957 National League of Nursing convention in Chicago, Thurman considers some of the more troubling tendencies of the new professional managerial class. He counsels these freshly minted young medical professionals that beyond the demands placed upon them by the society, there is the need always to return to the inner spiritual and moral resources that make for moral accountability, integrity, and a sense of reverence in public practices. He also cautions them against the class antagonism and overspecialization to which professionals can so easily fall prey.*

PERSONS WHO PRACTICE PROFESSIONS in any society do so by virtue of skills, techniques, and the knowledge which they have developed as a result of particular disciplines. Further, they practice the profession for considerations which would not be permitted them if they were not so equipped and trained. Society recognizes the necessity for making available for itself the skilled technical services of certain of its members in order to guarantee the general welfare and maintenance of social and individual well-being. Through many stages of growth and evaluation, a systemized plan of preparation is arrived at in order to guarantee a minimum basic equipment for the specialized services needed. Such a plan includes instruction given under certain circumstances and by qualified persons; materials that are to be used which will give to the individuals skill in their use under conditions that are as varied as the society affords; and the time interval for study and the tests by which society may be assured that skills have been learned.

Society's Concessions

Society makes certain important concessions to individuals who are selected to be trained to carry the unique responsibility of professionals. There is tacit agreement that individuals accepted as professionals may be excused from carrying the normal responsibilities so that their time, thought, and energy may be devoted specifically to the given ends of the profession. This is an important concession for it means that such individuals are literally taken out of circulation, and are not required to be functioning, active members of society. During this period their basic needs are guaranteed and underwritten by society. They do not have to work for a living. Often they are excused from political responsibility, and even at a time of universal military conscription, there are certain extenuating circumstances which temporarily relieve the individual from taking part, at this point, in the social process. He has a permanent excuse from participating responsibly as a working member of society.

Training stations, or more politely institutions of learning, are set up by society so that the best provisions possible may be made for guaranteeing the effectiveness and the efficiency of the profession. These training stations represent vast investments carrying important subsidies so that the person in training would not be required to pay to the institution what it costs society, through the institution, to train him. The amount of such a subsidy varies. The thing that does not vary is the subsidy itself.

In addition to general subsidy, there are special subsidies in terms of scholarships, grants, or perquisites to help insure that those of greatest promise will be relieved of maximum economic distractions from their work.

In addition to all of these, society gives the professional a preferred position by regarding him as a prestige bearing member of the community. There are subtle but strategic ego-satisfactions which are guaranteed to him by a grateful social order.

Society's Demands

Society makes certain demands of the professional aside from ability and intelligence. He must be committed to his profession as the avenue along which he chooses to find the fulfillment of his life as a responsible member of the community. This is very important. It says that he has made up his mind and is giving to this particular activity the nerve center of his consent. He undertakes his training under the aegis of this kind of moral commitment. Such a decision is apt to be perilous because of the very nature of the case. That is to say, no man can make a decision involving a life commitment on the basis of evidence that is quite conclusive and final. He may discover after the decision is made that there were certain things which he did not take into account and therefore the decision was for him a mistake. Fortunate, indeed, is the person who makes the discovery before he has gone too far. It is not easy to know how far is too far.

The professional in training must have definitive character. Character in the context in which I am using it has a specialized meaning. It has to do with the integrity of the act which the individual performs at the level of training as well as at the level of professional practice. When a person is sick and the skilled service of a nurse is indicated, what the patient wants to know above all else is not whether the nurse, as a person, is kind to her cat, or whether she buys presents for her nephews, or not even whether she observes the traffic laws in her town, as important as all these things are, but what the patient wants to know is, when she puts on her uniform and takes her place of responsibility, can she practice nursing? If there has been little integrity in the actions of her participation, whatever may be the intent of her heart and disposition, her failure at the crucial point of character as defined in this context may be disastrous.

There is a demand that is made with reference to compensation, or, what I choose rather to say, ability to pay. Society seeks to protect itself and its professionals by a series of general agreements about compensation. These agreements represent various stages of the evolution of the social process. I pass no judgment on their validity except to point out that the principle of payment for services rendered is an accepted one. From within the context of this principle a very important factor must be held in mind. It is that due consideration must be given to the fact that there is an original economic and social investment which society has made in the preparation of the professional which must be taken into account. This is especially true for institutions that place primary emphasis on teaching and training. In many hospital schools of nursing, apprenticeship training is still the order of the day. I would hazard the guess that most of the young people in these schools earn every penny of their education.

Every person who receives professional services is a member of the society who made the training of the professional possible in the first place. The professional has not paid what it costs society to train him and this fact must be borne in mind, not only in terms of the quality of performance, but in terms of the compensation for performances. There is a sense, of course, in which any compensation is a *recognition* of services rendered rather than *payment for* services rendered.

Principle of Concretion

Both the professional and society are under the necessity for the most creative exercise of the principle of concretion in dealing with each other. In the use of the term professional and society, I am employing two abstractions. Society does not exist; it is a fiction. Society has a name and the name of society is the name of people who make up the society. These people are individuals who eat and sleep and die. The term professional is an abstraction; it is a fiction. It is made up of people who have names who eat and sleep and die. The peril for anyone who speaks on behalf of society is that he will refer to the professionals as "they." The peril of anyone who speaks as a professional is that he will refer to society as "they." Such references breed contempt and antagonisms. It is the violent material out of which class and group struggles arise. It makes of human relations an armed camp.

Let us examine the difference that is made when the principle of concretion emerges. The moral responsibility of nonprofessionals is to remember that the professional is a human being first and, as such, is a member in good standing of the human family. The professional must remember that the person to whom he administers is a human being first and, as such, is a member in good standing of the human family. Each has a responsibility to the other to keep each reminded of this basic fact.

What is involved when the professional applies to himself the principle of concretion? First of all, he is a human being whose life is private, personal, and intimate. The professional has needs of various kinds which must be met if, as a human being, the professional is to be healthy. It is a person of emotional and physical health and well-being that he practices his profession. There is, therefore, a primary responsibility which every one has to, and for, himself in this regard. To neglect one's emotional and physical well-being because of one's commitment as a professional is to undermine the integrity of function and betray the social contract.

The professional has to be a person who is acquainted with the resources needful for carrying on one's work with maximum effectiveness. He must not overlook all of the resources of his profession upon which he may draw both as a professional and as a person. Obviously, this means keeping abreast of developments, advances, and the cumulative wisdom of the profession as it becomes more and more effective in the fulfillment of its appointed task. There is no valid excuse for being out of touch with such resources.

The professional must be alive to resources that are available in the society outside of the things that are unique to his profession. There is a general accumulation of resources that are a part of the growth and development of the common life upon which he should draw. Resources in the fine arts, in literature, the spoken word, as well as the overtones that seep into society from other professions.

Inner Resources

What about the resources that are in one's self? What kind of human be-ing is the professional? For him there must be springs of living water to which he turns for the renewal of his inward parts in times of barrenness and desolation. The major resource of this sort upon which mankind in all ages has drawn comes under the general category of religion. Here I make no special plea for any particular expression of religion. This is a private and personal matter. My insistence is that there is a hunger in the human spirit that can only be met by drawing upon a resource that is greater and more abiding than the individual life of man.

The professional is not exempt from finding in terms of spiritual values that which will do three simple things for him: (1) give him a fundamental validation for his life which can only come by finding the most worthful object of devotion and worship in the experience with which his life as a man is not dependent upon the vicissitudes of fortune or the incidents of fate; (2) give him a basis for the integrated behavior of his life out of which the context of his sense of values, the meaning of right and wrong will emerge enabling him to bring to his functioning, both as a human being and as a professional, an abiding integrity; and (3) give him in his work and in his play, in his joy and in his sorrow, in his success and in his failure, a sense of not being alone but rather sharing a comradeship and fellowship which makes the living of his life a hallowed and sacred experience.

CO | *The Public and Private Results of Collegiate*
Education in the Life of Negro Americans (1967)

*Thurman delivered the following speech at the Centennial Banquet of Morehouse Col-
lege on February 15, 1967, where he shared the rostrum with his lifelong colleague and
friend, President Benjamin Mays and President-elect, Dr. Hugh Gloster.* [122] *Here, Thurman reflects on the illustrious history of Morehouse College as an exemplar of the role of
historically Black colleges and universities in shaping the past and future of American
society.* [123] *In his inimitable oratorical style, Thurman suggests that while the educational process is justified, in part, by its public outcomes, the most significant measure of
higher education among African Americans has been its private results. Always concerned with the sanctity and integrity of the individual, Thurman concentrates on the
ways Morehouse College, since its humble beginnings during Reconstruction, has in-
stilled in young black men core values of self-validation and self-respect against the on-
slaught of an often violent, segregated culture. Implicit in his argument is a call for maintaining the private and public functions of education in an ethical society.*

I WOULD LIKE TO ASK US TO STAND in silence as a tribute to those men during the past hundred years who are no longer living in the flesh. May we
stand. "We died but you who live must do a harder thing than dying is, for
you must think and ghosts shall drive you on. Amen."

Mr. Toastmaster, President Mays, President-elect Gloster and all these prestigious persons at the two guest tables, ladies and gentlemen:

There are many things that go through a man's mind on an occasion like this, but we did not gather together to reminisce altogether. My remarks will be limited, and they will fall within the time limit that has been given me. Now the fact that it is ten minutes after ten has nothing to do with the time limit that was given me.

My address tonight is divided into two parts, and in order that certain things will be clear and direct, I want to read something as a background taken from *The Inward Journey* and then I want to read in summary the heart of what I want to say. When I finish that, then I am sure that you would have heard what I want to say. But I won't stop. Then I will talk with you for awhile.

[*Thurman reads "It Is a Strange Freedom."*]

Now the summary. The educational process is only partially justified by its public result. This public result is important and is often noteworthy because it has to do with the tangibles, the excellencies of faculties, facilities and equipment, standing or rating in the academic community, the public image which it maintains as a social institution dedicated to the training of the minds of those who are admitted into its particular academic community. During this year of centennial many competent voices will make a good and often dramatic case for the public results of Morehouse College, growing out of its first 100 years, and will give a sensitive prophecy concerning its future in American society during the next 100 years. However, I do not conceive my role to be in this area of the meaning of Morehouse College. In the time allotted me tonight I want to think with you somewhat about the private results of the existence of our college during the past century, and perhaps dare to make a judgment about the future.

My essential idea is that the educational process that was set in motion a hundred years ago in Augusta, Georgia, as the creative genius of a school for Negro men, is justified by its private result. That is, by its result in the lives of the generations of men who have been touched by its glow. The most important thing in life for any man at any time is the development of his own best self, the incentive to actualize his own potentials. The central emphasis of the past was on the intrinsic worth of the individual student; the necessity to experience himself as a human being in a climate in which he had no standing as a human being. Thus the incentive was man – the student must during this pass be in competition with himself.

The time and place of a man's life is the time and the place of his body but the meaning and the significance of his life are as vast and creative as the powers of his mind, the sensitivity of his spirit, and the ethical dimension of his commitment can make it. The insistence that the Morehouse student from that far off past, up through what does not seem to me the past, but it is the past . . . (Just as a sort of parenthetical something, it is amazing when I think about it that forty-eight years ago I was a freshman at Morehouse. It is incredible. Well, forgive me.) . . . the insistence was that the student must experience himself as a human being. Now this may seem to be something highly theoretical or speculative or perhaps just simply academic, but think of what was involved a hundred years ago when the four men who were the first students with the smell of slavery all over them, were called into the kind of intimate primary encounter that insisted that is was their prerogative and that is was mandatory to experience themselves as human beings. It is overwhelming that they were under some kind of judgment passed upon them by life to actualize their potential; not to recognize that they had potential, but to actualize their potential: to get on the scent of their own potential and follow it all the way.

We can't grasp easily. Now it was the same dimension moving in accordance with the categories that belonged to the shifting generation that obtained through the first twenty-five, thirty, forty years of this century at Morehouse. Think of what it meant for the president of Morehouse College every Tuesday morning in chapel, and other mornings when is seemed necessary, to lean over on the podium and say, "Young gentlemen." Not students, not fellows, not boys. Always young gentlemen. I remember the first time I went to chapel, fresh from Florida, and the president of the college said, as he addressed all the students who were in chapel, "Young gentlemen." Think about it. And this was symbolic of the emphasis that surrounded the college like a gentle climate, to protect us from the anonymous violence of the Atlanta environment, so that we as a college had very few primary, radical exposures to the climate of Atlanta.

As a matter of fact, so immunized were we from aspects of the climate that when I went to Divinity School from Morehouse, and in my first year I took a course in sociology and the assignment that the professor gave to me was to do a paper on the interracial commission of Atlanta, Georgia, I had never heard of it. This was, I think, by conscious and unconscious design, to hold an environment around you while you worked at the business of helping the men to experience themselves as human beings, and once this happened, then they could manage the environment.

I remember – and I do not wish to embarrass anyone about what I am going to say now, we were having a football game, and those of you who go far enough back to recall a certain policeman whose name was Mr. Chamberlain. He loved Morehouse in his way and that was a good way, because when you had an encounter with the Pharaoh who didn't know Moses, you were glad to know that Mr. Chamberlain was around. He always volunteered to be the policeman for Morehouse football games because Morehouse played good football and he enjoyed it. He and Dean Archer were standing just inside the gate and I was trying to make up my mind whether or not I would stay at the game or go back to work. Two little ragged boys came under the fence and started running across the field and Mr. Chamberlain said, "You little niggers get back under the fence." And "Big Boy" said, "Oh, don't call them 'niggers.'" And Mr. Chamberlain said, "I am not talking about your nice clean niggers, I am talking about . . ." And Dean Archer said, "But you don't call any of them niggers." This is what I am talking about. And one other simple illustration.

Mr. Harrold always called you "son." Now you might be forty or fifteen, but when he called you son, this was the notice that you were in the business of experiencing yourself as a human being.

Dr. Loomis at Teacher's College and Union tells a very interesting story that will illustrate the feeling and the tremendous impact of the private results of Morehouse College. He tells the story of a lady and her daughter and her son who went into a restaurant to get something to eat. The mother gave her order and the daughter gave her order and then the waitress said, "Young man, what will you have?" The boy started to order and then his mother said, "I will order for him." The waitress was very perceptive. She insisted, "Young man, what will you have?" and the daughter said, "If Mother will not order for him I will order for him because if

Mother were not here, I would order for him." But the waitress insisted, "Young man, what will you have?" and he said with a sort of soft, muted voice, "A hamburger." And she said, "With onions, and catsup and mustard, and relish – the works?" And he whispered after her, "Onions, catsup, mustard, and relish – the works." She gave the mother's order, then the daughter's order and then with full voice she said, "One hamburger – the works." And the boy in utter amazement looked at his mother and said, "Mother, she thinks I am real." This is what I am talking about, and the overwhelming impact down in the quiet places where the ultimate decisions as to self-validation and affirmation remain. There the private result of Morehouse College spoke, and when it spoke men began to feel themselves pass through themselves and get a taste of their own flavor and accent, so that they would know how it is to be a man. And this is the private result coming out of the past.

Just one little step about this present and I will simply salute the future. In the present the emphasis has shifted, not a fundamental shift, but a shift that is a radical and creative derivative from the original emphasis. That is a shift from the competition with one's self to competition with one's fellow. And it is the tremendous contribution of Bennie Mays at this point. We had some prophetic indication of this when he was a teacher and he would stand at the door with his watch in his hand. When the last bell sounded, he would reach for the knob and if you were turning the corner to come in he would stand full-grown in the door and say. "You are one minute late and you can't come in." This is the experience of one's mind as one's own. The first experience of one's self as a human being and this had to be rooted and stabilized and grounded. And this is the private result of the educational process which I am calling Morehouse College.

The second phase – the experience of one's mind as one's own, and this has manifested itself quite sensitively, and I think creatively, by Bennie Mays in trying to create a working facility in terms of all of the things that should go into the complete exposure of the young mind to the educational process – teachers, equipment, all of this – and calling attention to the fact that the Morehouse man has to work his way out of the area when he is on the defensive. I want you to think with me just for a moment. You are very nice, you haven't left me yet. What I mean by this is that as you begin to experience your mind as your own, you are apt to feel that around you because of superior advantages, because of a longer chance at the learning process, – all the things that one might think of – that because of this the burden of proof is on you. You must find external validation for the integrity of your own experience of your own mind. This is what I am trying to say. So that it becomes important, then, to get into the best graduate schools; it becomes important to enter into active competition in the whole arena of ideas; and we have heard tonight about the number of men who have received Ph.D. degrees, the number who have done this and this and this. All of this is a part of the process through which we are passing that makes it mandatory for us to try to discover an other-than-self reference for the validation of our own experience of our own mind. This is what I am talking about; and as we work through this we will make at last the great discovery that the experience of one's mind is its own validation, and when this happens we are ready to release all that we have experienced in training and discipline and equipment to the problems and the issues and the demands of our times. Now I am through – the private result of the college.

The time and the place of man's life is the time and place of his body. The time interval is body but the significance of his life is as vast and creative as the powers of his mind, the sensitivity of his spirit and the quality of his dedication to his time can make it. So in the language of the "Song of the River" in the "Blue Cat of Castletown," let me end with the words:

> Sing your own song, said the river
> Sing your own song
> Out of yesterday's song comes
> It goes into tomorrow
> Sing your own song
> With your life fashion beauty
> This, too, is a song
> Riches will pass and power
> Beauty remains
> Sing your own song
> All that is worth doing

Do well said the river
Sing your own song
Certain and round be the measure
Every line be graceful and true
Time is the mold, time the weaver
Because time and the workman together
Sing your own song, sing well, said the river, sing well.[124]

⚭ | *Excerpt from* The Luminous Darkness (1965)

Written against the backdrop of the early sixties, published in the year of the historic Voting Rights Act (1965) and following the March on Washington (1963) and the Public Accommodations Act (1964), Thurman's 1965 treatise The Luminous Darkness *outlined the anatomy of segregation and the basis for hope among races in American society.*[125] *In this excerpt, Thurman frankly addresses the place of religion and moral imagination in healing racial discord. Building on themes addressed in many of his earlier writings and public speeches, he underscores the fundamental issues at stake for a nation in crisis. In so doing, he distinguishes between the role of law, human conscience, and will and the role of religious institutions, namely Christian churches, in providing the spiritual and moral resources that insure the ethical ends of political and legal processes. Beyond its glaring realities and destructive practices, he argues, segregation is fundamentally the manifestation of a state of mind and mood of the human spirit. Like the younger visionary, Martin Luther King, Jr.,*[126] *Thurman counsels that desegregation is only a first step in a long and difficult process of establishing an integrated society. Laws are limited in that they can only establish the climate for fellowship with contact, but they can not guarantee the spiritual and moral requisites of community. Rather, true integration begins with a process of moral practices that must be worked out over "a time interval of sufficient duration" in a mood of grace and compassion without which the hope for an integrated society remains only symbolic. Once historical structural barriers are removed,*

there must be in place both symbolic and practical resources for building the new com-
munity. For Thurman, this was both a prophetic warning and an invitation to create in
private life the spiritual necessities for a viable and meaningful public future. He ex-
tends a summons to Christian churches to move beyond sectarian practices which in-
hibit their witness and to resurrect symbols and practices that make for peace and justice
in an unrelenting quest for true community.

DESPITE ALL THAT HAS BEEN SAID about the pattern of segregation in our society, it is my conviction that time is against it. In fact, much of the current effort to hold the line may be viewed as a back-against-the-wall endeavor. The more the world becomes a neighborhood in which time and space are approaching zero as a limit, the more urgent becomes the issue of neighborliness. Man can now circle the entire earth's surface in a matter of minutes. Communication is now instant! This means that the external symbols of segregation – the wall, the ghetto, the separate locale as a mandatory restriction binding upon groups of people because of race, color, creed, or national origin – cannot survive modern life. The emphasis here is upon the two words "external symbols." When I suggest that time is against the pattern of segregation, I am referring to the symbols. The walls are crumbling – this is one of the dramatic facts of our world. The fact itself is very frightening to many who have lived always behind the walls, within the walls, or beyond the walls. It is deeply disturbing also to those who have found the existence of the walls essential to their own peace, well-being, and security. Out of sight, out of mind – this can no longer be the case.

So much emphasis is placed upon the fact of the existence of the walls that the symbolic fact of the walls is ignored or is an unknown quantity. It must be remembered that segregation is a mood, a state of mind, and its external manifestation is external. The root of the evil, and evil it is, is in the human spirit. Laws which make segregation illegal may or may not attack the root of the evil. Their great function is to deny the binding character of the external symbol by giving it no legal standing. They alert the body politic to the variety of external manifestations of the mood, the state of mind, and declare that wherever such manifestations appear, they are not to stand. This is most important because it calls attention to that of which segregation is the manifestation. As such it becomes a tutor or a guide for the human spirit. The law cannot deal with the human spirit directly. This is not within its universe of discourse.

What happens when the external symbol is outlawed and the walls of segregation are razed to the ground is a concern of the law only at the point that safeguards are being erected against other external symbols. And this is of vast importance – though negative basically. The reaction of the human spirit that has lived under the pattern of segregation on both sides of the wall, when the wall is removed, is apt to be one of panic and profound mental and spiritual distress. When my family and I lived on the campus of Howard University, our front yard was enclosed by a picket fence along the outside of which was a sidewalk leading from the main walk of the campus to the street. We had a dog whose name was Beariemore. It was his chief-in-the-yard sport to lie upon the steps facing the direction of the main walk, watching for the appearance of a Western Union boy coming toward the fence on his bicycle. Beariemore would wait for him at the corner of the fence, bark him all the way, the full length of the yard, and send him on his way. Then he would return to his former waiting position. One day after a very heavy snowfall, there were snowdrifts four to five feet high in one corner of the yard. Beariemore began his game as usual. Only this time when he chased one of the boys he did not take the snowdrift into account. I heard him yelp as if he were in great pain. I ran to the door, thinking that someone had hurt him. He was all right except that when he found himself over the fence with no barrier between him and the Western Union boy, he panicked. People who are conditioned to living behind the walls and those whose emotional security is dependent upon the stability of the walls are apt to be seized by a sense of panic, not only if the walls are removed, but if their removal is imminent. Such a condition is spiritual.

At such a time the real task of making or building a decent society of equality will emerge. Since segregation is the manifestation of a state of mind and mood of the human spirit, in a situation of threat a new and more subtle manifestation of the mood may appear. The wall is in the mind and in the spirit.

The situation is apt to be aggravated by the fact that the wall has existed so long that it may no longer be regarded as a symbol but as the thing itself. Wherever this is the case, the removal of the wall is thought to be the riddance of segregation. When I was a college boy in Atlanta, our football team played a team of regular army men from a Negro regiment. At dinner in the evening before the game, the behavior of the soldiers was very crude and somewhat embarrassing. At the next chapel service, the dean of the college, in commenting on the behavior of the soldiers, said, "It is a long way from slavery to a sense of freedom and no former slave or former slaveowner can make it in fifty years."

The issue then is twofold. The walls that divide must be demolished. They must be cast down, destroyed, uprooted. This is beyond debate. There must be ceaseless and unrelenting pressure to that end, using all the resources of our common life. These barriers must be seen for what they are, a disease of our society, the enemy of human decency and humane respect. In many ways, they are so much a part of our landscape that they seem to belong to the landscape and as such are regarded as germane to the American way of life. The resistance against their reversal is so rooted that it has created a new term in the current vocabulary – backlash. As has been suggested earlier, the walls seem so permanent that to advocate their removal must be conditional: those who are the obvious sufferers because of their presence must prove themselves worthy of such action. In other words, the walls are sacrosanct and to tamper with them can be done only out of a mood of grace and compassion. In fine, the walls have an established right to be, even though what this right is, is never quite clear and he who would remove the walls must show cause. Their destruction is such a monumental undertaking and is calling for such huge costs in human lives, resources of money, time, and energy, that an ever-widening weariness is apt to sweep over the land in the wake of the crumbling of the walls. And this is the danger. When the walls are down, it is then that the real work of building the healthy American society begins. The razing of the walls is prelude – important, critical, urgent, vital, but prelude nevertheless. About this there must be no mistake.

The removal of the walls is the first step in the attack on the mood of which they are a manifestation. Care must be exercised to see to it that new walls will not be built. One of the things that will make it easier to build new walls of segregation in the form of new kinds of discrimination is what has been aptly called the discrimination gap which is the huge burden of the American Negro. This aspect of the issue has been effectively described by Whitney Young, the executive director of the National Urban League, in his recent book *To Be Equal:* "For at this moment in history, if the United States honestly drops legal, practical, and subtle racial barriers to employment, housing, education, public accommodations, health and welfare facilities and services, the American Negro still will not achieve full equality in our lifetime." He goes on to say that "more than three centuries of abuse, humiliation, segregation, and bias have burdened the Negro with a handicap that will not automatically slip from his shoulders as discriminatory laws and practices are abandoned. The situation is much like that of two men running the mile in a track meet. One is well-equipped, wears track shoes and runs on cinders. The other is barefoot and runs in sand. Seeing that one runner is outdistancing the other with ease, you then put track shoes on the second fellow and place him on the cinder track also. Seconds later it should surprise no one to see that the second runner is still yards behind and will never catch up unless something else is done to even the contest."[127]

All the damage done by the existence of the walls must be repaired and healed. It is not a part of the work of this essay to suggest such a program. I know of no more comprehensive, clear, and creative blueprint to this end than is set forth in Whitney Young's book.

The other aspect of the issue has to do with the mood, the state of mind out of which discrimination and the response to discrimination come in the first instance. The issue is a moral and spiritual one and falls within the broad and specific scope of morality and religion. The point of departure for this final aspect of my discussion is to be found at the beginning of the essay where reference is made to the fact that Negroes and white persons are often excluded from each other's magnetic field of value. The first step in giving the kind of new orientation that will bring one into moral focus is the loss of fear. When the relationship between the groups is devoid of fear, then it becomes possible for them to relate to each other as human beings and have far more that unites them than divides them.

The burden of being black and the burden of being white is so heavy that it is rare in our society to experience oneself as a human being. It may be, I do not know, that to experience oneself as a human being is one with experiencing one's fellows as human beings. Precisely what does it mean to experience oneself as a human being? In the first place, it means that the individual must have a sense of kinship to life that transcends and goes beyond the immediate kinship of family or the organic kinship that binds him ethnically or "racially" or nationally. He has to feel that he belongs to his total environment. He has a sense of being an essential part of the structural relationship that exists between him and all other men, and between him, all other men, and the total external environment. As a human being, then, he belongs to life and the whole kingdom of life that includes all that lives and perhaps, also, all that has ever lived. In other words, he sees himself as a part of a continuing, breathing, living existence. To be a human being, then, is to be essentially alive in a living world.

> I like to feel that strange life beating up against me. I like to realize forms of life utterly unlike mine. When my own life feels small, and I am oppressed with it, I like to crush together, and see it in a picture, in an instant, a multitude of disconnected unlike phases of human life – a mediaeval monk with his string of beads pacing the quiet orchard, and looking up from the grass at his feet to the heavy fruit trees; little Malay boys playing naked on a shining sea-beach; a Hindu philosopher alone under his banyan tree, thinking, thinking, thinking, so that in the thought of God he may lose himself; a troop of Bacchanalians dressed in white, with crowns of vine-leaves, dancing along the Roman streets; a martyr on the night of his death looking through the narrow window to the sky, and feeling that already he has the wings that shall bear him up; an Epicurean discoursing at a Roman bath to a knot of his disciples on the nature of happiness; a Kaffir witch doctor, seeking for herbs by moonlight, while from the huts on the hillside come the sound of dogs barking, and the voices of women and children; a mother giving bread and milk to her children in little wooden basins and singing the evening song. I like to see it all: I feel it run through me – that life belongs to me; it makes my little life larger; it breaks down the narrow walls that shut me in.[128]

In a conversation with three Indian chiefs in one of the Canadian provinces, I was deeply impressed particularly by the reply of one of them to the query, "Are you a Canadian and then an Indian, or are you an Indian and then a Canadian?" His reply, as it came through the interpreter, was essentially this: "I come from some miles near the Arctic circle in the north country. I live with the snow, the ice, the sharp wind in the winter; with the streams, the flowing waters, the sun and the blossoms in summer. These flow into me and I flow into them. They keep me and I keep them. I am a part of them and they are a part of me. I am not sure what you mean when you say Indian or Canadian."[129]

What he is saying is that he has a sense of being a part of an extended life that belongs to him and to which he belongs. Instead of its spreading him out so that all the margins of the self fade and vanish away, it deepens and intensifies his essential sense of uniqueness without the devastation of a sense of being different. The same basic principle was manifested by an experience in Nigeria. At the close of a lecture before the Press Club, to which reference has been made, I was invited to a small room for refreshments. I asked for a kind of soft drink called ginger beer. My host opened the bottle, poured a little on the floor as he said, "For my ancestors," and then he filled my glass.[130] In this concept of the extended family, as I saw it, there is a variation of the same theme. To experience oneself as a human being is to know a sense of kinship with one's total environment and to recognize that it is this structural relationship that makes it possible for one to experience himself as a human *being*. Being white or black becomes merely incidental and is of no basic significance. Does this seem far-fetched and speculative or unrealistic?

What is meant here can be most clearly understood if we look at the conditions that obtain when differences of race, culture, ethnic, or national origin are sloughed off, when the essential fact of being a human being in the world is brought sharply into focus. In times of disaster, when the only thing that is relevant is that a man is stripped of all superficial categories that separate and divide, one gets some notion of what it means just to be a human being in the world among other human beings who are all structurally bound together by a total environment. Flood, earthquakes, disaster, know nothing of race or class. "God causes his sun to shine on the just and the unjust, his rain to fall on the evil and the good."

In our own country, when the national life is threatened, we make common cause in which for the moment everybody is counted in as an essential human being, possessed of certain resources that are needful for the survival of the common life. Despite the fact that this is an act of desperation and convenience, which act may be so interpreted by all, nevertheless the salutary effect obtains in the lives of those who are counted *in* merely because they are needed. As ironical as this is, nevertheless, the national registration during the last World War made an important impact on the life of Negroes, particularly in the South. A man who had been called "J. B." all his life and who knew no other name had to make a name for himself out of the initials. Think of what it meant to this man who had been regarded by his society as without name or significance to find himself suddenly on the receiving end of personal attention from the vast federal government. Now his name was known, his address duly noted, and his *intention* to be a consumer of certain goods such as meat, sugar, gasoline, and automobile tires was registered.[131] An entirely fresh dimension of personal awareness opened out before him. He began to experience himself as a human being. The fact that the new status was crisis-created must not obscure what was really at work here. The new experience did not know anything about a crisis situation.

But it is not only the situation of the collective crisis that creates a climate in which the individual human being emerges with an experience of himself as a human being. Here at last we come face to face with the original claim of religion and here I refer especially to the ethical insight brought into the stream of contemporary life by the Judaeo-Christian tradition.

It is most unfortunate that the trustees of this insight, namely the religious institutions, have failed singularly to witness to the insight. The impact upon the individual when he experiences himself as a human being is to regard himself as being of infinite worth. Such a sense of worth is not confined by narrow limits of the self so that worth may be determined by contrast with something or someone of less worth. No, this is a specious basis for ascertaining worth. Such a sense of worth is rooted in one's own consciousness which expands and expands until there is involved the totality of life itself. As important as is the clue to one's self-estimate, as found in the attitude of others in the environment, this is not now what is at issue. To experience oneself as a human being is to feel life moving through one and claiming one as a part of it. It is like the moment of insight into a new idea or an aspect of truth. What initially is grasped by the mind and held there for meaning begins slowly or suddenly to *hold* the mind as if the mind itself is being thought by a vaster and greater Mind. It is like the thing that happens when you are trying to explain something to a child and you finally succeed in doing so. Then the child says, "I see." In that moment you are no longer there in fact. The barrier that stood between the child's comprehension of the idea and the idea itself has been removed. There is a flowing together, as if the child and the idea were alone in all the universe!

The ultimate meaning of experience is felt in such a way that all of oneself is included. It is total, it is unified and unifying. It is not the experience of oneself as male or female, as black or white, as American or European. It is rather the experience of oneself as *being*. It is at such a time that one can hear the sound of the genuine in other human beings. This is to be able to identify with them. One man's response to the sound of the genuine in another man is to ascribe to the other man the same sense of infinite worth that one holds for oneself. When this happens, men are free to relate to each other as human beings – good, bad, mean, friendly, prejudiced, altruistic, but human beings. Whatever may be the nature of the shortcomings, they are seen from the view on the other side where the person lives whose shortcomings are being encountered.

This is the precious work of the imagination. There is an apt quotation in Russell Gordon Smith's Fugitive Papers: "On the seventh day, therefore, God could not rest. In the morning and the evening He busied Himself with terrible and beautiful concoctions and in the twilight of the seventh day He finished that which is of more import than the beasts of the earth and the fish of the sea and the lights of the firmament. And he called it Imagination because it was made in His own image; and those unto whom it is given shall see God."[132]

The place where the imagination shows its greatest power as the agent of God is in the miracle which it creates when one man, standing where he is, is able, while remaining there, to put himself in another man's place. Many years ago I was the overnight guest in the house of a friend. I was seated the next morning in the living room reading the morning paper. His little boy rode into the room in his kiddy car, stopped it in front of me, and said, "Mr. Thurman, will you please help me change my tire, I just had a blowout." I helped him jack up his car, take the old tire off, replace it with a spare, and then remove the jack. He sat in his car, stepped on the starter, but the motor would not start. He pulled out the choke; nothing happened. He got out of the car, opened each side of the hood, tinkered a little, then tried again with the same results. Then a strange thing happened. His shoulders became very stiff, a grim look swept over his tender countenance, and words flowed forth from his lips that were taken verbatim from his father under such circumstances. Still nothing happened. He got out of the car and came around to me. "Mr. Thurman, lend me your pencil." With my pencil in hand, he opened the gas tank of his car, put the pencil down into it, held it up to the light. "Ah, the tank is empty. No wonder it wouldn't start." He rushed out to the kitchen, came back with a glass of water, sat in his kiddy car, drank the water, started the motor, and rode out of the living room, through the dining room and into the kitchen.

This is the idea. A man can send his imagination forth to establish a beachhead in another man's spirit, and from that vantage point so to blend with the other's landscape that what he sees and feels is authentic — this is the great adventure in human relations. But this is not enough. The imagination must report its findings accurately without regard to prejudgments and private or collective fears. But this too is not enough. There must be both a spontaneous and a calculating response to such knowledge which will result in sharing of life and resources at their deepest level.

This is to experience oneself as a human being and to have that essential experience illumined and underscored by experiencing one's fellows as human beings. This is what every person seeks to have happen to himself. Every man lives under the necessity for being at home in his own house, as it were. He must not seem to himself to be alien to himself. This is the thing that happens when other human beings relate to him as if he were not a human being or less than a human being. It is possible for a man to declassify whole groups of people on the basis of certain criteria which he establishes or which he inherits. For instance, it may be to denigrate all people who come from a particular country, locale, or region, or all who speak a certain language, or all whose skin has pigmentation of any kind or a particular kind, or all who claim a different religious faith.

It may be that the experience of which we speak is not possible unless

and until the individual sees himself as being contained or held by something so much more than he is that his life is brought into a focus of self-
conscious meaning and value. Such an experience is possible only in the
light of ultimate values and ultimate meanings. And this is what religion
undertakes to guarantee; the extent to which Christianity is religious is
the extent to which it would guarantee such an experience for the individual.

Once when I was very young, my grandmother, sensing the meaning of
the constant threat under which I was living, told me about the message
of one of the slave ministers on her plantation. Whatever he developed as
his theme on the rare occasions when he was able to hold services for his
fellow slaves, the climactic moment came in these exhilarating words:
"You are not slaves; you are not *niggers* condemned forever to do your master's will—you are God's children." When those words were uttered a
warm glow crept all through the very being of the slaves, and they felt the
feeling of themselves run through them. Even at this far distance I can
relive the pulsing tremor of raw energy that was released in me as I responded to her words. The sense of being permanently grounded in God
gave to the people of that far-off time a way to experience themselves as
human beings.

But this is one side of the coin. The community of believers must be involved in the same kind of experience. The normal reaction to experiencing oneself as a human being is to seek to experience other people as human beings. This does not have to be in the name of religion exclusively.
Such a reaction is automatic unless there is some kind of intervention
which short-circuits the process. The thing that determines the character
of how one relates to one's fellows in any manner that has personal meaning in it, is shaped by how the individual defines others. This is but another aspect of the issue as discussed earlier. The community of Christian
believers are under the judgment of a command to love God, which is the
response to the awareness that God cares or loves the individual and one
must love one's neighbor as oneself.

There has emerged in the tradition of the Christian movement a secondary consideration, which is that the Christian must love especially those

who are Christians. Here is a tie that binds all Christians as members of the Body of Christ. If this is the case, then to be a part of the Body of Christ is to share the love of all those who are a part of the Body of Christ. To spell it out: not only would a Baptist be under the demand to love all other Baptists and a Methodist to love all other Methodists, etc., but it would be binding upon each one who claimed to be a Christian, and therefore a part of the body of Christ, to love all others who make such a claim. It would follow then that the Christian would be unique among other men in that the Christian is secure in the love of other Christians. Indeed at one time in the history of Christianity it was this that separated the Christian from the world. "Behold how the Christians love each other." The formula can be stated categorically: the Christian has a special sense of being loved by God because he accepts the idea that God loved him by giving His son for his redemption. His response to the redemptive giving of God is to love God. "I love him because he first loved me." All Christians are involved in this relationship with God, therefore all Christians must give love to one another as a part of the giving of love to God.

The tragedy is that even among those whose profession of faith subscribes completely to the above, the total relationship gives evidence of another kind. In fact, it is precisely accurate to say that the church, which is the institutional expression of the doctrine, has given little indication that being a member of the Body of Christ has any bearing on how one member relates to the other members. Granted it may be less evident among those who are a part of the same sectarian tradition. There is much to indicate that the further a particular group may be from the so-called mainstream of the convention of the doctrine, the more apt we may be to find the practice of love of all who belong to the household of faith. One of my earliest memories is of greeting people at our door who asked for my parents because they wanted to talk to them about religion. Two things I remember: they called themselves Russellites,[133] and despite the fact that they were white they made themselves at home in the living room. Nothing entered into what they did or what they said that drew the color line.

Until most recently, no one expected the white Christian to love the black Christian or the black Christian to love the white Christian. Historically in this country, the church has given the sweep of its moral force to the practice of segregation within its own community of believers. To the extent to which this has been done, the church has violated one of the central elements in its own commitment. It has dared to demonstrate that the commitment is not central, that it does not believe that Christians are bound to love one another.

The effect of its position with reference to Christians of other races is far-reaching. It is to be noted that the doctrine has to be accommodated and dealt with in a manner that will hold the doctrine secure and at the same time tolerate its profound violation. How is this accomplished? With reference to the Negro, the church has promulgated a doctrine that makes the Negro the object of its salvation while at the same time it denies him the status of a human being, thereby enhancing the difficulties he must face in his effort to experience himself as a human being. Time after weary time, the church has dishonored its Lord. When I asked Mr. Gandhi, "What is the greatest handicap that Jesus has in India?" instantly he replied, "Christianity." And this is what he meant.

The purpose here is not to indict but rather it is to lament the fact that such is the situation. The point must be clear that the commitment to love as it stands at the center of the Christian doctrine of God has not prevented the Christian from excluding Negroes from his Christian fellowship, nor has it prevented the Christian who is Negro from excluding white people from his Christian fellowship. To the extent that this is true, being Christian may not involve a person either in experiencing himself as a human being or in relating to others so as to experience them as human beings. The sad fact is that being Jewish, Catholic, or Protestant seems to make little difference in this regard.

If being Christian does not demand that all Christians love each other and thereby become deeply engaged in experiencing themselves as human beings, it would seem futile to expect that Christians as Christians would be concerned about the secular community in its gross practices of prejudice and discrimination. If a black Christian and a white Christian, in encounter, cannot reach out to each other in mutual realization because of that which they are experiencing in common, then there should be no surprise that the Christian institution has been powerless in the presence of the color bar in society. Rather it has reflected the presence of the color bar within its own institutional life.

On the other hand, if Christians practiced brotherhood among Christians, this would be one limited step in the direction of a new order among men. Think of what this would mean. Wherever one Christian met or dealt with another Christian, there would be a socially redemptive encounter. They would be like the Gulf Stream or the Japanese Current tempering and softening the climate in all directions. Indeed the Christian would be a leaven at all levels of the community and in public and private living. Of course, such a situation may lend itself to all kinds of exploitation and betrayals – but the Christian would be one of the bulwarks of integrity in human relations in an immoral society.

If the Christian limited his practice to other Christians, thereby guaranteeing that the church, wherever it existed, at whatever cost, would not tolerate segregation within its body, then there would be a kind of fierce logic in its position. It would be consistent within itself because it would practice brotherhood without regard to race, color, and all the other barriers. It would make for a kind of arrogance and bigotry toward those who were not fortunate or wise enough to put themselves in the way of being Christian. This would narrow the basis of the faith deliberately, while at the same time providing enough room for the outsider to come in and belong. But the church has historically tended to reject this alternative.

It is true and freely acknowledged that there are many changes afoot. Here and there through the years the Gospel has been at work despite the prohibition placed upon it by many denials. There is a power in the teaching which, when released, goes on to work its perfect work. Slowly there have emerged certain ingredients in the social climate that have had a softening effect. Much of this is due to the introduction of the teachings of Jesus and the Christian religious experience into society.

In recent time it has become increasingly a part of the public policy and private practice of the church to put itself squarely on the side of cleaning its own house of the evils that separate the brethren. It has become more and more aggressive in attacking the presence of those same evils wherever they are in our society. It is a prestige factor in the church to take a challenging position in the matter of the treatment of Negroes. Very often when I am visiting in a city, clergymen and laymen proudly announce that their particular church is "integrated," or they may complain that they are wide open in the welcome of Negroes but that Negroes do not come. One is glad to witness the changes that are taking place and may regard the changes as delayed reactions to the impact of the Gospel in the church itself. But the thought persists that this is the response of the church to the pressure of the secular community upon it, rather than the response of the church to the genius of the Gospel which it proclaims. Perhaps it is both. Even the church cannot be in the position of establishing the ground rules by which God works in the development of the good life for His children.

But why has the church been such a tragic witness to its own Gospel? It does seem to me at times that it is because the church is not sufficiently religious. By this I mean that it is not wide open to the Spirit of the living God. Its genius as an institution has to be sectarian in character. Perhaps there can be no such thing among men as the Church of God; it is the nature of institutionalism to be adjectival; some qualifying word must always precede the word "church." It has to be some *kind* of church, and this gives it its unique character and position.

This fact creates a terrible dilemma. How important is the limiting and defining character? It may be that the church as such is an abstraction which only becomes concrete when a peculiar pattern or style of worship, etiquette, or doctrine emerges to define the character and give context to the abstraction. Nothing is ultimately admissible that may threaten the institutional structure that gives to the Christian religion its form and substance. But suppose as a part of the form and substance of the church all believers must commit themselves to loving all men, believers and nonbelievers, as children of God and therefore members one of another? Then the tremendous resources of such a church would be at the disposal of the performing ethic. Under such a circumstance, the whole missionary-conversion process would be reversed – men would knock at the door of the church to find out what they need to do to become what, in evidence, the Christian is. The life that the church lives in the world would "bring the world to Christ." This surely means first of all to go ye into one's very own world, one's very own life, to go into every part of one's very own being and proclaim the good news that one can be free to experience oneself as a child of God and to experience all other men as children of God. Of such is a part of the miracle of Jesus. Men came to him with the searching

question, What must I do? How may I? He made the life of God contagious!

The problem may not be so simple. It is too easy to say or to believe that
the church has not been true to its own Gospel. The question that de-
serves probing is Why? Is it because of human frailty? Is it because man
has not evolved to the point that he is sufficiently human to deal justly and
to promote the common good? Is there some inherent limitation in the
nature of man that works against his doing for himself and with and on
behalf of others that which makes for harmony, wholeness, love? Is it because of what the church recognizes as original sin? If not, precisely from
what is the believer saved by the death and resurrection of Christ? Are the
roots of conflict deep into a long forgotten past?

Why is it that in many aspects of life that are regarded as secular one is
apt to see more sharing, more of a tendency for human beings to experience themselves as human beings, than in those areas that are recognized
as being religious? There seems to be more of a striving toward equality of
treatment in many so-called secular institutions in our society than has
characterized those institutions whose formal religious commitment demands that they practice the art of brotherhood. When I was in college, I
heard two Negro men arguing on this very issue. We were on an all-day
train ride in the third of the day coach designated for Negroes. Finally, one
of the men, to clinch his point, said, "If I had committed a crime and was
being tried in court, I would much rather have a jury made up of gamblers,
race track men, pimps, than one made up of people who profess Christianity. I know I'd get much fairer treatment."

There is something out of line somewhere. Can it be that matters
which have to do with human relations are not the legitimate concern of
religion? Hardly. The fact cannot be ignored that generally our society
does not expect the church to be any kind of guide in these matters. It
seems to me that one of the really tremendous things that is happening
before our very eyes is that the religious community is now being judged
by the same standards of human relations as the secular institutions in our
society. This means that the church is slowly winning the right to be regarded as an institution that has a stake in the earthly fate of mankind. It
has always concerned itself with charity, with good works, with the meet-

ing of the creature needs of man; it has always concerned itself with the preaching of a doctrine of salvation which addressed itself to the spiritual condition as far as the soul was concerned; bur for some reason that has puzzled me all of my life, the religious community tended not to concern itself with the total needs of a man as a human being. And that, after all, is what matters most. Always it is a human being who hungers, who is sick, who is ignorant, who suffers. And he cannot be touched in any way that counts unless the word gets through to him that he is being experienced as a human being by the person for whom he is the object of good works.

Perhaps there is something inherent in the religious experience that always pulls back toward the personal center out of which the individual operates and the religious context that gives existential meaning to the experience itself. It is this latter frame of reference that creates the categories out of which the dogma of a particular faith comes. In this sense it may seem an unrealistic demand that religious experience be universal. If this is a true picture, then such notions or concepts as brotherhood, reverence for life, respect for personality, do not rightfully belong to the behavior pattern of the religious devotee. Such ideas would then invade the religious man's life from the wider context of his living, the areas of his life that are beyond and outside of the parochial and the sectarian character of his religious faith. I have often pondered the fact that men of different faiths may share common experiences which are outside of their specifically religious fellowship, and that on behalf of such demands they may make tremendous sacrifices, without feeling under any necessity to share the intimacy of their experience of God.

Or it may be in order to raise a question about the universality of an ethic which grows out of a sectarian or parochial religious experience. Could it be that we are face to face with an inherent weakness in religious experience, as such, that it is private, personal, and binding upon the individual only to the extent that he identifies himself with another and thereby becoming one with him at all the levels and all the ways that are significant? Here may be a clue, for wherever the Christian religious experience has made a difference in the one-to-one relationship of the believer, one sees this kind of private, personal identification at work. When I identify with a man, I become one with him and in him I see myself. I remember a quotation out of the past – the statement "know thyself" has been taken more mystically from the statement "thou hast seen thy brother, thou has seen thy God." This is the true meaning of the reference earlier about listening for the sound of the genuine in another. Such an experience cannot become a dogma – it has to remain experiential all the way. It is a probing process trying to find the opening into another. And it requires exposure, sustained exposure. One of the great obstacles to such exposure is the fact of segregation.

The religious experience as I have known it seems to swing wide the door, not merely into Life but into lives. I am confident that my own call to the religious vocation cannot be separated from the slowly emerging disclosure that my religious experience makes it possible for me to experience myself as a human being and thus keep a very real psychological distance between myself and the hostilities of my environment. Through the years it has driven me more and more to seek to make as a normal part of my relations with men the experiencing of them as human beings. When this happens love has essential materials with which to work. And contrary to the general religious teaching, men would not need to stretch themselves out of shape in order to love. On the contrary, a man comes into possession of himself more completely when he is *free* to love another.

I have dwelt at length upon the necessity that is laid upon the church and the Christian because the Christian Church is still one of the major centers of influence in the American community. Too, the Christian Church claims to be under the judgment of God as it fulfills itself in human history. But it must be remembered that what is true in any religion is to be found in that religion because it is true, it is not true because it is found in that religion. The ethical insight which makes for the most healthy and creative human relations is not the unique possession of any religion, however inspired it may be. It does not belong exclusively to any people or to any age. It has an ancient history, and it has been at work informing the quality of life and human relations longer than the records and the memories of man. Just as scattered through the earliest accounts of man's journey on this planet are flashes and shafts of light illuminating the meaning

of man and his fellows, so in our times we find the widest variety of experiments pointing in the same direction and making manifest the same
goals. Men are made for one another. In this grand discovery there is a disclosure of another dimension: this experience of one another is not
enough. There is a meaning in life greater than, but informing, all the immediate meanings – and the name given to this meaning is religion, because it embodies, however faintly, a sense of the ultimate and the divine.

There is a spirit abroad in life of which the Judaeo-Christian ethic is
but one expression. It is a spirit that makes for wholeness and for community; it finds its way into the quiet solitude of a Supreme Court justice
when he ponders the constitutionality of an act of Congress which guarantees civil rights to all its citizens; it settles in the pools of light in the face
of a little girl as with her frailty she challenges the hard frightened heart of
a police chief; it walks along the lonely road with the solitary protest
marcher and settles over him with a benediction as he falls by the assassin's bullet fired from ambush; it kindles the fires of unity in the heart of
Jewish Rabbi, Catholic Priest, and Protestant Minister as they join arms
together, giving witness to their God on behalf of a brotherhood that transcends creed, race, sex, and religion; it makes a path to Walden Pond and
ignites the flame of nonviolence in the mind of a Thoreau and burns
through his liquid words from the Atlantic to the Pacific; it broods over the
demonstrators for justice and brings comfort to the desolate and forgotten
who have no memory of what it is to feel the rhythm of belonging to the
race of men; it knows no country and its allies are to be found wherever
the heart is kind and the collective will and the private endeavor seek to
make justice where injustice abounds, to make peace where chaos is rampant, and to make the voice heard on behalf of the helpless and the weak.
It is the voice of God and the voice of man; it is the meaning of all the strivings of the whole human race toward a world of friendly men underneath
a friendly sky.

᧒ | *Whitney Young: What Can I Do? (1971)*

Whitney Young, a social worker by profession, was one of the most controversial leaders
of the modern Civil Rights movement.[134] *As executive director of the National Urban*
League during the turbulent decade of the 1960s, he reoriented the older, moderate orga-
nization's mission from one of providing social services to urban black communities to
one of pursuing civil rights. Yet throughout the period he also preserved close ties with
white corporate and political leaders whose funding and political clout enabled the
NUL to continue to resource poor black communities; pressed civil rights activists to
maintain "respectability" and lawfulness; and broke with King and others over their op-
position to the Vietnam War. Only late in his tenure with the NUL did he publicly op-
pose the war and lend partial support to the Black Power movement's call for greater self-
determination and autonomy within black communities. When Young died in 1971 at
the relatively young age of 49, the black freedom struggle was passing through a period
of fragmentation and intense self-examination. Thurman was called upon to deliver the
eulogy for his friend at Riverside Church in New York City, which he expanded a few
weeks later into the following address delivered at San Francisco's First Unitarian
Church. Through the prism of Whitney Young's life Thurman chose to examine the hard
choices one is forced to make, especially during the heat of social turmoil, which inevita-
bly lead to controversy and even enmity. This is why it is essential to ground one's short
life in love of God's world and to take seriously the cultivation of virtues and practices
that reflect self-respect.

IN THE PRESENCE OF DEATH there are no rich or poor, good or bad, black
or white, educated or uneducated – just human beings without defenses
and pretensions. All poses tend to fade away, and in the great stillness surrounding the silent corpse each man knows that the days of his life are
numbered and the time of his living is measured. What he must do with
his life or what he is doing with this life becomes at once an urgent and
dramatic question.

This thought came upon me with overwhelming intensity as I studied
the faces of many people in the vast congregation at Riverside Church,
gathered to celebrate the life of Whitney Young. I could think of no other
occasion which, by choice, would bring together the very rich and the
poor, the black separatist and the white segregationist, those who had
abandoned all hope for the internal reordering of society on the basis of
equality of opportunity and privilege, and those who were dedicated to an
orderly reshuffling of priorities which would give maximum participation
to all in the fruits of a good society; those who had some grasp of the magnitude of the loss in the passing of this man, feeling that once again the
contradictions of life were not only persistent but final, and those who
wept silently because a personal friend, a wonderful husband, lover, and
father would no longer come home with the smell of the world upon him,
to find quiet rest and the deep restoration of great love; those who were a
part of the organization identified with his name who knew him as a
worker and chief, and those who had little grasp of the function of the Urban League but only knew that some measure of their self-respect had
been restored through membership in a Street Academy or through a job
which had given them a toe hold up the economic ladder. These, and
many others, were there on that fateful Tuesday because Whitney Young
had asked and answered the central question, What can I do in the time
that I have?

In seeking an answer to the question, What can I do? we may get important clues from sober reflection on the life of Whitney Young. In the first
place, he knew what we all know: all a man has is a life, all that a man is
given is a life. It has been wisely said, "We must understand that the social
problems in America are people. It is time to understand that you are
people and that there is a direct connection between these problems and

the way you choose to live. For those social problems are nothing more than the way Americans choose to live; and if you want to speak to those people's lives, then you have to speak to them with your life. You can do that."

Whitney Young spoke with his life to Americans of power and authority, who were in temporary control of the economic and political structure. How did he do it? In the first place, he refused to separate his destiny from their destiny and their destiny from his. Every move he made of challenge, or negotiation, or joint or separate commitment was within the framework of a sense of common destiny. He refused to accept the status of an outsider in America society. He insisted on being regarded as an insider who had the same stakes in the society as those who felt that they could say "yes" or "no" with the power to make it stick.

Always he did his homework. It was his job to know as much about the issues as any man around the conference table. Singularly, this kept him from being on the defensive. No man could look him in the face and feel sorry for him because he had his hand out as a beggar. Because he had done his homework, he could challenge, confront, and convince. He was eloquent, but he did not depend upon rhetoric. Always he tied men irrevocably to the hard facts of the problem from which they could not extricate themselves, until they put their imaginations and resources and their lives at the disposal of the issues even as Whitney Young was doing. Many persons in government and business and philanthropy, present on the fateful Tuesday, regarded the silent figure in the bronze coffin as the one man who had helped them discover what they could do from within the citadels of power and control in which they lived. A man speaks to his time with his life, it is all that he has, it is all that is given him. That is one clue.

What can I do? Given the fact of his life, a man has to decide where he will take his stand, being mindful that all that is given him is his life. Sometime ago a friend sent me this quotation – I do not know the author –

"You say the little efforts that I make
Will do no good,
They never will prevail
To tip the hovering scale where justice keeps in balance.
I do not think I ever thought they would.

But I am prejudiced beyond debate
In favor of my right,
To choose which side shall feel
The stubborn ounces of my weight."

It was Whitney's personal decision to become first a social worker, as the simplest and most direct way to equip himself technically for relating the resources of society directly to the needs of people within the society. After securing his professional equipment he had to decide through which existing agency he would have the fullest scope for growth, development, and personal and professional fulfillment. For him, the choice was the Urban League. Sometime later there came the opportunity to put his field experience at the center of a training institution where maximum scrutiny could be given to a detached look at the complexities involved in the life of the poor, the defenseless, who at the same time were faceless and anonymous because they were black. To be poor in an affluent society was a catastrophe, to be black in and poor was a disaster. For this meant that the insidious climate of poverty was internalized, with the result in hopelessness and despair. It was not an accident that the city was Atlanta, that rare urban community in which the bitter fruits of segregation had, in some strange way, nourished a black consciousness confined largely to the expression of an academic and economic aristocracy deep within the heart of the segregated community. Here Whitney could observe the strength and the ultimate weakness of a black economy within the larger American economy, a black society within the larger white society. As long as these were separate units with the Great Divide between, the imperative of a common cause and a common destiny would have no meaning and existential reality. It is out of this experience, during the long days behind the segregated walls of the Atlanta School of Social Work within the larger segregated community of the Atlanta university system, that the conviction grew in him, as he put it: "We need a generation of people who have the commitment and creativity to try integration – to explore the creative possibilities of diversity." Continuing, he insists; "But I don't think it rests in the hands of the Negro. He has already said in a thousand ways that he believes in America. Now the time has come for America to say, "I believe in you."

Of course, as the civil rights struggle came more and more into focus, it could have been very easy for him to be sidetracked, confused, and a wanderer in search of a vision which he once saw. Just as he had refused to allow white society and its leaders to determine both how he felt and how he functioned, he refused to allow black society and its leaders to determine how he felt and how he functioned. To the end of his life he was his own man. From Atlanta he moved onto the national scene as the chief of the National Urban League. It was from that position that he catapulted into national and international prominence. But those who observed him closely or knew him well recognized the same hard-headed purpose that dominated his life: to put the resources of the society at the disposal of the needs of the society.

A man speaks to his time not only with his life but by making a choice as to where he will stand and live a life of social as well as private responsibility. Where can I put my skill, my imagination – limited as they may be – at the disposal of my time, my society, that my life will say clearly, "It is for this that I stand and it is against this that I stand. I shall put my little resources at the disposal of the needs of the society of which I am a part." "I am prejudiced beyond debate in favor of my right to choose which side shall feel the stubborn ounces of my weight." And this is his word to us. What can I do? I can always put the resources of my life at the disposal of the needs of the society of which I am a part.

At this critical period in American society, Whitney wrestled with the central dilemma in the mind of every thoughtful black man. At the risk of going back to an earlier part of my statement and thereby seeming repetitious, I close my remarks with a brief discussion of how, as it seems to me, Whitney Young dealt with this central dilemma. For it is here that we see, in clearest focus, his rare gifts of creative leadership. It was always his insistence that a man had to be at home somewhere before he could feel at home everywhere. He was a black man, identified in his roots with his own black people. But he did come to rest there. It was clear to him that the black man in America is also an American, profoundly involved in and a part of the development of an American society in which the walls that separate and divide black and white brothers would have no final relevancy. In order for this to be achieved, there was need for many techniques, many strategies. He saw strategy as people working very hard to make their own lives a commitment to something which they regarded as both crucial and critical. Added to all this was the use of a creative imagination and an infectious sense of humor. Thus, in our time, he became the symbol of hard headed, clear minded reconciliation between black and white, between rich and poor – often as an unenviable role, fraught with frustration, sometimes vilification and the profoundest misunderstanding. But Whitney chose this role as the most creative approach to the dilemma created when the will to separateness as a technique both for identity and survival was challenged by the *will* to community as a concept big enough to provide for the widest divergencies within the creative synthesis which is at once the genius of the democratic dogma. Whatever may be our reaction to his solution to this central dilemma, we are challenged to answer this basic question of our times with the intelligence, wisdom, and courage which he brought to a hopeful solution.

It may be that what he did not or could not accomplish in his living may be revealed to us in his dying. What can I do? was always his question. I have only my life. I shall speak to my times with its meaning and integrity. What can I do? I have only my life. "You say the little efforts that I make will do no good, they never will prevail to tip the hovering scale where justice keeps in balance. I do not think I ever thought they would. But I am prejudiced beyond debate in favor of my right to choose which side shall feel the stubborn ounces of my weight." The choice is ours, yours, and mine.

∞ | *America in Search of a Soul* (1976)

"America in Search of a Soul," delivered in the year of the bicentennial celebration of the United States, captures the essence of Thurman's understanding of America's role in world history and what he perceives to be its divinely sanctioned mission.[135] For Thurman, the Declaration of Independence, the Constitution, and the Emancipation Proclamation are the pivotal documents of the American civic and moral experience.[136] These civil documents hold out the hope of individual freedom and equality under God and remind Americans of their role as stewards of the democratic ideal. In this piece he also refers to Lincoln's famous Gettysburg Address as a mandate for the rejuvenation of a "new nation" entrusted with the moral responsibility of realizing the democratic ideal in the world with other nations. Composed during the infamous 1975–76 Boston busing crisis, this lecture underscores Thurman's concern with racism as an obstacle to Americans' realization of democracy at home and in the world.[137] With the potential for nuclear devastation wrought by the creation of the atomic bomb and, presumably, the rapid development of nuclear technology in the 1970s, however, Thurman also strikes a note of fear that it may be too late to realize the American Dream. The lecture has been transcribed from audiotape for reproduction here, giving readers some sense of Thurman's extemporaneous speaking style. However, the editors have not included his opening reading of the Gettysburg Address and "A Strange Freedom," the latter which appears at the beginning of this volume.

I BEGIN MY THINKING WITH YOU tonight from a background and out of the insight of a man who is earnestly engaged in an effort, an exercise, a commitment to be a religious man. I do not deal with the subject as one in a political field, but as one in the world of religion. I begin then my thinking about the subject from within the framework of certain basic religious affirmations. It is these that I want to state as directly and simply as possible.

It is my affirmation, my faith, that God is the Creator of Life. And not merely Life, but the Creator of the living substance out of which all particular manifestations of life emerge in the first place. Further, I believe that God is the Creator of existence, that God bottoms existence. So that from within the framework of my thought the totality of life on this planet—with all of its limitations, its fresh starts, its false starts, its rising and its falling—all of this is a lung through which the Creator of Life is bringing His breath into particular beings and manifestations. Therefore, I feel that Life is alive. Now this concept is so simple that perhaps the mind has some difficulty in reducing it to a manageable unit as an object of thought. But to me it is the aliveness of Life that provides the creative, churning continuum out of which all existences arise in the first place. The mind is so overwhelmed by the massive attack of all of these particular representations of vitality, that the simplest fact of all is overlooked, that Life itself is alive, is a living, breathing, pulsing, universal, total experience. When I think of America, when I think of the American "dream" if dream is the right word, I do not think of it outside of a structure of the kind that I have stated.

I begin with the simple fact that America, however we may define it for ourselves, is an expression of one creative process coming into being more and more as its inner mystery, which is inherent in Life, begins to unfold as process, as laws, as constitutions. Therefore, my first notion for your consideration, with all of this as a background, is that the soul of America is being sought as a part of its unfolding with the soul of America as a part of the given. It is not an accident to me that at a particular time in the history of our world, there came to this continent, in a most extraordinary way, groups of people with different backgrounds, with different interests, with different cultural idioms to land themselves among a people who were as different in terms of ethos, in terms of dreams, hopes, aspira-

tions as one could possibly imagine; and that without any apparent intentions of initially establishing a new order, a new way of living, a new series
of expressions of the common life, there emerged, as a result of that experience, something that was referred to in Lincoln's famous Gettysburg address as "a new nation," conceived as a new idea for a nation.

We have developed a society in which the experience of community
springing out of a common commitment which grew out of a common crisis, is the binding factor. At first, apparently, there was no intention to establish any kind of new world, any kind of new order, so that from my
point of view it seems to me that the fact that America became America,
a new people, a new order, a new political arrangement, was a part of the
revelation of the Creator working itself out in the time-space relationships between men in a strange and awkward world. But the thing that appeals to me most directly is that these people who came from Europe and
from other parts of the world were knit together by political ideas and ideals which were not created by them, but which represented a creative synthesis which revealed a projection of their own hopes and fears, dreams
and aspirations. It found formal statement in a Declaration of Independence, in a Bill of Rights, in a Constitution, in a form of government
unique in many ways. As circumstantial as that may be, there is something still more circumstantial which, from my point of view, is miraculous. It took place in North America – a land isolated from the stable civilized communal arrangements in Europe, and protected by two oceans, in
a climate almost ideal. Even Californians must share with the rest of the
country the glory of this idyllic natural circumstance.

Now get the picture. Here was a cross section of people with a medley
of cultural backgrounds and orientations, but all within a broad European
pattern, landing in the midst of what seems to have been an indigenous
people, isolated by two oceans, in a climate in which all of the basic creature needs and demands of life could be fulfilled by minimal effort. This
cross section of people was inspired by a political idea and a political theory which could only be developed within a sufficient time interval to test
whether or not they, the people of the colonies, could accommodate
themselves not only to each other, but also to the Indians whom they
found here. It was as if the Creator of Life and existence was anticipating

another moment in time far removed from this moment in history of which I speak.

They were a diverse people in a fertile land, a benevolent and beneficient land, brooded over by a political theory rooted in a certain way of thinking about the nature of life and the nature of existence – brooding over it as the spirit of the hives broods over the places where the bees make honey. (Once the spirit of the hive is no longer brooding, the bee cannot make honey, he's just another insect.) This was a political theory inspired by a fundamental way of thinking about the nature of life and the nature of man, with a time interval of sufficient duration to provide the opportunity, not the necessity, mark my word, but the opportunity, for growth in relatedness, for primary face-to-face discovery of the secret of a life far removed from one's own background and culture. In other words, the opportunity to experience community, an inner sense of relatedness defined by the external boundaries within which life is being lived. It was as if the Creator of existence wanted to discover whether or not a certain ideal could be realized in time and space, in anticipation of a time when time and space would be reduced to zero; when the whole planet would be as one little neighborhood in one little town.

This meant that somewhere on the planet there would be a primary unit of human beings being tutored in the graces of communal relatedness, crossing lines of race, of color, or creed, or background, of enforced or restricted neighborhoods. Nowhere else on the planet was this taking place. Nowhere else. And all of this would occur *before* the creative mind of modern man was to grapple with the stubborn and unyielding and recalcitrant stuff or nature, until at last by his intensive and sophisticated science, grudgingly, the secrets of nature would be revealed and the mind would seize upon the secrets and use them in pursuit of private ends. Suppose that man had developed the secret of the atom, and all of the other devices by which we have reduced time and space to zero, before there had been this colossal experience, this exposure to neighborliness? We live in panic now lest some man whose digestion goes awry will, in a moment of pain or panic, reach out and touch the wrong button. But the anxiety and fear that dog the footsteps of modern man is not to be compared with what would have happened if the whole process had been reversed –

if nowhere on this planet there had been the opportunity to experience growth in community day by day, hard year by hard year, in the midst of all kinds of struggle. But the Creator of existence, I think, was trying to see if it were possible for Him to realize Himself, to come to Himself, not in an individual expression of His creation, but in the *collective* sense; not by mindless instinct-bound creatures – but by those created in His own image.

So He said, "I wonder if I dare do this?" He tested it in all ways His great creativity could figure out: "I'll set up somewhere a school and I'll call that school, America." (Now don't be upset by what seems to be a doctrine of manifest destiny.[138] Don't be bothered by that.) "But I'll set up a school somewhere and I'll time it well, so that it will pre-date some other secrets that I'm going to give to my children, the secret of my energy, so that there will be a backlog of accumulated social and political experience, ethical, moral, religious experience if you please, upon which my children may draw totally and I'll make some dry runs while I'm doing this."

Now, school is out. School is out and it's been out for some time. And the soul of America that is seeking to realize itself in the life of America, is revealed by the degree to which the enforced experience of neighborhoods, which represents our 200 years, can be a living, practicing part of neighborliness, which is the fulfillment of the dream.

We have worked at this. I think the two principles that have been guide-posts for this as they emerged in the great Declaration, which is a sort of mandate, have to do with definitions – pragmatic definitions, practical definitions, empirical definitions – of equality and freedom, equality and freedom.

One comment about the first. When I think about the meaning of equality against this background, I think of many kinds of definitions. Some, the result of the fact that I'm a child of these times: Equality of opportunity, Equality of privilege, Equality of gifts. But in every one of these there is the germ of a cult that seeks to nullify this equality. This is the Cult of Inequality. So that I am stripped to what seems to me to be the literal essence of my own pulse beat in which the sense of equality is grounded – that is the sense of my own self, my own self. My own self as distinguished from your self. My own self, of infinite worth and significance. This may be, perhaps, the only authentic equality that there is. I've been worrying over all of this for a long time. *The equality of infinite worth.* That is my truest experience of myself. That is not a derivative from any judgment external to myself, that is not located in any extension of myself, not located in any extenuating circumstances with regard to myself, not related to any definition that does not arise out of that, out of which, at last, the true grounds of my own self-respect arise. This definition of equality is implicit then in that aspect of the soul of America that is still in the process of realizing itself, in institutions, in communal relations, in social arrangements and in the security of its laws.

In the winter of the middle thirties my wife and I travelled some 16,000 miles in India, Burma and Ceylon visiting colleges and universities. It was a difficult time because whenever we came down to tight, analytical discussions with Indian students, whether they were Hindu, Buddhists or Christians, they always said to us, "We are so much better off than you are." They were still under British rule. "We are so much better off than you are because" and then go on to give a variety of reasons. Then I would say that one important difference between their society and ours was that brooding over all of the inequities in our society is a Supreme Court. And therefore the final interpretations of the genius of the democratic dogma was given into the hands of men whose job it was to monitor the life of the nation by the profoundest interpretations of the meaning of the Constitution and the Bill of Rights. This the students did not have. There was always the possibility for me, which for the Indians simply wasn't true, that there was at work in the structure of American society that which is always involved in condemning that which violates the spirit and the genius of the democratic dogma itself.

The second summary statement bearing on all of this has to do with freedom. When I think about freedom it is always from the point of view of the true distinction between freedom and liberty. As I interpret the American story, liberty has to do primarily with elements of the social contract. It can be given, it can be taken away. It can be wiped out. It is related to external but very important agreements within the structure of the society itself. Therefore, it can be altered by law, improved, destroyed, prostituted, or glorified. But that was not what was meant by freedom orig-

inally. Freedom, as defined in the slow development of the language of the
Constitution, had to be redefined many times. What was finally being said
was that freedom is a quality of being. It cannot be given and it cannot be
taken away. Liberty can be taken away. But freedom! Freedom is the process by which, standing in my place where I am, I can so act in that place
as to influence, order, alter, or change the future – that time is not frozen,
that life is not so fixed that it cannot respond to my own will, my own inner
processes. Standing in my place I can so order my life and varied dimensions of my environment as to influence, and often determine and shape,
the future.

But it is more than this. It is the private, intimate, primary exercise of
a profound and unique sense of alternatives. Now this is very important.
Freedom, as it was thought of in that far-off time, and as it has been working itself out at least two hundred years – freedom is the sense of option.
Mark you, I do not say that freedom is the exercise of option. That may not
be possible. But freedom is the sense of option, the sense of alternatives
which only I can affect. And this is the thing that threatens all dictator-
ships, all tyrants, because there is not any way which the external forces in
the environment can reach inside and cause the individual human spirit
to relax and give up its sense of option.

Let me illustrate. When I was a boy, living in Florida, I went with my
sister one summer day out into the woods near our house to pick huckle-
berries. I was younger than she. I was always trying to grow up and she was
always trying to cut off my growth. As we walked along the country road I
noticed a baby snake about the length of my foot. I knew how she felt
about old snakes, young snakes, baby snakes, any kind of snake. I saw it
before she did and I said to myself, "Now is my chance." And so I said,
"Henrietta look at this." And she reacted. And then I said, "Oh, I'm not
afraid of it. To show you I'll stand on it." So I put one of my feet on top of
this little creature and the weight of my body made it impossible for him
to move. Then I felt a series of simple, quiet, rhythmic spasms under my
foot. The snake couldn't move, but he could do this wiggle. He kept alive
the sense of option. Even though he couldn't opt the options. Now this is
what I mean: that freedom is a sense of option, and wherever this dies,
wherever elements in the environment are internalized by people so as to

paralyze this sense, then all the lights go out and the soul of the people begins to rot.

Now this carries with it very definite responsibilities, and these responsibilities are the safeguard against the degradation of the democratic dogma. One is a sense of responsibility for one's own actions. [Without this], something is cut off, the oxygen is taken out of the air and the person dies, perishes. That is why I think the myth of George Washington and the cherry tree has remained in our culture. "I did it with my little hatchet. I did it!"

There is the second aspect of freedom that belongs in any discussion about it, and that is that freedom is my own responsibility for my own reactions *to* the events, the forces, the influences that impinge upon my life, that are not responsive to my will, however good that will may be – impersonal forces that don't even know that as an individual I am here. But I must deal with them at the point at which they touch my life. And I can say, you see, that it is not my fault that forces, alien to my mind and spirit, created this situation that results in my predicament. True this may be, but I'm not relieved if I would be free. I must take the responsibility for how, mark my word, *how* I react to the forces that impinge upon my life, forces that are not responsive to my will, my desire, my ambition, my dream, my hope – forces that don't know that I'm here. But I know I'm here. And I decide whether I will say *yes,* or *no,* and make it hold. This indeed is the free man, and this is anticipated in the genius of the dogma of freedom as a manifestation of the soul of America, born in what to me is one of the greatest of the great experiments in human relations.

> Heir of the kingdom 'neath the skies
> Often he falls yet falls to rise
> Stumbling, bleeding, beaten back
> Holding still to the upper track
> Playing his part in Creation's plan
> God-like in image, this is Man
> This is Man.

∞ | *The Search in Identity (1971)*

In the final chapter of The Search for Common Ground, *Thurman's most extended
philosophical exposition of community, he explores the idea of identity, most of which is
reprinted here.*[139] *Composed during the waning years of the modern Civil Rights movement and the ascendency black identity politics, this piece outlines Thurman's perspective on the place of race, religion, and culture in the new public and religious narrative
he believed was in the making. Identity is not an isolate, but is forged within the values of
one's culture, he argues, transmitted through the family and, in modern times, the state.
But in a contemporary world "fouled" by pollution and marked by geographical tran-
sience, the young have difficulty developing identity in the context of community and, as
a result, experience "acute alienation" and rootlessness. The disintegration of the family
and the failure of the "state" to abide by its own ethical ideals affects the quest for identity
among African-American youth with special intensity, he argues, for without familial
protection and with democracy reduced to international "power politics," young black
men and women encounter the realities of racism with a harshness unknown to Thurman's generation. Thurman recognizes the appeal of "Black Power" under these circumstances. But he carefully details his reasons for thinking the movement is misguided, and
at best serves a temporary historical need.*

... THE PLACE TO LOOK for the emergence of community in human life is in the primary social unit, the family. It is here that the child first becomes aware of himself as a person. It has often been said that a child is not born human but becomes human only in a human situation or context. I take this to mean that in the intimacy of the family the profound process of the unfolding of potential is set in motion. The goal of fulfillment appears on the far horizon and persists as the pull of the long-timed emotion of the ideal. The child may fail both within and without, but against that failure something wars, always pushing, always making its claim felt. It is the claim of the building blocks, the built-in demand of the mind, the insistence of the organism, the upward push of the racial memory, the glow of the prophets' demand and the dream of the seer; it is what in religion is often called the will of God as touching the life of man.

What happens if in the life of the child there is in the family no pivotal point around which positive self-awareness emerges? The child is apt to become permanently crippled. This period of the child is also characterized as a time of innocence. In that sense there is the recapitulation of the story of the race as found in the various creation myths or query stories. For the child, very important things are happening in his organism, for the track is being laid [for] the life journey of the body. In terms of community, this means that if the child is forced by the circumstances of his life to cope with his environment as if he were an adult, his very nervous system becomes enraged and an utter sense of alienation is apt to become the style of his life. Because he is rejected by life he begins to reject himself. The process of withdrawal and alienation begins its deadly operation before the child has any tools for assessing or interpreting what is happening to him. As an unconscious windbreak against this kind of communal suicide, provisions are made within the scope of the culture for giving children an early sense of belonging to the group as a whole and to a primary group within the larger relationships that give character to the total society.

There seems to be a built-in resistance in all human beings against the threat of isolation. It is a major safeguard against the disintegration of the self, for we cannot abide being cut off. And it is in the primary experience of family that the stage is set for the constant renewing and sustaining of the private life of the individual. Here the raw materials are provided for establishing an inner climate for the growth of personality and for giving full scope to the inner urge for whole-making that in turn increases the possibility for actualizing the potential of the individual. For in such a setting the individual not only has an awareness of being cared for, but also the way is opened for him to emerge as a person in an enlarged relationship of persons, the family.

In some societies, for what may be a wide range of reasons, the concept of the extended family has developed. This means that no member of the family, in substance, is ever lost. One evening in Nigeria, Mrs. Thurman and I were being entertained after a public address by an official of the Western Region. Our host offered us a soft drink, ginger beer. When he opened the bottle, but before serving us, he poured just a little on the floor, saying, "To my ancestors." For just one swirling moment I felt as if I were surrounded by a host of others who were suddenly a part of this moment of celebration. In modern life such a concept bristles with intense complications. However it is but another manifestation, in fine, of the need for belonging, for being cared for, which, in turn, is instinctive to life itself and therefore cannot be ultimately affected by death. A way has to be found for honoring this urgency of life and the human spirit. The frustration of this tendency to wholeness in man is the withering blight that is making so much of modern life a wasteland.

The recognition of the continuing sense of belonging is not only present in the so-called ancestor but is also to be found in the total etiquette surrounding the experience of death. In some parts of the world I have seen the graves of deceased members of the family in the front yards of the family house. This symbolizes their continuing presence that even death cannot sever. Many funeral rites are suggestive in the same way. There are clues to this insistence in the sustaining way that mourning for the dead honors their presence in the midst of the living.

To be remembered is the point that the family group is a part of a larger social unit in an ever-widening circle of belonging. The importance of place, of territory, of the earth takes on special meaning. Man is a child of nature; he is rooted and grounded in the earth. He belongs to it, and it belongs to him. I remember hearing an Indian Chief from northwestern

Canada say: "I come from away up North near the Arctic Circle. I am a part of the snow, ice, and wind in winter. These flow into me and I flow into them." Man cannot long separate himself from nature without withering as a cut rose in a vase. One of the deceptive aspects of mind in man is to give him the illusion of being distinct from and over against but not a part of nature. It is but a single leap thus to regard nature as being so completely other than himself that he may exploit it, plunder it, and rape it with impunity.

This we see all around us in the modern world. Our atmosphere is polluted, our streams are poisoned, our hills are denuded, wildlife is increasingly exterminated, while more and more man becomes an alien on the earth and a fouler of his own nest. The price that is being exacted for this is a deep sense of isolation, of being rootless and a vagabond. Often I have surmised that this condition is more responsible for what seems to be the phenomenal increase in mental and emotional disturbances in modern life than the pressures – economic, social, and political – that abound on every hand. The collective psyche shrieks with the agony that it feels as a part of the death cry of a pillaged nature.

Nevertheless, the importance of territory in the experience of community remains. Territory is one of the perennial guarantors supporting man's experience of community. Man has to *feel* at home if he is to be nurtured; home means place and the place means territory.

In modern life the symbol of homeland that has emerged in full significance is that of sovereignty. Thus the state becomes the rallying point for establishing the meaning and the significance of the life of persons within its boundaries. This is the larger unity that guarantees the smaller primary and secondary units within its boundaries. This symbol of belonging seems to meet a deep need in the life of modern man in a manner somewhat unique in modern history. As such, it unifies the individual and supersedes all other integrating symbols; this is particularly true in a society where there is no state religion to share the sovereignty of the state. It provides a common tie for its citizens and a technical ground for rejecting aliens. It formally defines an outsider and establishes rites and rituals for belonging. Even where there are birthrights unique to those who are born within its boundaries, provisions are made for "categories of belonging" established by custom and guaranteed by laws that govern. In modern life it is sovereignty that finally has the power to veto and certification over the individuals who make up the common life.

Thus the state takes on a transcendent role, thereby fulfilling one of the basic requirements of a religion. It seeks to answer three basic needs of the human spirit: for a supreme object of devotion and therefore worship, for a way of thinking about and believing in the object of devotion, and for a way of life in which the spirit of the object of devotion is expressed. The assumption is that the citizen who is loyal to sovereignty experiences community. He lives in a climate in which it is reasonable to assume that his potential can be actualized or that life can under the circumstances or condition be given a maximum opportunity to realize itself in him.

Such a notion of sovereignty does something more. It gives the citizen an integrated basis for his behavior so that there is always at hand a socially accepted judgment that can determine for him when he is lost, when he has missed the way – that is, when he is out of community. It defines the meaning of civic character and determines the kind of civic responsibility that may develop it. It may withhold such responsibility and thereby determine who may develop civic character, the true symbol of membership. Again, such a notion inspires a basis for a definition of self-sacrifice, not only of possessions, but also of life itself. If the sacrifice of life is made in defense of sovereignty, a man is given a special place of honor and recognition. If in defense of the integrity of sovereignty he takes the life of another, his guilt is short-circuited by the paeans of praise accorded to the hero. A curious and specious distinction is made between murder at the behest of sovereignty and murder without such sanction. Finally, the notion inspires a sense of participating in a collective or communal destiny, thus reaffirming in crisis a sense of belonging to a transcendent entity in which the individual life is somehow transformed into something so much more than itself.

There are many symbols and rituals of sovereignty by which the sense of community is kept current, fluid, and viable. Symbols such as a national flag and a national anthem or hymn come to mind. There is the ritual that is a part of the voting ceremony or etiquette, the varied celebrations to commemorate the nation's founding, the spontaneous or struc-

tured emotions surrounding the crises due to war with other sovereign-
ties, etc. . . .

It can be very readily understood how the sovereignty of the state may
create a major problem for the man of religion, the assumption being that
such a man has a commitment and a sense of loyalty that may transcend
his loyalty to the state, leading to an inescapable and fundamental conflict
in loyalties. The very concept of sovereignty cannot accommodate itself
to a divided loyalty in any sense that is absolute. Such a position is intoler-
able to both its integrity and stability. One of the practical though silent
agreements between the state and religious institution is the recognition
of separate spheres of influence over the life of the individual. Within the
total territory for which sovereignty is responsible certain limited areas
may be recognized as temporarily out of bounds for the state. In our country such a provision is made in the separation of church and state, as defined in the Constitution. The important thing here is to indicate that
such a dualism is limited, and ultimately the power of veto and certification of the life of the individual rests with the state. An individual may
abide by the judgment and take the consequences. There is a long history
of those who reserved the right of veto and certification over their own
lives, the authority of sovereignty to the contrary notwithstanding. But
despite the varied avenues of appeal, of adjustment, of adjudication, the
prerogative of sovereignty is finally to say "yes" or "no," and to make it hold.
The rationalization covering such an eventuality is that the sovereign *is*
the people.

It becomes clear that if there are any citizens within the states who by
definition, stated or implied, are denied freedom of access to the resources of community as established within the state, such persons are
assailed at the very foundation of their sense of belonging. It reaches in to
affect what takes place even within the primary social unit, the family,
where community is first experienced. The term "second-class citizen" is
often used to describe such a status. This means that such persons are
"outsiders" living in the midst of "insiders," required to honor the same demands of sovereignty but denied the basic rewards of sovereignty. This
collective or communal denial of the rights and the "rites" of belonging
cuts deep into the fabric of the total life of the state. In the first place, it

creates a condition of guilt in the general society that has to be absorbed in order to keep life tolerable within the body politic in general.

This becomes an increasingly critical issue as the relationships between sovereign states themselves become more competitive in the terrific crucible of power politics. It is here that the search for the jugular vein of one state is sought by another state of relatively equal strength and power on a steadily shrinking planet. The basic commodity in the play of power politics is for the extension of community of the particular states. The aim here is to bring those who are out of community into a vigorous sense of their own importance, thus inspiring the hope that in such acquiescence they will be able to realize their own potential. This is the essence of the critical struggle for the conquest of the minds and emotions of modern man. Given the loyalty and devotion of these, all other things follow: acceptance of standards of value, new wants for consumer goods immediately available, thereby making new markets – the list is endless. It is seen that the issue turns on the rewards for belonging. But if within the competing powers it can be clear, or is known, that within a given sovereignty there are those who are by birth insiders but are regarded or defined as outsiders notwithstanding, then those who stand in candidacy for belonging may be deterred, stymied, or sidetracked. In the light of this analysis, for instance, it is quite possible that in the major struggle between the Soviet Union and the United States of America the future belongs to that power which is the most convincing witness to the fact that it makes available to all its citizens the freedom of access to a social climate in which the individual not only has an authentic sense of belonging, but in which it is a reasonable hope for him to actualize his potential, thereby experiencing community within himself as part and parcel of the experience of community within the state.

The role of minorities in the modern state is crucial not only for the state as a community among world states, but also for the experience of community on the part of the minorities themselves. As suggested earlier, wherever citizens are denied the freedom of access to the resources that make for a sense of belonging, a sense of being totally dealt with, the environment closes in around them, resulting in the schizophrenic dilemma of being inside and outside at one and the same time. Or worse still, they are subject to the acute trauma of not knowing at any given moment whether they are outsiders or insiders. Such is the terrifying fate not only of the Afro-American but also of the Mexican-Latin American, the American Indian, and all those ethnic strains that make up the so-called Third World.

I shall permit myself two comments – one brief, the other extended – concerning the bearing of my thesis on community in the life of two of these minority groups.

I

The American Indian is the only indigenous people within the confines of American sovereignty. The merciless and ruthless attack on the ground of community in the life of the American Indian is completely amoral: To uproot him from territory that gave him a rare sense of belonging, in which he could actualize his potential within a frame of reference that was totally confirming, and at the same time to keep him in full or relative view of his devastated and desecrated extension of self that the land signified is a unique form of torture, a long, slow, anguished dying. The original insider is forced to become an outsider in his own territory. There are some things in life that are worse than death – surely this must be judged as such. The Indian wanders homeless and rootless as a fleeting ghost in and out of our dreams and like Banquo, is an invisible guest at both our times of feasting and our times of prayer. An unconscious guilt has entered namelessly into the very fiber of the American character and there is no catharsis to be found. Every time in our sovereign power we champion the cause of those who are uprooted in their own land and are forced to watch their souls wither and die without communal nourishment, there he stands in full view before our spirits while our words falter and our claim to challenge falls limp at our feet.

II

The search for community on the part of the Afro-American minority within the larger American community reveals still another facet of the inside-outside dilemma. Those interested in a more elaborate statement of my views should read my book *The Luminous Darkness*, an analysis of the anatomy of segregation and the ground of hope. Unlike the American Indian, the African slave was uprooted from his land, his territory, and brought forcibly several thousand miles away to another land completely alien to his spirit and his gods. All ties that gave him a sense of belonging, of counting, of being a person nourished by a community of persons were abruptly severed, lacerated, torn asunder. Bodies that were emotionally bleeding hulks were set down in the new world of the Americas. Initially he had no standing, even of that of outsider. In terms of his access to the sources of nourishment for community, initially he had none. No, not even the status of being a human being. It is no accident that the New Testament Greek word for slave is *soma,* which means body, a thing.

He was a part of the land, the territory. To that extent – and this is crucial – he was a part of the *ground* of community, the land by which the slaveowner sought to realize his potential in community. Thus some measure of well-being to the slave could not be separated from the well-being of the slaveowner. They were bound by the same chains. To some readers, such a distinction may seem merely academic and therefore unreal. For the slave, the primary social group, the family, rested always upon an unpredictable contingency. Most often the existence and the integrity of the family were ignored or destroyed when on the slave market all familial ties were like flotsam and jetsam on the tide of the angry waters of bartering. Those who lived on a given plantation were forced into a primary social group and gave what was available to the children in their midst, while their little wary egos squeezed their experiences for whatever could be found to nourish and sustain.

There were three currents flowing through the communal life of the plantation slave from which survival, sustenance, and nourishment could be drawn. The first was his tendency toward whole-feeling, to which much of our earlier discussion was devoted. It is one with the endless search for nourishment, inherent in even the simplest forms of life. Here there was no exception – the inner necessity to stake a claim for the self not only to nourish but also to sustain. Second, he needed some all-encompassing dimension to life, native to the spiritual needs of the human spirit and the raw materials brought into focus and synthesis by the religious mood. Third, he felt the drive, the tendency or urge expressed in aggression. Aggression cannot be separated from the urge for and to community. It may be that we get a grand and awesome preview of these two in the incipient ground of human behavior in what has been discovered about the behavior of the cell in seeking its own nourishment and rejecting, by an uncanny directed spontaneity, any intruder that is sensed as a threat to the inner cohesiveness of the structure of the cell. No understanding of the significance of community can escape the place and significance of aggression. Thus it was the operation of this trilogy in the life of the slave that made the forebears of the Afro-American of today endure the long night and greet the dawn with ancient awareness.

In the weary isthmus connecting the slave to the present there were many cataclysms: the War between the States, centering on the issue of slavery – a wide range of legal statutes defining and redefining the status and rights of the slaves and their descendants, which have continued down to the latest times; at least two world wars, in which finally no distinction was made between combatants and noncombatants; the rise of communism and the appearance on the world scene of two world powers involving more than half of the earth's population, dedicated to one form or another of the dialectic of materialism, economic determinism, and the overthrowing of state religions; the rise and fall of two great fascist states committed to the armed conquest of the world; the ushering in of the atomic age by initiating the use of the atomic bomb in war and the creation of stockpiles of atomic weaponry sufficient to provide the equivalent of 30,000 tons of TNT explosives for every human being on the earth; the mechanization of life by phenomenal advances in technology; the real possibility of the discontinuity of life on the planet – the explorations of inner space; the immoral war in Vietnam – the list seems endless!

While all these things were happening, and not fundamentally unconnected with them, there was the general revolt of youth and their disenchantment with the society into which they were born. The result is that more and more they regard themselves as outsiders in the midst of the land of their roots and culture. In their acute alienation, they have a diminishing sense of belonging, do not feel themselves cared for and nurtured in a climate that makes the possibility of actualizing their potential remote, if at all possible. Two things characterize their mood and temper: one, they have no sense of place and are therefore rootless and disoriented in their contemporary environment, and two, the future has little if any meaning, for it is jeopardized by war and the threat of wars, with the fateful consequences of full-scale atomic racial suicide and the destruction of nature itself, without whose sustenance even the thought of survival comes to a grinding halt.

All these things have had a terrific impact on the life of the Afro-American in society. They have crucially affected his sense of belonging, which was always tenuous and fragile. Several considerations should be noted here. Together with the rest of America he is experiencing the collapse of the family structure – that primary womb out of which emerges the self-conscious urge to community – as a sense of belonging and support. It must be remembered that notwithstanding the family life's survival of the ravages of slavery, the struggle for individual economic survival in the turbulent waters of the period of Reconstruction, the acute vulnerability of the family structure under the constant attack of lust, lasciviousness, and often secret affection of many of the white men of the South, and, from the turn of the century, the personality damage wrought by mounting segregation in the region and in the country as a whole, something very creative was at work deep within the social structure of Negro life. It was a counterdefense. The individual began to feel himself part of a larger primary structure in which kinship by blood was not a criterion for the claim of belonging. For a long time the Negro adult in the community stood *in loco parentis* to any Negro child. It was not necessary to know who the child was or where he lived. This gave the child an immediate sense of being cared for, with positive results in his own personality. The individual life could not be easily separated from the whole. Any stranger who came into the community had to be given hospitality, for all doors outside of the Negro community were closed to him. Thus there was the constant experience of overall identification. And this was good.

It broke down decisively and with devastating results, however, at one crucial point – with the white community. The residue that accumulated in the collective and individual psyche of the black man from the awful sense, *that always, under any and all circumstances, his life was utterly at the mercy of the white world, is the most important, single clue to the phenomena of the present.* The most vicious, cruel, and amoral manifestation of this fact was lynching. The heartrending years when hundreds of Negroes were lynched, burned, and butchered by white men whose women and children were often special spectators of the inhuman ceremony are conveniently forgotten. It is scarcely remembered how long it took to pass antilynching legislation. The *bodies* of Negroes remember, and their psyches can never forget this vast desecration of personality. The boundaries of any sense of community, the effectiveness of one's life as a person, the breakdown of the instinctual tendency toward whole-making, the personality violence from aggression, thwarted and turned in on one's self, the searching felt in the presence of the humiliation of heroes, the guilt inspired by anonymous fears that live in the environment – these are some of the shadows, the unconscious reaction to which must be understood as we try to find community in the presence of the grim confrontations facing American society.

Concerning the society as a whole, much has been written and there will be much more as perspective is gained on the social events of the present time. As the older generation, we have suddenly become aware of our youth, as if for the first time. We are angered by their anger, even though secretly we marvel at the courage of their anger. We are frightened by their violence, even as we ponder it. We are shocked by their failure to respond to our values, even as we are humiliated by our own sense of failure and inadequacy. Nothing seems to hold. Nothing seems adequate to the crisis that is upon us. In our extremity we are tempted to take refuge in old shibboleths that we ourselves long since abandoned. We find ourselves using words that have been forsaken by meaning. At last it is beginning to dawn upon us, that at some time in the past – when, we are not sure – we became separated from our absolutes. It is from the life of our youth that we discover that we have lost our way. We, too, have little sense of belonging; our feel for whole-making has included less and less of the world, of the wide range of human life, until we are only sure of it as touching our family, particularly our children. Now, it often seems to us, they turn and rend us because we have sought to nourish them with the sense of our failure.

All of this applies to the older generation of Negroes, but with even greater intensity. In many ways they have tried to shield their children from naked exposure to the worst and most damaging aspects of white society. They have stood guard on the walls that separate and divide, seeking always how to make a virtue of social necessity. Often with sacrifices of which they dare not speak, they have bought time for their youth to prepare for effective living with tools, skills, and knowledge of which they sometimes dreamed but could never realize. Many of them uprooted themselves from a life that they knew, under circumstances with which they had learned to cope, in order that their children might have a wider range of opportunity and a cleaner chance to actualize *their* potential. Now they are faced with the bitter judgment of their own youth, denouncing them as cowards and fools because they were duped and betrayed by the very society from which they sought to protect them. This they sought to accomplish either by reducing the exposure of their youth to that society or by equipping them with a facility that might be exchanged in that society for certain prizes or immunities not available to the rest of their kind.

Meanwhile, these older ones were seeking ways and means for pushing back the boundaries by removing the walls that shut them in. What a long and often unrewarding struggle! The cry in the heart was for more room, more opportunity, more of a sense of belonging. Thus the circling series of confrontations, within and without any zones of agreement – the ballot, better schools, equal schools, the same schools, the freedom of access to the total life of the community on the same basis as other citizens – the list is long and wearisome, but whatever may have been the contradictions, they were never regarded as final. Many tried to keep before their view heroes and heroines of the past to bolster a sagging self-estimate in the present. But there was ever the insinuating circumstance, the heroes failed where they themselves had failed – they were outsiders – the walls, sometimes bold and direct, often soft-spoken and indirect, were ever present.

The heroic *quality* of life was not missing. But the precious ingredient had never been found to protect or immunize the hero from the final assault that would send him crashing to the ground! The hero had to be a man of courage, possessing the acumen of mind and the discipline of training that could stand up under the scrutiny of the sharpest critics who guarded the citadels of power upon which society based its security, prowess, and control. In addition he must be one whose sense of community was deep in the throb of Negro life so that between his heart and theirs there would be a swinging door that no man could shut. His thinking, his feelings, and his deeds must transcend all that separates and divides. He must know hate and conquer it with love; he must know fear and conquer it with strange new courage.

As a result of a series of fortuitous circumstances there appeared on the horizon of the common life a young man who for a swift, staggering, and startling moment met the demands of the hero. He was young. He was well-educated with the full credentials of academic excellence in accordance with ideals found in white society. He was a son of the South. He was steeped in and nurtured by familiar religious tradition. He had charisma, that intangible quality of personality that gathers up in its magic the power to lift people out of themselves without diminishing them. In him the "outsider" and the "insider" came together in a triumphant synthesis. Here at last was a man who affirmed the oneness of black and white under a transcendent unity, for whom community meant the profoundest sharing in the common life. For him, the wall was a temporary separation between brothers. And his name was Martin Luther King, Jr.

His star shot across the heavens like Halley's comet, making a mighty radiance in the light of which ancient dwellers in darkness could find their way to brotherhood. A fresh, cool wind blew across the desert places and the tired, the weary, the fearridden, the hated, and the haters could find a bold new courage. At last there was available a personal and collective catharsis. Here was a new hero who gave the assurance of succeeding at the very point that had proved so vulnerable to all the heroes of the past. As a special kind of grace, he had achieved this by the time the assassin's bullets struck him down. Never again would the boundaries be as established as they were before his coming. In his own short and intense life, the announcement was made to all and sundry, far and near, that the life of the black man was not at the mercy of white people. That for better or for worse they were tied together. No black man could be what his potential demanded unless the white man could be what *his* potential demanded. No white man could be what his potential demanded unless the black man could be what *his* potential demanded. For him this was literal truth and therefore literal fact. The elements of a new residue began building up in the psyche of the black man. And this was good.

It is not my purpose here to discuss the deep polarizations within the black community that began to emerge; however, there are two important aspects in the subsequent unfolding of the whole-making tendency operative in Negro life. First, there was the emergence of other heroes. The psychological condition for testing the hero had been set forth in the dynamics of the social experience of the race. One of the characteristics of the awakening that followed the emergence of Martin Luther King was a search for other heroes whose magic would make room for the vital and fundamental place of aggression, that deep drive in life so central to the life of the species. It is not merely protective, shielding to life, but it also has a prowling quality that can scarcely be distinguished from belligerence. In the light of this need, the drive could not be ignored – it had to be utilized, if not on behalf of community, then it was mandatory that a different concept of community must be created. Just as nonviolence had become the watchword of community in the first instance, violence became the watchword of the new concept.

What emerged as the new concept of community? The tendency toward whole-making was at once self-defeating if it did not establish clear-cut and fixed boundaries. Without such boundaries freedom itself had no significance, so the reasoning ran. Therefore, it was only within fixed boundaries, *self-determined* – and that is the key word – that the goals of community could be experienced, achieved, or realized. The natural lines along which the boundaries should be set would be to separate those who had been historically victimized by society from those who had victimized them. The bankruptcy of trust stood fully revealed. What had been whispered for so long behind closed doors about the real relation between black and white was now shouted in the streets and in the public forums, followed by the demand for radical separation between black and white. There was the strident insistence that any notion of inclusiveness was merest illusion, and the term "brainwashed" was applied to anyone with a contrary point of view. Such a separation was distinguished from segregation because it was voluntary and deliberate. Psychologically, it would utilize aggression in a manner positive and creative rather than positive and destructive. The way was clear now for the emergence of a new kind of hero, one who would be a new symbol – a profoundly angry man, hard and unyielding. Black now took on a new meaning and the term "Black Power" became a fresh rallying point for a sagging self-estimate. Nothing must be as it was before in school, church, marketplace, and territory. The winds blew sharp and fierce across the regions of American life.

This kind of self-estimate sent the believers back into the past, as far as human records extended. Africa became symbolic of the ideal, an ancient, yet historical expression of the new center for the integration of the human spirit. Many rituals appeared in varied forms – new styles of dress, of hair grooming and new forms of old culinary delights. Fresh words also entered the vocabulary – soul food, dashikis, and the Afro Hair dress, etc. In fine, the new sense of community made for the rejection *of* the white community rather than being rejected *by* the white community. A cause was made out of the latter rejection and a new offensive was born. The heroes were men and women who became at once the voices of that rejection. They were local, national, and international. The dream of a new sovereignty within the larger sovereignty became apparent. A new political structure within the larger political superstructure put in its challenging appearance.

There were other forms that the mood of the new sense of community found acceptable. The use of language became a complete mythology. Niceties and refinement of speech became anathema, for they were symbols of the world that was being rejected. "Vulgarity" became the trademark of many who had freed themselves of the contamination of the white society. Often those who stood for the old sense of community and continued to work on its behalf were regarded as "Uncle Toms." The man who was concerned about such things as goodwill and love beyond the new community was seen increasingly as a "traitor" to the new order. "Black is beautiful" became not merely a phrase – it was a stance, a total attitude, a metaphysic. In very positive and exciting terms it began undermining the idea that had developed over so many years into a central aspect of white mythology: that black is ugly, black is evil, black is demonic; therefore

black people are ugly, evil, and demonic. In so doing it fundamentally attacked the front line of defense of the myth of white supremacy and superiority. The point at which to start would be with the children. Thus there
would be a penetration into the seedbed where ideas are planted, nurtured, and developed. There began to appear new centers for black children that were not much concerned about the traditional tools of learning – reading, writing, and arithmetic – as they were about uprooting and
replanting. That is fundamental.

In order to document this new mood for a radically different sense of
community, a rereading of history became urgent. Such a concern was not
new in itself nor was it particularly novel. There were many voices from
the past that had insisted upon correcting the distortions of the story of
the black man in the western world and in the Americas. But the voices
did not carry far because they were confined largely to the sophisticated,
the most literate, and, above all, to the specialists. Now all of this had to
be changed; the fresh word about the past had to take to the streets, giving
rise to an informed public mind both within and beyond the black community. It had to be a common knowledge that would generate mass enthusiasm for building a different collective self-image, thus providing
stature for the design to stake out territory in the domain previously dominated and controlled by white society. Such a reexamination of the roots
of history did not exclude the origins of the common religion, Christianity. This emphasis found its most arresting statement in the Black Manifesto delivered to the churches, and in the concepts of the Black Jesus and
the Black Madonna. Overall, there has been the reaction of stubborn resistance, shudders of guilt, wary capitulation, and desperate efforts to understand and comprehend. The behavior of the cells of the body in the
presence of the radical invasion of other cells from foreign bodies as seen
in organ transplants *may be* mute testimony to the ground of such behavior in personality.

The summary above must suffice to indicate the profound seriousness
of the new concept of community as it emerged in Negro life. The recognition of the instinctual tendency to whole-making and the utilization of
the equally basic drive manifested in aggression were both being expressed in establishing and defending the boundaries separating black

from white. It cannot be overemphasized that the emergence of the new African states in the arena of world states and their place of influence in the United Nations must not be separated from the new concept of community appearing in the black community.

Let my meaning be clear. What we see happening is the deliberate, carefully delineated effort to create within white society a community of separateness within which an attempt is being made to establish a dependable sense of black autonomy, to make articulate a collective sense of self, capable of nourishing and supporting the individual as he works out his destiny in American society and the world. In order to do this, it has seemed necessary to reduce exposure to all white persons to a minimum and to recognize, in fact, that the white man is the *enemy*, as is indicated by his historic treatment of the black man. The assumption is that such a pragmatic possibility is quite realistic. It can be carried out with or without his cooperation, peacefully if possible, violently if necessary. Inasmuch as he has used fear most effectively in the past, in his effort to establish and maintain throughout his society artificial and arbitrary boundaries between himself and nonwhites, others may use the same instrument to establish and maintain self-determined boundaries between black and white. The white community has held the black community in place by the threat of violence, backed always by the power to implement it and to carry it out. This means that he is psychologically and precisely vulnerable to the same tactical maneuver. Violence is his most acceptable instrument for both control and social change as he may determine it. The difference in access to and the availability of the tools of violence between the black and white communities *must* not be permitted to blunt the appeal or deflate the enthusiasm. So the argument runs.

One more step in this rather long summarizing critique must be taken. What has been the overall effect of this concept of community on American society in general? I suppose the social historian or psychologist would have an impressive and exhaustive list. I would make this observation. There have been far-reaching effects in accommodating the impact on white society. Many doors that have been closed and sealed are now open. This is true not merely because of the impact of the new pressure, but also because the pressure itself has provided opportunity for doing

what apparently could not have been done before without good, sufficient, and defensive reasons. Vast areas of society that have been aware of
but not affected by Negro life have let such awareness become effective in
many changes within the social patterns and structures.

In many ways the antiblack hatemongers have become legitimatized
and, in many instances but by no means in all, violence and brutality
against Negroes have been given moral and social sanction. By vocal and,
most often, silent consent the cry for Law and Order is given a specific, racially sinister meaning. The sanctity of sovereignty, as discussed earlier,
expressed in the power of the state to exercise veto and certification over
the lives of its citizens, is declared to be in jeopardy, and Order is separated
from and given precedence over Justice. The will to segregate that is inherent in the structure of American society is more and more stripped of
its disguises and making itself felt without its customary facades; at the
same time all kinds of people in the larger society are being aroused to
make their voices heard and their power felt on behalf of the creation of an
American society inclusive of all. Such persons make the rejection of the
more narrowly fixed and self-determined boundaries of the black community their strength and incentive. Up to and including the present time, no
creative way has been found to accomplish the specific ends of identity
and healthy self-estimate that is devoid of the negativisms that seem to be
inherent in the present struggle.

There are those who interpret what is happening as the work of a few
radicals and hotheads. They cannot see in the stirrings anything that is
symptomatic of the shifting of the ground of society that makes for cata-
clysm and upheaval. The notion suggests that if the leaders can be elimi-
nated, jailed, or even killed, it would restore what is regarded as a lost harmony among the races. Others declare that a sickness has overtaken the
society as a whole, and what we are observing is but symptomatic of something far more disturbing in the common life. There are still others – they
are always to be found – who seek to exploit the unrest and the zeal for the
sense of limited community on behalf of ideologies that are foreign to the
soil of America; a new kind of outsider from another social climate is
busily at work carrying out his evil design. This sense of jitters allows hidden anxieties to surface themselves with many hideous, ugly, and threat-

ening faces. It is the time and the moment when the alarmist comes into his own, but the cry is far removed from the real source of the ferment.

It is not amiss to be reminded that there may be many areas of life within the black community that are disturbed at the turn of events. Perhaps the sharpest criticism is the seeming ignorance of the champions for self-determined separateness concerning the struggles of the past. The paradox is as cruel as it is apparent. On the one hand there is the insistence of reinterpretation of, and at the same time, a rejection of past history. This evident lack of a sense of history is a most damaging criticism. There seems to be no recognition of the relentless logic tying present events and ideas with what has preceded them and from which they can never be separated. The cavalier manner in which this seems to be ignored is seen as being the merest stupidity and ignorance. There is general alarm over the way in which the aggression turns on itself, inflicting havoc and wreckage on Negroes themselves. There are many who have lived deep in the heart of American society and know with certainty that to undertake to build community as a closed entity within the large society is not only suicidal but the sheerest stupidity, because it plays directly into the hands of those persons and elements in society who have stood as defenders against any and all inclusiveness as the true (American) basis of community. What they were unable to accomplish after three hundred years is now being done for them without their having to lift a finger. They are willing to encourage, to support with their money and their power all moves toward separating black from white. At last, their message has gotten through to Negroes and is being implemented by them in a manner not to be envisioned by the wildest flight of the imagination.

One of the most disturbing features of this total activity is its effect on youth. There is widespread feeling and thought that the youth are being used by clever men, many of whom are motivated by unselfish concerns and dedication, to sacrifice the youth while their minds are undeveloped and they have no survival skills that enable them to cope with their environment in the future. The notion that such youth are expendable is as cruel as it is self-defeating.

But there is one indictment against the older generation that the present movement brings into focus: Black youth have not been given a binding sense of identity – this is not confined to them exclusively – and there have been few avenues open to them for having a sense of membership in society as a whole. But the new and limited sense of community, whose boundaries are self-imposed, has provided two things: (1) *a basis for identity with a cause and a purpose more significant to them than their own individual survival, and* (2) *a feeling of membership with others of common values with whom they can experience direct and intense communication.* When they hear that call they drop their tools and answer! No amount of logic, argumentation, intimidation, or appeal has meaning where those precious ingredients are lacking. I feel that here is the clue to the appeal that the new community makes to youth. Among the youth are not merely to be found those who are not standing in immediate candidacy for higher learning, whose direct prospects for the actualizing of their potential is without promise of fulfillment. There are others who have the skills already, whose minds are disciplined for finding some measure of fulfillment in society as it is now constituted. Two of the most important tests of community are met here – a basis for integrated action or behavior with which the individual may, can, and, finally, must identify and a sense of membership in and belonging to a company of others who are held together by common values, ideals, and commitments. White society has not only shut them out of such involvements (except at times when the stern Voice of Sovereignty sends forth the call to arms in defense of ideas or ideals to which they do not have the freedom of access and therefore with which identification is not easy), but also it has robbed them of any sense of belonging in the present or in any imaginable future. Therefore, the new sense of community within self-determined boundaries seems the most realistic and immediately practical solution to a cruel and otherwise seemingly insoluble problem.

It is my considered judgment that the present solution is a stopgap, a halt in the line of march toward full community or, at most, a time of bivouac on a promontory overlooking the entire landscape of American society. It is time for assessing and reassessing resources in the light of the most ancient memory of the race concerning community, to hear again the clear voice of prophet and seer calling for harmony among all the children of men. At length there will begin to be talk of plans for the new city – that has never before existed on land or sea. At the center of the common life there will be strange and vaguely familiar stirrings. Some there will be whose dreams will be haunted by forgotten events in which in a moment of insight they saw a vision of a way of life transcending all barriers alien to community. Among the elder statesmen will be those through whose blood the liquid fires of Martin Luther King's dream swept all before it in one grand surge of beatific glory. They will remember and wonder at what they see about them. It will be discovered, how long and under what circumstance will remain among the mysteries, that the barriers of community can never be arbitrarily established, however necessitous it may be to seek to do so for good and saving reasons. Here and there will be those who will walk out under the stars and think lonely thoughts about whence they came and the meaning that their presence in the heavens inspires. They will wonder and ponder heavy thoughts about man and his destiny under the stars. One day there will stand up in their midst one who will tell of a new sickness among the children who in their delirium cry for their brothers whom they have never known and from whom they have been cut off behind the self-imposed barriers of their fathers. An alarm will spread throughout the community that it is being felt and slowly realized that community cannot feed for long on itself; it can only flourish where always the boundaries are giving way to the coming of others from beyond them – unknown and undiscovered brothers. Then the wisest among them will say: What we have sought we have found, our own sense of identity. We have an established center out of which at last we can function and relate to other men. We have committed to heart and to nervous system a feeling of belonging and our spirits are no longer isolated and afraid. We have lost our fear of our brothers and are no longer ashamed of ourselves, of who and what we are – Let us now go forth to save the land of our birth from the plague that first drove us into the "will to quarantine" and to separate ourselves behind self-imposed walls. For this is why we were born: Men, all men belong to each other, and he who shuts himself away diminishes himself, and he who shuts another away from him destroys himself. And all the people said *Amen*.

 *Section Four*

MEDITATIONS FOR "APOSTLES OF SENSITIVENESS"

ᑳ | *Saddle Your Dreams*

Saddle your dreams before you ride them.

IT IS THE NATURE of dreams to run riot, never to wish to contain themselves within limitations that are fixed. Sometimes they seem to be the cry
of the heart for the boundless and the unexplored. Often they are fashioned out of longings too vital to die, out of hankerings fed by hidden
springs in the dark places of the spirit. Often they are the offspring of
hopes that can never be realized and longings that can never find fulfillment. Sometimes they are the weird stirrings of ghosts of dead plans and
the kindling of ashes in a hearth that has long since been deserted. Many
and fancy are the names by which dreams are called – fantasies, repressed
desires, vanities of the spirit, will-o'-the-wisps. Sometimes we seek to dismiss them by calling their indulgence daydreaming, by which we mean
taking flight from the realities of our own world and dwelling in the twilight of vain imaginings.

All of this may be true. But all their meaning need not be exhausted by
such harsh judgement. The dreams belong to us; they come full-blown
out of the real world in which we work and hope and carry on. They are not

imposters. They are not foreign elements invading our world like some solitary comet from the outer reaches of space which pays one visit to the sun and is gone never to come again. No! Our dreams are our *thing*. They become *other* when we let them lose their character. Here is the fatal blunder. Our dreams must be saddled by the hard facts of our world before we ride them off among the stars. Thus, they become for us the bearers of the new possibility, the enlarged horizon, the great hope. Even as they romp among the stars they come back to their place in our lives, bringing with them the radiance of the far heights, the lofty regions, and giving to all our days the lift and the magic of stars.[140]

☯ | *The Narrow Ridge*

FOR SOME MEN there can be no security in life apart from being surrounded by the broad expanse of country in which all landmarks are clear and the journey is along a well-worn path. Day after day they must be able to look up at any moment and know exactly where they are. Their lives feed on the familiar tidbits concerning those to whom one long adjustment has been made, and the possibility of the sudden shift in temperament or behavior almost never occurs. There is a strange comfort in the assurance of the commonplace and familiar. Everything is in its place and all things are arranged in a neat pattern of stability. The one great fear is the fear of change, the one great dread is the dread of strangeness.

Of course there is strength in this kind of security. Living can become routinized and reduced to the dignity of the behavior pattern. Thus the shock of the sudden encounter has a constant absorption. It is as if one's life were lived behind a sure and continuous windbreak. Days come and go and each one is as the one before. At length the monotony folds its wings and stirs no more. There is not even the pith of endurance, only the settling in and the dimming of all lights.

Buber says that life for him is at its very best when he is living on what he calls "the narrow ridge." It is a way of life that generates zest for each day's round because it is lived with anticipation. There is the full recognition of the necessity for routines and even the inner provisions for the simple monotony which is a part of all human experience. The commonplace remains the commonplace and the ordinary remains the ordinary – but this does not exhaust the meaning of the days. Each day's length is rimmed round with a margin of the joy of the unexpected, the anticipation of the new and the significant. It is to give to living a whiff of ammonia. The accent, the bias, of such a life is on the side of the margin, the overtone, rather than a mere acceptance of the commonplace and the ordinary. If such is one's prevailing attitude, then even the commonplace becomes infused with the kind of vitality that gives it a new meaning. This is not merely a matter of temperament or special gift. Such a possibility lies within reach of every man. It stems out of a conviction about the meaning of life as a whole, a faith that affirms that Life can be trusted to fulfill itself in the big Moment *and* the ordinary event, that what a man demands of life must never be more than what he is willing to believe about life. In each of us there is a "Cascade Eagle," a bird that is higher when soaring in the gorge than the highest soarer above the plains – because the gorge is in the mountains. To give this eagle wings is the call to every man.[141]

∞ | Contradictions Not Final

TWO MEN FACED EACH OTHER in a prison cell. They belonged to different countries, their roots watered by streams from different cultures. One was under sentence of death, scheduled to be executed within a few short hours. The other was a visitor and friend – this, even though months before they had been enemies in a great war. They bade each other farewell for the last time. The visitor was deeply troubled, but he could not find his way through the emotional maze in which he was caught to give voice to what cried out for utterance. This is what he wanted to say but could not:

"We may not be able to stop and undo the hard old wrongs of the great world outside, but through you and me no evil shall come either in the unknown where you are going, or in this imperfect and haunted dimension of awareness through which I move. Thus between us we shall cancel out all private and personal evil, thus arrest private and personal consequences to blind action and reaction, thus prevent specifically the general incomprehension and misunderstanding, hatred and revenge of our time from spreading further!"

The forces at work in the world which seem to determine the future and the fate of mankind seem so vast, impersonal, and unresponsive to the will and desire of any individual that it is easy to abandon all hope for a sane and peaceful order of life for mankind. Nevertheless, it is urgent to hold steadily in mind the utter responsibility of the solitary individual to do everything with all his heart and mind to arrest the development of the consequence of private and personal evil resulting from the interaction of the impersonal forces that surround us. To cancel out between you and another all personal and private evil, to put your life squarely on the side of the good thing because it is good, and for no other reason, is to anticipate the Kingdom of God at the level of your functioning.

At long last a man must be deeply convinced that the contradictions of life which he encounters are not final, that the radical tension between good and evil, as he sees it and feels it, does not have the last word about the meaning of life and the nature of existence, that there is a spirit in man and in the world working always against the thing that destroys and cuts down. Thus he will live wisely and courageously his little life, and those who see the sunlight in his face will drop their tools and follow him. There is no ultimate negation for the man for whom it is categorical that the ultimate destiny of man on this planet is a good destiny.[142]

∞ | Keep Open the Door of Thy Heart

> *Keep open the door of thy heart.*
> *It matters not how many doors are closed against thee.*

IT IS A WONDROUS DISCOVERY when there is disclosed to the mind the fact that there may be no direct and responsible relation between two human beings that can determine their attitude toward each other. We are accustomed to thinking that one man's attitude toward another is a response to an attitude. The formula is very neat: love begets love, hate begets hate, indifference begets indifference. Often this is true. Again and again we try to mete out to others what we experience at their hands. There is much to be said for the contagion of attitudes. There are moments in every man's life when he tries to give as good or as bad as he gets. But this presupposes that the relation between human beings is somehow mechanical, as if each person is utterly and completely separated. This is far from the truth, even though it may seem to square with *some* of the facts of our experienced behavior.

There is a profound ground of unity that is more pertinent and authentic than all the unilateral dimension of our lives. This a man discovers when he is able to keep open the door of his heart. This is one's ultimate responsibility, and it is not dependent upon whether the heart of another is kept open for him. Here is a mystery: If sweeping through the door of my heart there moves continually a genuine love for you, it bypasses all your hate and all your indifference and gets through to you at your center. You are powerless to do anything about it. You may keep alive in devious ways the fires of your bitter heart, but they cannot get through to me. Underneath the surface of all the tension, something else is at work. It is utterly impossible for you to keep another from loving you. True, you may scorn his love, you may reject it in all ways within your power, you may try to close every opening in your own heart – it will not matter. This is no easy sentimentality, but it is the very essence of the vitality of being. The word that love is stronger than hate and goes beyond death is the great disclosure to one who has found that when he keeps open the door of his heart, it matters not how many doors are closed against him.[143]

∞ | On Viewing the Coast of Africa

FROM MY CABIN WINDOW I look out on the full moon, and the ghosts of my forefathers rise and fall with the undulating waves. Across these same waters how many years ago they came! What were the inchoate mutterings locked tight within the circle of their hearts? In the deep, heavy darkness of the foul-smelling hold of the ship, where they could not see the sky, nor hear the night noises, nor feel the warm compassion of the tribe, they held their breath against the agony.

How does the human spirit accommodate itself to desolation? How did they? What tools of the spirit were in their hands with which to cut a path through the wilderness of their despair? If only death of the body would come to deliver the soul from dying! If some sacred taboo had been defiled and this extended terror was the consequence – there would be no panic in the paying. If some creature of the vast and pulsing jungle had snatched the life away – this would even in its wildest fear be floated by the familiarity of the daily hazard. If death had come, being ushered into life by a terrible paroxysm of pain, all the assurance of the Way of the Tribe would have carried the spirit home on the wings of precious ceremony and holy ritual. But this! Nothing anywhere in all the myths, in all the stories, in all the ancient memory of the race had given hint of this torturous convulsion. There were no gods to hear, no magic spell of witch doctor to summon, even one's companion in chains muttered his quivering misery in a tongue unknown and a sound unfamiliar.

O my Fathers, what was it like to be stripped of all supports of life save the beating of the heart and the ebb and flow of fetid air in the lungs? In a strange moment, when you suddenly caught your breath, did some intimation from the future give to your spirits a wink of promise? In the darkness did you hear the silent feet of your children beating a melody of freedom to words which you would never know, in a land in which your bones would be warmed again in the depths of the cold earth in which you will sleep unknown, unrealized and alone?[144]

∞ | Meaning Is Inherent in Life

INHERENT IN LIFE IS MEANING. This is a quality, independent of the way in which outside forces may operate upon life. The life in the seed bursts forth in root and stalk and fruit – the whole process takes place within. Many forces may operate upon it from without – cramping the roots, making the shape of the stalk into a caricature of itself – but always with whatever life there is, the built-in purpose is never given up. Concerning this meaning there is no doubt, wherever life appears. This is the integrity of life, it is the commitment of life; this is the singular characteristic of all aliveness; this is the miracle, the shaping of matter from within: the materializing of vitality. The total experience seems to take place in a manner so pervasive that we look in vain for the center, the location of the secret.

Can life's experience of itself at the level of tree and plant, cat and dog, even in the body of man, be also life's experience of itself at the level of the mind? Is there a meaning inherent in the life of the mind itself that is the unfolding of an inner logic not to be accounted for in terms of stimulus from the outside or of response to the outside? May it be that all the dreams, the hopes, the creative flashes like summer lightning, which do not ever quite desert the human mind, are inherent in the mind itself as meaning characteristic of the life in the mind? Wherever life appears it carries with it meaning which is characteristic of all vitality – life means inherent order, built-in goals, purposes, patterns, or designs. These, however simple, determine the form of the life. When the form of life becomes more complex, this fact too is reflected in the pattern, the design, the purpose, the inherent aim.

It may be that in the mind of man, in the rich diversity and depth of human thought, in the searching restlessness for which the word "spirit" seems more appropriate, the life inherent is moving always toward goals and ends that are sensed only when realized. And beyond all these there may be a life of mankind which is more than individuals and groups but in which there is the built-in purpose, aim, and goal. Such purposes, aims, and goals may have increasing creativity as their inherent characteristic. Perhaps this is why we seem always to be presented with goals that can never be realized and ends which can never be fulfilled. Thus the ultimate word which is reserved for God is Creator – the creative act must ever be the personal act.[145]

∞ | The Horns of the Wild Oxen

> *From the horns of the wild oxen*
> *Thou hast answered me.*

THE HORNS OF THE WILD OXEN. I recognize the panic and the sharp pain of sheer brutality. Upon each of us there may come the cruel visitation. It may come in the form of a sudden illness, a quick tragedy, or an unexpected loss. It may be a dramatic disappointment, a complete failure or an overwhelming disaster. It may be a radical sense of helplessness in the presence of the sheer agony of a beloved's need or the inspired awareness of a blanket of misery covering the wretchedness of nameless men, women, and children. "The horns of the wild oxen," the symbol of unpremeditated destruction from which, at last, none may find sure refuge or adequate protection.

"From the horns of the wild oxen, Thou hast answered me." Here is the Ultimate Protection against final agony. Here is the Steadying Assurance which addresses the central point of the individual's aliveness. Here is the Hand that reaches out to hold and in holding, rescues. Here is the Animated Confidence that undergirds and sustains. In the quietness of this hour, I saturate myself with the spirit of the living God which is THE answer to all the shocks that await me on tomorrow.[146]

> From the horns of the wild oxen
> Thou hast answered me.

ᙦ | Keep Alive the Dream in the Heart

AS LONG AS A MAN has a dream in his heart, he cannot lose the significance of living. It is a part of the pretensions of modern life to traffic in what is generally called "realism." There is much insistence upon being practical, down to earth. Such things as dreams are wont to be regarded as romantic or as a badge of immaturity, or as escape hatches for the human spirit. When such a mood or attitude is carefully scrutinized, it is found to be made up largely of pretensions, in short, of bluff. Men cannot continue long to live if the dream in the heart has perished. It is then that they stop hoping, stop looking, and the last embers of their anticipations fade away.

The dream in the heart is the outlet. It is one with the living water welling up from the very springs of Being, nourishing and sustaining life all of life. Where there is no dream, the life becomes a swamp, a dreary dead place and, deep within, a man's heart begins to rot. The dream need not be some great and overwhelming plan; it need not be a dramatic picture of what might or must be someday; it need not be a concrete outpouring of a world-shaking possibility of sure fulfillment. Such may be important for some; such may be crucial for a particular moment of human history. But it is not in these grand ways that the dream nourishes life. The dream is the quiet persistence in the heart that enables a man to ride out the storms of his churning experiences. It is the exciting whisper moving through the aisles of his spirit answering the monotony of limitless days of dull routine. It is the ever-recurring melody in the midst of the broken harmony and harsh discords of human conflict. It is the touch of significance which highlights the ordinary experience, the common event. The dream is no outward thing. It does not take its rise from the environment in which one moves or functions. It lives in the inward parts, it is deep within, where the issues of life and death are ultimately determined. Keep alive the dream; for as long as a man has a dream in his heart, he cannot lose the significance of living.[147]

 | *The Growing Edge*

LOOK WELL TO THE GROWING EDGE. All around us worlds are dying and new worlds are being born; all around us life is dying and life is being born. The fruit ripens on the tree, the roots are silently at work in the darkness of the earth against a time when there shall be new leaves, fresh blossoms, green fruit. Such is the growing edge! It is the extra breath from the exhausted lung, the one more thing to try when all else has failed, the upward reach of life when weariness closes in upon all endeavor. This is the basis of hope in moments of despair, the incentive to carry on when times are out of joint and men have lost their reason, the source of confidence when worlds crash and dreams whiten into ash. The birth of the child – life's most dramatic answer to death – this is the growing edge incarnate. Look well to the growing edge![148]

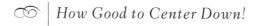 | *How Good to Center Down!*

How good it is to center down!
To sit quietly and see one's self pass by!
The streets of our minds seethe with endless traffic;

Our spirits resound with clashings, with noisy silences,
While something deep within hungers and thirsts for the still moment and the
*   resting lull.*
With full intensity we seek, ere the quiet passes, a fresh sense of order in our
*   living;*
A direction, a strong sure purpose that will structure our confusion and bring
*   meaning in our chaos.*
We look at ourselves in this waiting moment – the kinds of people we are.
The questions persist: what are we doing with our lives? – what are the motives
*   that order our days?*
What is the end of our doings? Where are we trying to go?
Where do we put the emphasis and where are our values focused?
For what end do we make sacrifices? Where is my treasure and what do I love
*   most in life?*
What do I hate most in life and to what am I true?
Over and over the questions beat in upon the waiting moment.
As we listen, floating up through all the jangling echoes of our turbulence, there
*   is a sound of another kind –*
A deeper note which only the stillness of the heart makes clear.
It moves directly to the core of our being. Our questions are answered,
Our spirits refreshed, and we move back into the traffic of our daily
*   round.*
With the peace of the Eternal in our step.
How good it is to center down![149]

 ## Let Us Remember the Children

THERE IS A STRANGE POWER inherent in the spirit of man. Sitting or
standing or lying in one place, he can bring before his presence those long
separated from him by distance or by death, those whose plight he understands but whose faces he has never seen and whose names register in
him no meaning.

Let us bring before our spirits the children of the world! The children
born in refugee camps where all is tentative and shadowy, except the hard-
ness of the constant anguish and anxiety that have settled deep within the
eyes of those who answer when the call is "Mommy" or "Daddy" . . . the

numberless host of orphans corralled like sheep in places of refuge where the common conscience provides bread to eat, water to drink, and clothes to cover the nakedness and the shame . . . the inarticulate groan of those who are the offspring of hot lust held in its place by exploding shells and the insanity of war – these are the special wards of the collective guilt of the human race, the brood left behind when armies moved and the strategy of war made towns into a desolation. The illegitimate children of peacetime, who have no peg upon which to hang the identity of meaning, whose tender lives are cut adrift from all harbors of refuge and security – these are choked by a shame not of their making and who look upon their own existence with heartache and humiliation. The children in families where all love is perishing and they cannot even sense the awareness that their own lives are touched by love's gentleness and strength. The sick children who were ushered into the world as if their bodies were maimed and twisted by disaster which was their lot in some encounter before the fullness of time gave them birth among the children of men. Those who played and romped on the hillside but now will never walk again. Those who once enjoyed the beauty of sky and earth, who looked upon everything about them with unsullied wonder, but who are closed in darkness never to see again. The children of the halting, stumbling mind in whom some precious ingredient is lacking, leaving in its place the vacant mindless stare. The children of great and good fortune whose lives have been always surrounded by the tenderness of affection and the gentleness of understanding, across whose paths no shadows have fallen and for whom life is beautiful and free –

What we bring before our presence, our Father, we share with Thee in our time of quiet and prayer. We thank Thee for the gift to do this, the strange power inherent in our spirits. Grant that what we see in this way may not leave us untouched but may inspire us to be active, responsive instruments in Thy hands to heal Thy children, to bless Thy children, to redeem Thy children. Amen.[150]

∞ | A Prayer for Peace

OUR FATHER, FRESH FROM THE WORLD with the smell of life upon us, we make an act of prayer in the silence of this place. Our minds are troubled because the anxieties of our hearts are deep and searching. We are stifled by the odor of death which envelopes the earth because in so many places brother fights against brother. The panic of fear, the torture of insecurity, the ache of hunger – all have fed and rekindled ancient hatreds and long-forgotten memories of old struggles when the world was young and Thy children were but dimly aware of Thy Presence in the midst. For all this we seek forgiveness. There is no one of us without guilt, and before Thee we confess our sins: we are proud and arrogant; we are selfish and greedy; we have harbored in our hearts and minds much that makes for bitterness, hatred, and revenge.

While we wait in Thy Presence, search our spirits and grant to our minds the guidance and the wisdom that will teach us the way to take, without which there can be no peace and no confidence anywhere. Teach us how to put at the disposal of Thy Purposes of Peace the fruits of our industry, the products of our minds, the vast wealth of our land, and the resources of our spirit. Grant unto us the courage to follow the illumination of this hour to the end that we shall not lead death to any man's door, but rather may we strengthen the hands of all in high places and in common tasks who seek to build a friendly world of friendly men, beneath a friendly sky. This is the simple desire of our hearts which we share with Thee in quiet confidence. Amen.[151]

∞ | I Will Not Give Up

IT WAS ABOVE THE TIMBERLINE. The steady march of the forest had stopped as if some invisible barrier had been erected beyond which no trees dared move even in single file. Beyond was barrenness, sheer rocks, snow patches and strong untrammeled winds. Here and there were short tufts of evergreen bushes that had somehow managed to survive despite the severe pressures under which they had to live. They were not lush, they lacked the kind of grace of the vegetation below the timberline, but they were alive and hardy. Upon close investigation, however, it was found that these were not ordinary shrubs. The formation of the needles, etc., was identical with that of the trees farther down; as a matter of fact, they looked like branches of the other trees. When one actually examined them, the astounding revelation was that they *were* branches. For, hugging the ground, following the shape of the terrain, were trees that could not grow upright, following the pattern of their kind. Instead, they were growing as vines grow along the ground, and what seemed to be patches of stunted shrubs were rows of branches of growing, developing trees. What must have been the tortuous frustration and the stubborn battle that had finally resulted in this strange phenomenon! It is as if the tree had said, "I am destined to reach for the skies and embrace in my arms the wind, the rain, the snow and the sun, singing my song of joy to all the heavens. But this I cannot do. I have taken root beyond the timberline, and yet I do not want to die; I must not die. I shall make a careful survey of my situation and work out a method, a way of life, that will yield growth and development for me despite the contradictions under which I must eke out my days. In the end I may not look like the other trees, I may not be what all that is within me cries out to be. But I will not give up. I will use to the full every resource in me and about me to answer life with life. In so doing, I shall affirm that this is the kind of universe that sustains, upon demand, the life that is in it." I wonder if I dare to act even as the tree acts. I wonder! I wonder! Do you?[152]

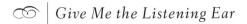 | *Give Me the Listening Ear*

> *Give me the listening ear*
> *The eye that is willing to see.*

GIVE ME THE LISTENING EAR. I seek this day the ear that will not shrink from the word that corrects and admonishes – the word that holds up before me the image of myself that causes me to pause and reconsider – the word that challenges me to deeper consecration and higher resolve – the word that lays bare needs that make my own days uneasy, that seizes upon every good decent impulse of my nature, channeling it into paths of healing in the lives of others.

Give me the listening ear. I seek this day the disciplined mind, the disciplined heart, the disciplined life that makes my ear the focus of attention through which I may become mindful of expressions of life foreign to my own. I seek the stimulation that lifts me out of old ruts and established habits which keeps me conscious of my self, my needs, my personal interests.

Give me this day – the eye that is willing to see the meaning of the ordinary, the familiar, the commonplace – the eye that is willing to see my own faults for what they are – the eye that is willing to see the likable qualities in those I may not like – the mistake in what I thought was correct – the strength in what I had labeled as weakness. Give me the eye that is willing to see that Thou has not left Thyself without a witness in every living thing. Thus to walk with reverence and sensitiveness through all the days of my life.[153]

> Give me the listening ear
> The eye that is willing to see.

∞ | The Kingdom of Values

IT IS A TRUTH recognized over and over again in various guises that the key to the meaning of life is found deep within each one of us. When Jesus insists that the Kingdom of God is within, he is affirming that which is a part of the common experience of the race. Incidentally, this is one of the unique things about Jesus: he calls attention again and again to that which is so utterly a part of the deep commonplace experience of life.

There is a story told of the musk deer of North India. In the springtime, the roe is haunted by the odor of musk. He runs wildly over hill and ravine with his nostrils dilating and his little body throbbing with desire, sure that around the next clump of trees or bush he will find musk, the object of his quest. Then at last he falls, exhausted, with his little head resting on his tiny hoofs, only to discover that the odor of musk is in his own hide.

The key to the meaning of life is within you. If you have a glass of water out of the ocean, all the water in the ocean is not in your glass, but all the water in your glass is ocean water. This is a characteristic of life. The responsibility for living with meaning and dignity can never be finally taken away from the individual. Of course, there is the fact of limitations of heredity and the like, which may circumscribe decidedly the area of awareness within the individual life; there is the total sphere of accidents which may alter the mind and the spirit by some deadly seizure. But the fact remains that the judgment which the individual passes upon life and by which life weighs him in the balance, finds its key within the individual and not outside of him. It is the great and crowning dignity of human life.

Man rates the risk that life takes by resting its case within his own spirit. How good God is to trust the Kingdom of Values to the discernment of the mind and spirit of man![154]

Notes

1. Howard Thurman, *The Luminous Darkness: A Personal Interpretation of the Anatomy of Segregation and the Ground of Hope* (New York: Harper and Row, 1965), x.

2. *Deep Is the Hunger: Meditations for Apostles of Sensitiveness* (New York: Harper and Brothers, 1951), ix and xi. To be an apostle of sensitiveness, for Thurman, is to have a sense of what is vital, a basic underlying awareness of life and its potentialities at every level of experience. Thurman first explored the concept, "Apostles of Sensitiveness," in an address delivered at the cathedral of St. John the Divine in New York City in February, 1946, under the auspices of the Interracial Fellowship of Greater New York. He later incorporated the term into the title of the first in a series of three popular collections of meditations, entitled *Deep Is the Hunger* (1951), *Meditations of the Heart* (1953), and *The Inward Journey* (1961).

3. Alton Pollard makes this point in "The Future of African-American Religion," in Mozella G. Mitchell, ed., *The Human Search: Howard Thurman and The Quest for Freedom: Proceedings of the Second Annual Thurman Convocation*, Martin Luther King, Jr., *Memorial Studies in Religion, Culture and Social Development*, 2 vols. (New York: Peter Lang, 1992), 2:150.

4. See Harold Cruse, *The Crisis of the Negro Intellectual* (New York: William Mor-

313

row, 1967); Christopher Lasch, *The Agony of the American Left* (New York: Vintage, 1969); Cornel West, *Race Matters* (Boston: Beacon Press, 1994). For contemporary commentary on the "crisis" in black intellectual leadership from a variety of perspectives, see for example, Eugene F. Rivers, 3d, "Beyond the Nationalism of Fools: Toward an Agenda for Black Intellectuals," *Boston Review* 20 (Summer 1995):16–18; Glenn C. Loury, *One by One from the Inside Out* (New York: Free Press, 1995); Adolph Reed, "What Are the Drums Saying, Booker? The Current Crisis of the Black Intellectual," *The Village Voice* 11 (April 1995): 31–36; Michael Eric Dyson, *Race Rules: Navigating the Color Line* (New York: Addison Wesley, 1996), 47–76; Kevin K. Gaines, *Uplifting the Race: Black Leadership, Politics, and Culture in the Twentieth Century* (Chapel Hill: University of North Carolina Press, 1996); and Joy James, *Transcending the Talented Tenth: Black Leaders and American Intellectuals* (New York: Routledge, 1997).

5. Thurman, *Luminous Darkness*, 3.

6. Quoted in Mary E. Goodwin, "Racial Roots and Religion: An Interview with Howard Thurman," *The Christian Century* 90 (May 9, 1973): 533–35.

7. Howard Thurman, *With Head and Heart: The Autobiography of Howard Thurman* (New York: Harcourt Brace, 1979), 160–61.

8. Sue Bailey Thurman, "Response to Tribute by Beth Rhude," Thurman Convocation Commemorating the Fortieth Anniversary of *Jesus and the Disinherited*, Vanderbilt Divinity School, October 26, 1989.

9. See Howard Thurman, *Footprints of a Dream: The Story of the Church for the Fellowship of All Peoples* (New York: Harper and Brothers, 1959), 144.

10. Ibid.

11. Howard Thurman, *Jesus and the Disinherited* (Nashville: Abingdon Press, 1949), 43–44. See also Cornel West, *Prophesy Deliverance! An Afro-American Revolutionary Christiantiy* (Philadelphia: Westminster Press, 1988), 54.

12. Howard Thurman Papers (1984 Gift), Boston University, Department of Special Collections, Writings: Box D, "Eulogy for Whitney Young (March 16, 1971)."

13. "Footprints of the Disinherited," student seminar, Howard Thurman Educational Trust, October 1979.

14. Darrell J. Fasching, "Holy Man for the Coming Millennium," in Mitchell, *The Human Search*, 191–203. See also Jan Corbett, "Howard Thurman: A Theologian for Our Times," *American Baptist Quarterly* (December 1979): 9–12; and Lerone Bennett, "Howard Thurman: Twentieth Century Holy Man," *Ebony* (February

1978): 68–70, 72, 76, 84–85. According to John Mangram, "Howard Thurman has been Mr. Black Theologian for a long time." See John Mangram, "Jesus Christ in Howard Thurman's Thought," in Samuel Lucius Gandy, ed., *Common Ground: Essays in Honor of Howard Thurman on the Occasion of His Seventy-fifth Birthday, November 18, 1975,* (Washington, D.C.: Hoffman Press, 1975), 65. J. Deotis Roberts places Thurman's contribution to African-American religious thought in the category of mysticism and religious philosophy. "In this category," he writes, "Howard Thurman has no rival and no second among his black brothers. It is surprising to me that he has been ignored almost completely in anthologies and works on mysticism. He is, indeed, one of the great mystics of all times. His mysticism is not "introverted," nor is it a mysticism of withdrawal from human problems. His mysticism is practical and urges us toward involvement and engagement in the real world where social and ethical issues are at stake." See J. Deotis Roberts, "The American Negro's Contribution to Religious Thought," in John Slabey Roucek and Thomas Kiernan, eds., *The Negro Impact on Western Civilization* (New York: Philosophical Library, 1970), 87. See also Martin Marty, "Mysticism and the Religious Quest for Freedom," in Henry J. Young, ed., *God and Human Freedom: Festschrift in Honor of Howard Thurman* (Richmond, Ind.: Friends United Press, 1983).

15. Thurman, *Inward Journey,* 110.

16. Howard Thurman, *Barren or Fruitful?* (Privately printed: Washington, D.C., 1932). See also Howard Thurman Papers (1997 Gift), Boston University, Department of Special Collections, Writings: Transcripts and Manuscripts Alphabetical File, Box 4, "Barren or Fruitful?"

17. Howard Thurman, "What Shall I Do With My Life?" *Christian Century Pulpit* (September 1939): 210–11.

18. Margaret Stanton, "A Prayer." This poem is among many Thurman recorded in poetry scrapbooks that are now scattered in fragments throughout his papers.

19. Howard Thurman, *Disciplines of the Spirit* (Richmond, Ind.: Friends United Press, 1977; 1963), 64–85.

20. Here Thurman appears to be summarizing the ethical thought of Albert Schweitzer, not that of Olive Schreiner.

21. Carl Ewald, *My Little Boy, My Big Girl,* Beth Bolling, trans. (New York: Horizon Press, Inc., copyright 1962), pp. 81–85. Used by permission of the publisher. [Citation reprinted from the original.]

22. See Eugene Marais, *The Soul of the White Ant,* trans. Winifred de Kok (New York: Dodd, Mead, and Co., 1937), 106–14.

23. C. S. Lewis, *The Problem of Pain* (London: Geoffrey Bles, 1940), p. 144. [Citation reprinted from the original.]

24. Simone Weil (1909–1943) was a French mystic, social philosopher, and activist in the French Resistance during World War II. Her posthumously published works, especially *Gravity and Grace* (1947) and her spiritual autobiography *Waiting for God* (1951) had particular influence on post-war French and English social thought. Her death, officially deemed a suicide, was the result of a hunger strike undertaken in Britain in solidarity with her French compatriots under German occupation.

25. Leslie Paul, *The Meaning of Human Existence* (London: Faber and Faber, 1949), p. 235. [Citation reprinted from the original.]

26. Margaret Kennedy, *The Feast* (New York: Rinehart, 1950).

27. W. W. Story, "Io Victus," from *Masterpieces of Religious Verse,* James D. Morrison, ed. (New York: Harper and Brothers, 1948), p. 288. [Citation reprinted from the original.]

28. Howard Thurman, *Deep River and The Negro Spiritual Speaks of Life and Death* (Richmond, Ind.: Friends United Press, 1975; 1945 and 1947, respectively), part two: 7–58.

29. Thurman, *With Head and Heart,* 216–17.

30. Willard Sperry (1882–1954) was dean of Harvard Divinity School, 1922 to 1953.

31. Bertrand Russell (1872–1970), controversial English philosopher and political activist, published "The Free Man's Worship" [*The Independent Review* 1 (December 1903): 415–24] shortly after an experience of "mystical illumination" prompted him to embrace pacifism. "In action, in desire, we must submit perpetually to the tyranny of outside forces, " Russell wrote in this famous essay, "but in aspiration, we are free, free from our fellow men, free from the petty planet on which our bodies impotently crawl, free even, while we live, from the tyranny of death. Let us learn then that energy of faith which enables us to live constantly in the vision of the good; and let us descend, in action, into the world of fact, with that vision always before us."

32. St. Augustine, Bishop of Hippo (354–430) established the intellectual foundations of the early Catholic Church in his major works, *Confessions* and *The City of God.* The quotation is from *Confessions,* Book 1, Chapter 1.

33. Thurman, *Disciplines of the Spirit,* 86–103.

34. The Sanhedrin consisted of the several official councils that governed the political, religious, and judicial life of the Jewish people in Palestine under Roman rule. It was destroyed after the abortive Jewish rebellion against Rome in 66–70 A.D.

35. Albert Schweitzer (1875–1965), German theologian, philosopher, famed organist, and mission doctor in equatorial Africa, received the Nobel Peace Prize in 1952. Influenced by his experiences in Africa and by the horrors of World War I, he wrote *Philosophy of Civilization* in 1923, in which he set forth his concept of "reverence for life." This ethical principle, with which Thurman felt a lifelong affinity, held that respect for all living things was essential to the survival of civilization.

36. Richard E. Byrd, *Alone* (New York: Putnam, 1938), p. 183. [Citation reprinted from the original.]

37. Meister Johannes Eckhart (1260–1327 or 28), widely-regarded as the greatest German speculative mystic, was a Dominican theologian concerned with understanding the journey of the human soul as it seeks union with God through worldly detachment. His major works include *Book of Divine Consolation, On Detachment,* and *The Nobleman.*

38. The practice of "centering down" is central to the Quaker worship tradition. Together in silence, those assembled in Meeting attentively and expectantly seek the hidden presence and will of Christ.

39. Zona Gale, "The Sky-Goer," from *The Le Gallienne Book of English and American Poetry,* Richard Le Gallienne, ed. (New York: Garden City Books, 1935), p. 293. Used by permission of the author's estate. [Reprinted from the original.]

40. Intercessory prayer petitions God to intervene on someone else's behalf, in contrast to prayers of supplication which request blessings for oneself.

41. Thurman, *Inward Journey,* 63.

42. Howard Thurman, *The Search for Common Ground: An Inquiry into the Basis of Man's Experience of Community* (Richmond, Ind.: Friends United Press, 1986; 1971), 1–7.

43. Reprinted by permission of Jeffers Literary Properties. [Reprinted from the original. The citation is Robinson Jeffers, "The Inhumanist," from *The Double Axe and Other Poems* (New York: Random House, 1948), 52–54.]

44. Howard Thurman, "Mysticism and Social Change," *Eden Theological Seminary Bulletin* 4 (Spring 1939): 3–34.

45. For a comprehensive survey of interpretations of mysticism, see Bernard

McGinn, *The Foundations of Mysticism: Origins to the Fifth Century,* Volume I (New York: Crossroads, 1995). Additional volumes are forthcoming.

46. B. Russell, *Mysticism and Logic,* p. 11. [Citation reprinted from the original.]

47. Leo Tolstoy (1828–1910) was a Russian author and one of the world's greatest novelists, perhaps best known for the epic of historical fiction, *War and Peace* (1865–69). In his later years, Tolstoy embraced Christian anarchism and devoted himself to social reform and communitarian living. William Ernest Hocking (1873–1966), an American philosopher of religion, explored the relative merits of non-Christian religions and stressed the similiarities among mystics of various traditions.

48. Heinrich Suso (1295–1366), a student of the great German speculative mystic Meister Eckhart and author of *Little Book of Eternal Wisdom* (1328), was a leader of The Friends of God, a circle of devout ascetics who opposed contemporary social evils. He was beatified in 1831 by Pope Gregory XVI. Thurman's source, "Principal Hughes," could not be determined.

49. Thurman erred in his reference to "Commodore Perry." He evidently intended to speak of Robert Edwin Peary (1856–1920), an American Arctic explorer usually credited with leading the first expedition to reach the North Pole in 1909. Roland Hayes (1887–1976) was the first African American vocalist in the classical tradition to receive international acclaim, particularly for his celebrated interpretation of German lieder. Walter Hampden (1879–1955) was an American actor, theater manager, and repertory producer of Shakespearean drama, whose fame was established in London in 1906 with his portrayal of Hamlet. The biblical passages appear in I Corinthians 9:6, Acts 26:19, and Luke 4:18–19. The Bible does not appear to make reference to Jesus unstopping "the ears of the deaf."

50. K. E. Kirk, *Vision of God,* pp. 445ff. [Citation reprinted from the original. See note 52 for complete cite.]

51. Vladimir G. Simkhovitch, *Toward the Understanding of Jesus* (New York: Macmillan, 1921), 60.

52. Kenneth E. Kirk, *The Vision of God: The Christian Doctrine of the Summum Bonum* (New York: Longmans, Green, and Co., 1931), 451.

53. Rufus Jones, *Social Law in the Spiritual World: Studies in Human and Divine Interrelationship* (Philadelphia: J. C. Winston Co., 1904), 154. Here, Jones makes what was for Thurman an all-important distinction between "affirmation mystics" and "negation mystics." Negation mystics (with whom the entire mystical

tradition had become identified by modern psychology) believe that God cannot be found in transitory human experience, but only through withdrawal from the world of the senses and the merging of one's personality with the reality of God.

54. Eugene Debs, "Social Reform," in *Labor and Freedom: The Voice and Pen of Eugene V. Debs,* ed. Phil Wagner (St. Louis: Phil Wagner, 1916), 89.

55. Allen, *The Choir Invisible.* [Citation reprinted from the original. The complete cite is James Lane Allen, *The Choir Invisible* (New York: Macmillian, 1897), 359.]

56. Howard Thurman, "Religion in a Time of Crisis," *The Garrett Tower* 18 (August 1943): 1–3.

57. See H. Richard Niebuhr, "War as the Judgment of God," *Christian Century* 59 (May 13, 1942): 630–33 and "War as Crucifixion," *Christian Century* 60 (April 20, 1943): 513–15.

58. Thurman to Abe Mellinkoff (October 10, 1969), Howard Thurman Papers (1994 Gift), Boston University, Department of Special Collections, Mixed Files, Box 8, "Fellowship Church, #2."

59. This is a loose paraphrase of 1 Kings 19:9–18. In this Old Testament story, Elijah exclaims to Yahweh that his fellow Israelites have abandoned the covenant and torn down the altars concluding, "I am the only one left and now they want to kill me." Yahweh tells Elijah to annoint Jehu King of Israel and to instruct the new leader to kill the worshipers of the idol Baal, but to spare "all the knees that have not bent before Baal, all the mouths that have not kissed him."

60. Famous Negro spiritual.

61. See note 54 for source of Debs quote, which Thurman used frequently in his early work.

62. In November 1931, Japan invaded the Manchurian city of Shenyang on Chinese soil. Within five months the Japanese had created a puppet state called Manchukuo out the three historic Manchurian provinces, which they occupied until 1945 when the long-contested area was conquered by the Soviet Union.

63. The Atlantic Charter was a joint manifesto issued on August 14, 1941 by British Prime Minister Winston Churchill and American President Franklin D. Roosevelt, which was subsequently incorporated into the Declaration of the United Nations on January 1, 1942. In brief, it declared their commitment to territorial sovereignty and self-determination, and to the principles of economic security and fair labor standards for all nations.

64. "Biddies" are chickens.

65. Thurman, *Jesus and the Disinherited*, 11–35.

66. Heinrich Weinel and Alban G. Widgery, *Jesus in the Nineteenth Century and Af- ter*, p. 405. [Citation reprinted from the original.]

67. Octavian Caesar, or Augustus, successor to his great-uncle Julius Caesar, ruled the Roman Empire from 31 B.C. to 14 A.D. Emperor Augustus ushered in a period of prosperity and bureaucratic stability for Roman citizens within the empire, including a more efficient system of tax collection within its far-flung territories.

68. Pp. 10–11. Copyright 1921, 1937, 1947 by the Macmillian Co. and used with their permission. [Citation reprinted from the original. See "Mysticism and Ethics" for a complete cite, and note 51.]

69. Thurman is referring to the Student Volunteer Movement convention held in In- dianapolis from December 28, 1923 through January 1, 1924. The S. V. M. was a loosely organized body of Christian student organizations, such as the YMCA, from around the world.

70. Korea was a political battleground in the early twentieth century, caught be- tween the imperial designs of both Japan and Russia. With the ending of the Russo-Japanese war in 1905, Japan's claim was recognized. Korea was made a Japanese colony by 1910, engendering a fierce Korean nationalist movement con- sisting of Christians and Confucians, those who remained in their homeland and those who fled, and a large number of students. In 1919, the March First movement organized a mass uprising, which was brutally suppressed by the Jap- anese Army. Koreans continued to fight for national independence until it was secured in 1945, though the country was then divided along the 38th parallel leading to the conflict resulting in the Korean War.

71. Famous Negro Spiritual.

72. *Toward the Understanding of Jesus*, pp. 60–61. Copyright 1921, 1937, 1947 by the Macmillian Co. and used with their permission. [Citation reprinted from the original.]

73. For an example of Thurman's youthful critique of Black Church practices – part of a generational revolt influenced by liberal modernism and that included such figures as Benjamin Mays and Mordecai Wyatt Johnson – see "Task of the Negro Ministry," reprinted in this volume.

74. See Acts 25:6–12.

75. Thurman, *Jesus and the Disinherited*, 58–73.

76. Thurman was deeply influenced while in seminary by Olive Schreiner's literary

style and found affinity with her belief in the unity of life and the redemptive role of personal responsibility in establishing common ground. But she is best-known for her book, *Women and Labor* (1911), which was widely acclaimed by the early twentieth-century women's movement.

77. The Equal Rights Amendment, first introduced to Congress in 1923, reads in its entirety: "Equality of rights under the law shall not be denied or abridged by the United States or by any state on account of sex." It has not yet been ratified.

78. The class of germs that causes tuberculosis.

79. Howard Thurman, "Leadership," *Torch and Trefoil*, 35 (February 1960): 4.

80. Olive Schreiner, *From Man to Man* (New York: Harper and Brothers, 1927), 158.

81. Source of quote undetermined.

82. Thurman, *Disciplines of the Spirit*, 104–27.

83. Mannequins, or models of the human body, are commonly used for displaying clothes.

84. *This Week Magazine*, "What Monkeys Are Teaching Science about Children," March 3, 1963, p. 18. [Citation reprinted from the original.]

85. "At Church Next Sunday," author unknown, from *The Best Loved Religious Poems*, James Gilchrist Lawson, ed., (Westwood, N.J.:Fleming H. Revell Co., 1933). [Citation reprinted from the original.]

86. Jose Ortega y Gasset (1883–1955), Spanish philosopher and humanist, is best known for *The Revolt of the Masses* (1929) in which he characterized twentieth-century thought as dominated by the mediocrity and violence of the "masses," whom he proposed should surrender leadership to a cultivated intellectual minority.

87. See discussion of Thurman's intellectual influence on King in Walter Earl Fluker, *They Looked for a City: A Comparative Analysis of the Ideal of Community in Howard Thurman and Martin Luther King, Jr.* (Lanham, Md.: University Press of America, 1988), 111–13; Lewis V. Baldwin, "Martin Luther King, the Black Church, and the Black Messianic Vision," *Journal of the Interdenominational Theological Center* 12 (Fall/Spring 1984–85): 103–4; Larry Murphy, "Howard Thurman and Social Activism," in *God and Human Freedom: A Festschrift in Honor of Howard Thurman* (Richmond, Ind.: Friends United Press), 154–55; John Ansbro, *Martin Luther King, Jr.: Making of a Mind,* (Maryknoll, N.Y.: Orbis Books, 1982); Lerone Bennett, *What Manner of Man,* 2nd rev. ed. (Chicago: Johnson Publishing Co., 1976), 74–75; Sudarshan Kapur, *Raising Up a Prophet:*

The African American Encounter with Gandhi (Boston: Beacon Press, 1992); and Greg Moses, *Revolution of Conscience: Martin Luther King, Jr. and the Philosophy of Nonviolence* (New York: Guildford Press, 1997), 144–46. See also Thurman's remarks on his relationship with King in, *With Head and Heart,* 255. Correspondence between Thurman and King, which was concentrated in the late fifties, will be published in Fluker and Tumber, eds., *The Sound of the Genuine: The Papers of Howard Thurman,* 3 vols., forthcoming from University of South Carolina Press, 2002.

88. See King sermons, "The Meaning of Hope," Dexter Avenue Baptist Church, 10 October 1967, 16–17 and "Is the Universe Friendly?" Ebenezer Baptist Church, 12 December 1965, 5–6. King Archives, Atlanta, Ga. Compare with Thurman, *Head and Heart,* 20–21. See Martin Luther King, Jr., "Antidotes for Fear," *Strength to Love* (Philadelphia: Fortress Press, 1981), 36; and King, "Knock at Midnight," in *Strength to Love,* 65–66.

89. Thurman, *Inward Journey,* 83.

90. Howard Thurman, "The Task of the Negro Ministry," *The Southern Workman* 57 (October 1928): 388–92. *The Southern Workman* was the official publication of the historically black college, Hampton Institute. Founded in 1871 to promote industrial education in the South, the journal had become by the 1920s the primary forum for discussion of economic conditions among African Americans.

91. See Howard Thurman, "Higher Education and Religion," *The Home Mission College Review,* 1 (November 1927): 23–26.

92. Olive Schreiner, *Trooper Peter Halket of Mashonaland* (London: T. Fisher Unwin, 1897). This quote appears in Howard Thurman, ed., *A Track to the Water's Edge: The Olive Schreiner Reader* (New York: Harper and Row, 1973), 129–30.

93. From the late nineteenth century to the first quarter of the twentieth, American Christianity underwent a movement to make churches more efficient. This mirrored a similar movement in American business culture, most evident in the work of Frederick W. Taylor, whose *The Principles of Scientific Management* (1911) had a profound impact on the way American enterprises, including churches, conducted their daily operations. By the late 1920s, the efficiency movement produced, among other things, an enormous religious bureaucracy that included countless organizations and buildings dedicated to Christian endeavors. The most well-known early twentieth-century indictment of these practices and others within the Black Church is Benjamin Mays, *The Negro's Church* (1938).

94. This is most likely a paraphrase of Friedrich Nietzsche: "What are these churches now, if they are not tombs and monuments to God?" Friedrich Nietzsche, *The Joyful Wisdom,* trans. Thomas Common (New York: Russell & Russell, 1964), 169.

95. Albert Parker Fitch, *None So Blind* (New York: Macmillan, 1924), 27.

96. Walter Rauschenbusch (1861–1918), author of *Christianity and the Social Crisis* (1907) among others, was the most prominent theologian of the Social Gospel movement. The integration of religion and life was a major tenant of the Social Gospel, as was the idea that salvation is achieved less through personal piety than through community service. Rauschenbusch joined the faculty of Rochester Theological Seminary, after pastoring a Baptist Church in New York City from 1886 to 1897. Although Rauschenbusch had already died by the time Thurman attended RTS from 1923 to 1926, his Social Gospel theology remained an important part of the seminary's curriculum.

97. Schreiner, *Trooper Peter Halket,* in Thurman, ed., *Track to the Water's Edge,* 120–21.

98. This case is more popularly known as the Scopes Trial (1925), named after John Scopes, a high school biology teacher who was bound over to a Dayton, Tennessee, grand jury for the crime of teaching evolutionary theory in a public school. This was a widely publicized case, in part because of the celebrity of opposing attorneys Clarence Darrow and William Jennings Bryan, in part because it dramatized the beliefs of the relatively new modern fundamentalist movement.

99. 2 Corinthians 3:6.

100. Thurman analyzed modern sexual morality, particularly the greater frequency of premarital sex, in his 1926 Rochester Theological Seminary Bachelor of Divinity thesis, "An Inquiry into the Attitude Toward Premarital Sexual Morality among Various Peoples and an Analysis of its True Basis," which will be published in full in Fluker and Tumber, eds., *Sound of the Genuine.*

101. Howard Thurman, "What We May Learn from India," *Report of the Eleventh Week of Work, 1936* (New York: National Council on Religion and Education, 1936), 25–28. See also Howard Thurman Papers (1995 Gift), Boston University, Department of Special Collections, Writings: Box 1, "What We May Learn from India."

102. Other members of the delegation were Mrs. Sue Bailey Thurman and The Reverend, later Bishop, and Mrs. Edward G. Carroll. They were guests of the Student Christian Movement in India, Burma, and Ceylon.

103. Francis Xavier (1506–1552), one of the original members of the Society of Jesus (or "Jesuits"), became known as the "Apostle of the Indies" for his early missionary work in India, the East Indies, and Japan. A native of Portugal, he was canonized in 1622.

104. "Mussulman" is an archaic term for Muslim. The Islamic Mughal Empire, established in 1526, encompassed the northern region of the Indian subcontinent, which was predominantly Hindu. The Mughals were not strict Muslims and did not rigidly enforce Muslim law especially under the reforms of its third emperor, Akbar (1542?–1605), who disestablished Islam as a state religion and ushered in a period of political, economic, and to some extent, cultural unification in northern India. With Akbar's death, interreligious conflict ensued, divisions between Hindu castes deepened, and the way was prepared for the domination of British trade interests. Britain succeeded in colonizing India in 1818 and preserved its rule until 1947.

105. Eli Stanley Jones (1884–1973), a Methodist Episcopal Church missionary to upper caste Indians, wrote *Christ and Human Suffering* (New York: Abingdon, 1933), among others. It was to this book that Thurman probably intended to make reference here.

106. Jarrell Waskom Pickett (1890–1981), a Methodist Episcopal Church pastor, missionary, and editor who served in various positions throughout India beginning in 1911, was elected bishop by the Central Conference of Southern Asia in 1935–36, a post he held until his retirement in 1956. Pickett earned his B. A. (1907) and M. A. (1908) from Asbury College in Kentucky.

107. Joseph Louis Barrow or "Joe Louis" (1914–1981), called the "Brown Bomber," was an African-American boxer and heavyweight champion of the world from June 22, 1937 to March 1, 1949, when he retired. He not only held this title for the longest period in the history of the heavyweight division, but stood as a cultural hero to millions of Americans opposed to racial discrimination.

108. Howard Thurman, "The Will to Segregation," *Fellowship* (August 1943): 144–46.

109. The Selective Service Training Act of 1940 banned racial discrimination in administering the draft, but preserved segregation. Segregated programs were established throughout the war for training black officers, pilots, and technicians, who were allowed to serve in combat units only toward the end of the war. In 1941 Roosevelt issued Executive Order 8802, which specified that defense contractors ban discrimination and open training programs to minorities and estab-

lished the Fair Employment Practice Committee to investigate violations. In 1943 unions were denied collective bargaining status if they practiced racial discrimination, and the War Labor Board outlawed race-based wage differentials.

110. The United States entered World War I "to make the world safe for democracy," only to find that the post-war settlement, which provided for large German reparations payments and fed the victors' economic ambitions, contributed to the hostilities that led to World War II. In his January 6, 1941 State of the Union address, Franklin D. Roosevelt set forth American hopes for a post–World War II settlement as the "Four Freedoms": "The first is freedom of speech and expression – everywhere in the world. The second is freedom of every person to worship God in his own way – everywhere in the world. The third is freedom from want – which, translated into world terms, means economic understandings which will secure to every nation a healthy peacetime life for its inhabitants – everywhere in the world. The fourth is freedom from fear – which translated into world terms means a worldwide reduction of armaments to such a point and in such a thoroughgoing fashion that no nation will be in a position to commit an act of physical aggression against any neighbor – anywhere in the world." The Four Freedoms proved primarily to be a wartime slogan, principles that were again severely eroded during post-war settlement negotiations.

111. Thurman is referring here to Japan's attack on Pearl Harbor on December 7, 1941, which destroyed the U.S. Navy's entire Pacific fleet and prompted the U.S. to declare war on Japan and its allies during World War II.

112. The International Fellowship of Reconciliation (FOR), a Christian pacifist organization, was established during the First World War. Its American section had long been especially interested in race relations. Under the leadership of A. J. Muste, most of the American FOR's leading activists had by the early forties become disciples of Mahatma Gandhi, whose Indian independence movement was at that time employing nonviolent resistance as both a tactic and a way of life. In 1942 FOR had established the Congress of Racial Equality (CORE), which inherited its parent organization's nonviolent "Christian idealism." See August Meyer and Elliot Rudwick, *CORE: A Study in the Civil Rights Movement, 1942–1968* (New York: Oxford, 1973), 4; and Jervis Anderson, *Bayard Rustin: The Troubles I've Seen* (New York: HarperCollins, 1997), 61–77.

113. Howard Thurman, "The Fellowship Church of All Peoples," *Common Ground* (Spring 1945): 29–31. For a book-length treatment of the formation and develop-

ment of Fellowship Church see Howard Thurman, *Footprints of a Dream: The Story of the Church for the Fellowship of All Peoples* (New York: Harper and Brothers, 1959).

114. The Church for the Fellowship of All Peoples represented a notable hybrid between the Fellowship Church movement, to which Thurman makes reference in this article, and the post-war Neighborhood Church movement. The early Fellowship Churches were ideologically committed to interracial worship, but held afternoon services in participating black and white churches. None of them established a permanent home until Thurman and Fiske founded Fellowship Church in San Francisco. The Neighborhood Church movement emerged in response to black migration to city neighborhoods abandoned by whites relocating to new suburban areas after the war. Instead of following their middle-class white congregations to the suburbs, Neighborhood Church movement leaders sought to establish a new base for church membership among their new black neighbors.

115. The American Friends Service Committee was founded by American and Canadian Quakers in 1917 to promote peace and reconciliation through projects such as referral services for conscientious objectors, student foreign exchange programs, refugee and migrant assistance, and programs intended to facilitate interracial understanding.

116. Albert Cleage (1913–), a 1943 graduate of Oberlin School of Theology, preceded Thurman as Fellowship Church's black pastor in February 1944 with the understanding that Thurman would assume the role at the end of the academic year. Cleage, who changed his name to Jaramogi Abebe Agyeman in 1970, later became well-known as the author of *The Black Messiah* (1968) and as the founder of the Shrines of the Black Madonna of the Pan African Orthodox Christian Church.

117. Those who joined Fellowship Church as national associates included First Lady Eleanor Roosevelt; the South African author of *Cry, The Beloved Country,* Alan Paton; jazz diva, Josephine Baker; and civil rights attorney, Pauli Murray, who later became a founding member of the National Organization of Women and the first black woman to be ordained a priest of the Episcopal Church in 1977.

118. Sun Yat-Sen (1866–1925) played a leading role in the overthrow of the Manchu dynasty in the early 1910s. The plaque on Beniamino Bufano's red granite and

stainless steel sculpture, created in 1937 with WPA funding, states that Sen was a "champion of democracy, father of the Chinese republic, and first president, 1921–22."

119. Beginning in 1942, on the basis of racial fears and suspicions of wartime disloyalty, virtually the entire Japanese-American population of the west coast – some 110,000 people – was rounded up and imprisoned in "relocation camps." Most of them were released in 1944. In most cases, the internees lost their property as well as their liberty. In San Francisco, many of the neighborhoods left vacant by these imprisoned Americans became occupied by African-American workers who had migrated to the area to participate in national defense and wartime industries. Fellowship Church was located in one of these neighborhoods.

120. Howard Thurman Papers (1994 Gift), Boston University, Department of Special Collections, Correspondence: San Francisco Correspondence, Box 6.

121. Howard Thurman, "The Responsibility of the Professional Person to Society," *Nursing Outlook,* 5 (June 1957): 334–35, the "Official Organ of the National League for Nursing."

122. Howard Thurman Papers (1997 Gift), Boston University, Department of Special Collections, Writings: Alphabetical Transcripts and Manuscripts, "Public and Private Results of Collegiate Education in the Life of Negro Americans."

123. John Hope (1868–1936), who served as president of Morehouse College from 1906–1931, attracted a new generation of faculty and administrators and is credited with establishing the school's tradition of educating black public leaders for all areas of American life. During his tenure, the college was renamed in honor of Henry L. Morehouse, the corresponding secretary of the Atlanta Baptist Home Mission Society. Thurman – one of the school's most outstanding students – received the benefits of this new era and the personal tutelage and friendship of President Hope, Dean Samuel Archer, and Professors Garrie More and Lorimer Milton. On the history of Morehouse College, see Edward O. Jones, *A Candle in the Dark: A History of Morehouse College* (Valley Forge: Judson Press, 1967).

124. Francis Xavier Hagney, *Blue Cat of Castletown,* "The River Song" [vocal score], words by Catherine Cate Coblentz (New York: Longmans, 1949).

125. Howard Thurman, *Luminous Darkness* (Richmond, Ind.: Friends United Press, 1989; 1965), 89–113.

126. See Martin Luther King, Jr., "The Ethical Demands for Integration (1963)" in

James M. Washington, ed., *A Testament of Hope: The Essential Writings of Martin Luther King, Jr.* (San Francisco: Harper and Row, 1986), 117–25.

127. New York: McGraw-Hill Book Company, 1964, pp. 22–23. [Citation reprinted from the original.]

128. Olive Schreiner, *The Story of an African Farm* (London: Ernest Benn, Ltd., 1951 ed.), pp. 201–2. [Citation reprinted from the original.]

129. As one of the first projects of his "wider ministry," Thurman traveled to Vancouver in mid-October 1962 to meet with the Federation of Saskatchewan Indian Chiefs. According to Thurman, this encounter was the first between these Canadian Indian leaders and an African American public figure. For fuller accounts of the meeting, see *With Head and Heart,* 242–47; "Annual Report: The Wider Ministry, 1962–1963;" and "Draft Report on Federation of Saskatchewan Indians." The latter two documents may be found in the Howard Thurman Papers (1984 Gift), Boston University, Department of Special Collections, B. U. Subject Files, Box 56, "Annual Report, 1962–63" and Box 65, "Federation of Saskatchewan," respectively.

130. In fall 1963, Thurman served as Visiting Lecturer in the Department of Religious Studies at the University of Ibadan near Lagos, Nigeria. For an extended treatment of his first and only trip to Africa, see *With Head and Heart,* 193–211.

131. During World War II all citizens of the United States were required to register with the federal government to receive ration coupons for certain foods and consumer goods in limited supply.

132. New York: Columbia University Press, 1930, p. 96. [Citation reprinted from the original.]

133. The "Russellites" was the former name – until 1931 – of the Jehovah's Witnesses, founded by Charles Taze Russell (1852–1916) in 1872.

134. Howard Thurman Papers (1997 Gift), Boston University Department of Special Collections, Alphabetical Transcripts and Manuscripts File, "Whitney Young: What Can I Do?" Whitney Moore Young, Jr. (1921–1971) was born and raised in Lincoln Ridge, Kentucky, and earned his B.A. from Kentucky State Industrial College (1941). After serving in World War II, he earned an M.A. in Social Work from the University of Minnesota (1947). He served in various local leadership positions with the National Urban League until 1954, when he was appointed dean of the Atlanta University School of Social Work, whose fortunes and reputation he dramatically increased. While in Atlanta, he was also involved in a

number of civil rights organizations and sat on the board of the Atlanta NAACP. In 1960, he was made executive director of the NUL, a post he held until 1969. A personal friend and consultant to President Lyndon Johnson, he greatly influenced the development of Johnson's Great Society antipoverty programs, participated in a special delegation to Vietnam in 1967, and was awarded the Medal of Freedom in 1969. Young authored several books, including *To Be Equal* (1964), a collection of his regular columns for the *Amsterdam News,* and *Beyond Racism* (1969). He sat on a number of corporate boards, including the Rockefeller Foundation and the Federal Reserve Bank of New York, and served as president of the National Conference on Welfare in 1967 and of the National Association of Social Workers from 1969 until his death. He died on March 11, 1974 in Lagos, Nigeria, while swimming, probably of a brain aneurysm.

135. Howard Thurman Papers (1994 Gift), Boston University, Department of Special Collections, Writings Series, "America in Search of a Soul."

136. See Thurman's "Human Freedom and the Emancipation Proclamation," *Pulpit Digest* 2 (December 1962), 13–16, 66; the five-part sermon series, "The Declaration of Independence" (July 29–August 26, 1951) Howard Thurman Papers (1997 Gift), Writings: Transcribed Sermons, "Declaration of Independence;" and *Creative Encounter,* 125–34.

137. Thurman had provided pastoral counsel to one of the families featured in J. Anthony Lukas's definitive account of this painful episode, *Common Ground* (New York: Vintage, 1986), as he had to so many others – black and white – struggling with racial injustice.

138. "Manifest Destiny," a term coined in the 1840s and officially invoked throughout the nineteenth century, alleged the inevitable territorial expansion of the United States to the Pacific coast. It was also invoked to justify U.S. involvement in Hawaii and the Philippines.

139. Thurman, *Common Ground,* 81–104.

140. Thurman, *Inward Journey,* 67.

141. Ibid., 85.

142. Ibid., 105.

143. Ibid., 42.

144. Thurman, *Head and Heart,* 193–4.

145. Thurman, *Inward Journey,* 14.

146. Thurman, *Meditations of the Heart,* 97.

147. Ibid., 36.

148. Ibid., 134.

149. Ibid., 28.

150. Thurman, *Inward Journey,* 109.

151. Ibid., 106.

152. Thurman, *Meditations of the Heart,* 123.

153. Ibid., 208.

154. Howard Thurman, *For the Inward Journey: The Writings of Howard Thurman* (New York: Harcourt, Brace, Jovanovich, 1984): 54–55. This meditation was selected by Anne Spencer Thurman.

ACKNOWLEDGMENTS

None of our work with the Howard Thurman Papers Project would have been possible without the unwaivering support and good humor of Mrs. Sue Bailey Thurman. As we began work on this collection, Mrs. Thurman fell ill, and on Christmas Day 1996, she "passed into the Elysian fields," as she had often characterized the inevitable. With love and profound respect, we dedicate this volume to her memory.

With pleasure and deep affection we would also like to thank Anne Spencer Thurman and Olive (Thurman) Wong, who gave us formal permission to publish their father's words in *A Strange Freedom*. Their many kindnesses, proffered even in the midst of personal sorrow and tremendous family responsibility, have sustained us in this undertaking.

Several people read drafts of the Introduction, and their criticism no doubt prevented us from committing a number of sins. The end result is, of course, entirely our own responsibility. Vincent Harding and Stephen Angell offered useful comments at the 1997 annual meeting of the American Academy of Religion. Luther Smith contributed painstaking commentary on both substance and style. Jim Tumber, Michael Sauter, Mara Kozelsky, and Rebecca Edwards each gave it a helpful read, too, and we are grateful to them all.

Rebecca Edwards provided the lion's share of research assistance – only a fragment of which is evident here – and Michael Sauter, Eileen Pollack, Mara Kozelsky, and Michelle Jones transcribed the documents for publication. We would also like to acknowledge the contributions of former Thurman Project assistant editors Quinton Dixie and Peter Eisenstadt, whose research, annotation, and historical knowledge provided the base for some of what appears here. Michael Sauter, the Thurman Project's Office Manager and Database Technician moved things along with intelligence, wit, and good cheer.

Our work simply would not have been possible without the cooperation and support of Howard Gotlieb and Margaret Goostray of Boston University's Department of Special Collections, along with the assistance provided to our staff by countless librarians and archivists at repositories across the country, whom we would like to thank individually upon publication of our forthcoming documentary edition of Howard Thurman's papers, *The Sound of the Genuine*. For this volume, we owe a special debt of gratitude to Sally McMasters and the staff of the University of Rochester Interlibrary Loan Department.

Thanks are also due to Martin E. Marty, whose thoughtful foreword graces these pages. Fred Kameny, our editor at University of South Carolina Press, kindly permitted us to include some of the documents that will later appear in *The Sound of the Genuine*. Tisha Hooks, our editor at Beacon Press, has been a sure guide – an intelligent and enthusiastic supporter. We are also grateful to our copy editor, George Lang, who professionally polished this apple.

From 1992 through 1997 the Howard Thurman Papers Project was a project of Colgate Rochester Divinity School in cooperation with the Howard Thurman Educational Trust. The Thurman Project will complete its work through the sponsorship of Morehouse College. It has received generous support from The Lilly Endowment, Inc., The Pew Charitable Trusts, the National Historical Publications and Records Commission, the Louisville Institute for the Study of Protestantism and American Culture, and the Henry R. Luce Foundation.

Finally, the editors are deeply grateful to Sharon Watson Fluker and Melinda Gaye Johnston for their radical social patience and personal support.